TEACHER TO TEACHER

TEACHER TO TEACHER

Strategies for the Elementary Classroom

Mary W. Olson
University of North Carolina at Greensboro

Susan P. Homan
University of South Florida

Editors

International Reading Association
Newark, Delaware 19714

Director of Publications   Joan M. Irwin
Managing Editor   Romayne McElhaney
Associate Editor   Anne Fullerton
Assistant Editor   Amy Trefsger
Editorial Assistant   Janet Parrack
Production Department Manager   Iona Sauscermen
Graphic Design Coordinator   Boni Nash
Design Consultant   Larry Husfelt
Desktop Publishing Supervisor   Wendy Mazur
Desktop Publishing   Anette Schuetz-Ruff
                 Cheryl Strum
                 Richard James
Proofing   Florence Pratt

The International Reading Association attempts, through its publications, to provide a forum for a wide spectrum of opinions on reading. This policy permits divergent viewpoints without assuming the endorsement of the Association.

Much of the material contained in this volume first appeared in *The Reading Teacher*, a copyrighted journal of the International Reading Association. Every attempt was made to contact authors of previously published work to inform them of this use of their material. The publisher welcomes correspondence from contributing authors concerning corrections or updated information that can be incorporated in subsequent editions of this publication.

Library of Congress Cataloging in Publication Data
Teacher to teacher: Strategies for the elementary classroom/Mary W. Olson,
    Susan P. Homan, editors.
        p.   cm.
Chiefly articles from The Reading Teacher, 1983-1991.
Includes bibliographical references and index.
    1. Language arts (Elementary)—United States. 2. Teaching—Aids and
devices. I. Olson, Mary W. II. Homan, Susan P.
LB1576.T367   1993   92-35883
372.6'044—dc20   CIP
ISBN 0-87207-382-3

Contents

Foreword

After reading the article "Home Writing Activities: The Writing Briefcase and the Traveling Suitcase" (In the Classroom, October 1991), I came up with three spin-off activities. My third graders love to take a suitcase home....

(Janice Wright, *The Reading Teacher*, February, 1992)

I was interested in Edward J. Dwyer's article, "Comprehending Figurative Language" (In the Classroom, December 1991), and was impressed that a kindergarten teacher was introducing this to her students. I strongly recommend this practice to other early education teachers....

For reinforcement, I would like to suggest the book *The King Who Rained* by Fred Gwynne. It...complements the approach used by Ms. Kelly....

(Grace G. McCaw, *The Reading Teacher*, September 1992)

These excerpts are from the "Encore" section of *The Reading Teacher*'s "In the Classroom" department. "Encore," a feature initiated by department editors Carolyn Colvin and Pamela Ross, provides readers with an opportunity to share uses and extensions of information found in earlier "In the Classroom" articles. Wright's and McCaw's comments typify the kind of response teachers have had to this long-running department of *The Reading Teacher*—praise for its pithy, practical instructional strategies and ideas, which are authored usually by preschool and elementary teachers themselves.

Thus, it is appropriate that Mary W. Olson and Susan P. Homan have collected some of the best of the best of these teaching ideas in *Teacher to Teacher: Strategies for the Elementary Classroom*. In this book, they and their editorial board have assembled tried and tested strategies for reading words, developing vocabulary, reading orally, comprehending text, learning from content materials, composing text, using literature, and promoting children's enjoyment of the written word. And Olson and Homan have succeeded with distinction in selecting useful, interesting, and engaging ideas for this collection. Anyone working with preschool children through middle grade students will find a wealth of practical teaching ideas in this volume.

In a *Reading Teacher* article written by classroom teachers who shared their experiences in writing for publication, Carol J. Fuhler wrote, "As classroom teachers, you are the experts whose personal endorsements count as we all try to perfect our skills and provide the best possible educational environment for our students. Share those ideas. I am looking forward to learning from you, a trusted colleague, as you publish in *The Reading Teacher*" (D'Alessandro, Diakiw, Fuhler, O'Masta, Pils, Trachtenburg, & Wolf, February 1992). Indeed, the authorities have spoken and shared many hundreds of their most valued and successful teaching ideas in *The Reading Teacher* over the years. *Teacher to Teacher* contains a rich selection of them. I am certain you will find in this book useful "expert to expert" information to savor and digest. So, read and enjoy. Bon appetit!

James F. Baumann
The University of Georgia and
The National Reading Research Center;
Editor, *The Reading Teacher*, 1989-1993

Preface

We have long admired *The Reading Teacher*'s regular column of teaching ideas, "In the Classroom" (called "The Classroom Reading Teacher" until May 1988 and, beginning in September 1993, "Teaching Reading"). We therefore decided to collect the best articles from "In the Classroom" in an easily accessible volume for preservice and inservice teachers. Even though teaching certainly involves much more than a series of classroom activities, we believe that a volume of suggestions from which thoughtful teachers can conveniently select appropriate practices for particular goals, contexts, and children might be very useful. (At this point, it is important to note that any book of teaching suggestions should be used with this notion of thoughtful selection in mind.)

Other reasons prompted our effort to put together this volume. Many classroom teachers are unfamiliar with or do not have access to *The Reading Teacher*, and we felt that one volume of classroom ideas could be helpful for those teachers. Even those teachers who do receive *RT* regularly may not keep their copies close at hand when they are planning future lessons. Furthermore, searching through dozens of issues for appropriate strategies is time consuming—and time is a scarce commodity for teachers. Finally, dissemination of the results of current research, as well as instructional strategies compatible with those results, is a long-standing problem for education. This volume is an attempt to address that problem.

Teacher to Teacher contains strategies and activities selected from the October 1983 to May 1991 issues of *The Reading Teacher*. Even though the strategies and activities were peer-reviewed by an editorial board for inclusion in the journal, the articles included in this volume were subjected to an additional review by a second editorial board of 11 classroom teachers and reading/language arts coordinators from across the United States. Members of the editorial board were as follows:

Carol Avery, Jean Frey, Kris Grantz, Kris Knudsens, Tamara Lindsey, John Logan, Lynn McKay, Molly McLauren, Donna Noyes, Sue Reisdorph, and Linda Scott.

We asked reviewers to identify the appropriate grade levels for each activity or strategy described in the "In the

Classroom" articles, to classify each by topic (vocabulary development, writing, study skills, word recognition, etc.), and to rate each on nine criteria. These criteria were as follows:

1. The strategy has a stated purpose and is appropriate for that purpose; implementing the strategy would achieve the stated purpose.
2. The strategy is consistent with current research.
3. The strategy has potential as a way for students to learn content.
4. The strategy has potential as a way for students to learn a skill.
5. The steps to implement the strategy are clearly described and carefully sequenced; it would be easy to implement the strategy and use it in the classroom.
6. The materials needed to implement the strategy are clearly described.
7. Teachers would find this strategy easy to implement and would probably use it.
8. The strategy has the potential to motivate students to pursue further learning.
9. The strategy could be used at several grade levels; changing only the content (e.g., choice of texts) would be required.

All of the reviewers on our editorial board were outstanding in their knowledge of reading and language arts, their judgments based on that knowledge, and the promptness with which they completed their task. Without their help and suggestions, this volume would not exist. We acknowledge that it was very difficult for them, and for us, to omit some excellent strategies from our final copy; nevertheless, because of their thoughtful ratings, we believe we have included many of the best articles from "In the Classroom." The authors of those articles are listed at the conclusion of this volume in the "Index of Contributors."

We would also like to thank the reviewers on the IRA Publications Committee. Their insights and suggestions were most helpful and appreciated. We owe special thanks to Susan Granda, Pat Joyner, and Ellen Summers for typing the manuscript.

This volume has nine chapters. Each chapter contains an introductory orientation to the chapter's focus, a list of suggested further readings, and the strategies recommended for inclusion by the editorial board. It is important to acknowledge that we created the chapters out of a need for structure; obviously many of the activities could fit in several chapters simultaneously. Teachers will rightfully reorganize to suit their particular needs.

It was a pleasure compiling *Teacher to Teacher: Strategies for the Elementary Classroom*. We hope that teachers find that it offers helpful, stimulating, creative, and sound practices for their classrooms.

MWO
SPH

Introduction

While reading is central to the focus of this book, it is important to recognize that reading is only one of the language arts, which together consist of writing, speaking, and listening, along with reading. Each of these components is grounded in language, and it is language that allows us to think about ideas, topics, events, and so on and to express our thoughts to others. In fact, Stoodt (1988) argues that thinking should be considered the fifth language art since it is so central to each of the language arts.

When we encounter various ideas or topics, we try to organize and make sense of those experiences using knowledge we already have; in this way we learn, or "make meaning." This process of pulling together what we already know and applying it elsewhere is what is usually called *critical thinking.* As knowledge is applied in other settings or contexts, it becomes *transformed knowledge* that is used to understand, solve, define, and judge (Scardamalia & Bereiter, 1986). The language arts are processes that provide a vehicle for teachers to help children become critical thinkers and thus, transform knowledge.

"Language arts instruction" implies that teachers use strategies that make connections among the language arts components as they plan activities for the children in their classrooms, activities whose ultimate aim is to foster critical thinking. Indeed, educators and researchers argue that the language arts are supportive of one another and that children benefit from an integration of reading, writing, listening, and speaking instruction (see, for example, Pinnell, 1988, and Dobson, 1988). In other words, children should frequently be engaged in speaking, listening, writing, and reading activities that involve and promote learning in all the language arts. This approach has a number of advantages over a segmented curriculum that assigns separate times for reading, writing, listening, or speaking instruction. For instance, integrated language arts instruction is sensitive to a real-world context whereas segmented instruction often is not. Teachers committed to an integrated approach frequently make extensive use of literature to create an authentic instructional context that, among other things, allows them to build in children a natural appreciation of different cultures as well as meet the needs of a diverse student population. Examples of school activities that provide opportunities for the integration of the language arts include notetaking (writing with listening or reading); summarizing (reading and writing); oral interpretation using Readers Theatre, plays, or poetry readings (reading, listening, and speaking); and language experience stories (speaking, listening, writing, and reading).

Each language arts component also carries with it an array of skills and concepts for children to master. For example, embedded in writing instruction may be instruction in spelling, usage, mechanics (punctuation and capitalization), and penmanship. Reading instruction might include learning to read and reading literature and subject texts, as well as learning researching and study skills. Speaking and listening instruction might include opportunities for the use of standard oral language patterns, oral interpretation of literature, or critical and accurate listening.

The fortunate children who experience a warm, supportive school environment have many opportunities for language use with an integrated language arts curriculum. They read and listen with understanding and write and speak with purpose. They use the language arts for clarifying, expressing, and gaining new knowledge across the curriculum (Copeland, 1984; Newell, 1984). These children are immersed in language-rich classrooms that allow them to use oral as well as written language while learning the forms and functions of language. Teachers in language-rich classrooms understand that language develops throughout the day, including during recess and at lunch.

Even though reading is the primary emphasis of this book, many strategies and activities that strengthen the connections among the language arts are included in each chapter. Because the relationships among the language arts are so interdependent, it was often difficult to assign strategies and activities to particular chapters; it is important to note, therefore, that the chapter assignments are suggestions only. Since many articles could have been assigned to more than one chapter, we simply made decisions based on the major emphasis of each strategy or activity.

References

Copeland, K.A. (1984). *The effects of writing on good and poor writers: Learning from prose*. Unpublished doctoral dissertation, University of Texas at Austin.

Dobson, L. (1988). *Connections in learning to write and read: A study of children's development through kindergarten and grade one* (Tech. Rep. No. 418). Cambridge, MA: Bolt, Beranek, & Newman. (ED 293 088)

Newell, G. (1984). Learning from writing in two content areas: A case study/protocol analysis. *Research in the Teaching of English, 18*, 165-271.

Pinnell, G.S. (1988). *Success of children at risk in a program that combines writing and reading* (Tech. Rep. No. 417). Cambridge, MA: Bolt, Beranek, & Newman. (ED 252 061)

Scardamalia, M., & Bereiter, C. (1986). Research on written composition. In M. Wittrock (Ed.), *Handbook of research on teaching* (3rd ed., pp. 778-803). New York: Macmillan.

Stoodt, B.D. (1988). *Teaching language arts*. New York: HarperCollins.

Chapter 1

Recognizing Words

Reading—the process of constructing meaning from text—requires interactions among various subprocesses, such as recognizing printed words, determining the meaning of words, dividing sentences into syntactic groups, and creating an overall meaning for the text. The foundation of the reading process is word recognition (Gough, 1984), or the ability to identify words in continuous text quickly, accurately, and effortlessly. The overall goal of reading is comprehension of text, but the ability to recognize words is a prerequisite for achieving this goal.

Phonological awareness has been identified as a strong predictor of children's word-recognition ability and, by extension, reading achievement. Phonological (or phonemic) awareness is a metalinguistic ability that allows children to reflect on and manipulate features of spoken language (Tunmer, Herriman, & Nesdale, 1988) as well as to understand spelling-to-sound correspondences of English words (Ehri, 1987). Stanovich (1986) defines phonological awareness as "conscious access to the phonemic level of the speech stream and some ability to cognitively manipulate representations at this level" (p. 362). In other words, children with a high level of phonological awareness can examine the phonemes that make up words and play with those sounds by segmenting or blending them.

The development of phonological awareness often begins when children become familiar with simple rhymes (Maclean, Bryant, & Bradley, 1987), followed by their recognition of syllable junctures and the understanding that one-syllable words have two parts (Trieman, 1985). (The *onset* is the initial portion of the word—*sh* in *shout*, for example—and the *rime* is the combination of the vowels plus the ending consonants—*out* in *shout*.) Finally, children begin to distinguish phonemes. Word-recognition instruction should build on children's development of phonological awareness. For example, children need to be able to hear separate phonemes to benefit from phonics instruction; if they are to discover word patterns they must be able to hear onsets and rimes. Children's ability to identify mulitsyllabic words in print depends on their awareness that spoken words can be segmented into syllables.

Other considerations also enter into word-recognition instruction. Children often seem to recognize easily words as whole units, and this ability can become the foundation for later letter-sound analysis and decoding. Instruction that starts with identifying known words helps children establish stronger connections among printed words and oral language. In addition, teachers use this "sight-word" instruction to help children quickly pick up words with irregular spelling patterns, high-interest or high-frequency words in a specific text, or words that children don't yet have the ability to decode. Teaching these words in the context in which they appear may help students remember what the words look like; in any case, if the words chosen for instruction are meaningful and useful to children, they will be able to learn to read them more successfully.

Phonics instruction builds on children's phonological awareness and helps them understand the letter-sound correspondence of words they already have in their oral vocabulary. Certainly many common words have irregular sound patterns and need to be taught as sight words, but letter-sound analysis is still a useful word-identification strategy. Usually consonant sounds are taught to children first, with reminders of alphabet letter names to help them learn the sounds. Children who learn to recognize these sounds in different positions in words and in different combinations will also learn the main concepts of orthography. Using phonograms to teach phonics capitalizes on the notion of onsets and rimes as well as letter patterns. That is, if *buck* is an unknown word but the child knows *truck* and the sound made by the letter *b*, he or she can substitute /b/ for /tr/ to sound out the new word.

Children also recognize words by analyzing their morphemic units and letter clusters. This sort of structural analysis is the process children use to identify multisyllabic words, contractions, words with inflections, words with affixes, and compound words. Cunningham (1975) believes that to analyze an unknown multisyllabic word, children search for word parts of the largest manageable unit and compare the chunks to familiar words, phonograms, or letter clusters. It does not appear to be important that children learn rules for dividing words, but the ability to pronounce syllable units rapidly, recognize familiar affixes and roots, and relate an unknown word to known words is necessary for reading multisyllabic words (Shefelbine, 1987).

Finally, skilled word recognition seems to depend on children's ability to use a combination of strategies and to monitor their deductions when reading to be sure that the words they identify make sense in the context of the story. Rereading a text helps improve both word recognition and monitoring skills, as does frequent writing.

This chapter contains strategies and teaching ideas designed to strengthen children's word-identification abilities—

whether through sight-word instruction, phonics instruction, structural analysis, or monitoring.

References

Cunningham, P. (1975). Investigating a synthesized theory of mediated word recognition. *Reading Research Quarterly, 11*, 127-143.

Ehri, L. (1987). Learning to read and spell words. *Journal of Reading Behavior, 19*, 5-31.

Gough, P.B. (1984). Word recognition. In P.D. Pearson (Ed.), *Handbook of reading research* (Vol. 1, pp. 225-253). White Plains, NY: Longman.

Maclean, M., Bryant, P., & Bradley, L. (1987). Rhymes, nursery rhymes, and reading in early childhood. *Merrill Palmer Quarterly, 33*(3), 255-281.

Shefelbine, J. (1987). *Syllabication reading strategies: A model for assessment and instruction.* Paper presented at the National Reading Conference, St. Petersburg, FL.

Stanovich, K.E. (1986). Matthew effects in reading: Some consequences of individual differences in the acquisition of literacy. *Reading Research Quarterly, 21*, 360-406.

Trieman, R. (1985). Onsets and rimes as units of spoken syllables: Evidence from children. *Journal of Experimental Child Psychology, 39*, 161-181.

Tunmer, W.E., Herriman, M.L., & Nesdale, A.R. (1988). Metalinguistic abilities and beginning reading. *Reading Research Quarterly, 23*, 134-158.

Further Reading

Carnine, D.W. (1977). Phonics versus look-say: Transfer to new words. *The Reading Teacher, 30*, 636-640.

Cunningham, P. (1988). When all else fails.... *The Reading Teacher, 41*, 800-805.

Ehri, L.C., & Wilce, L. (1980). Do beginners learn to read words better in sentences or in lists? *Reading Research Quarterly, 15*, 451-476.

Fry, E., & Sakiey, E. (1986). Common words not taught in basal reading series. *The Reading Teacher, 39*, 395-398.

Johnson, D.D., & Baumann, J.F. (1984). Word identification. In P.D. Pearson (Ed.), *Handbook of reading research* (Vol. 1, pp. 583-608). White Plains, NY: Longman.

Just, M.A., & Carpenter, P.A. (1987). *The psychology of reading and language comprehension.* Needham Heights, MA: Allyn & Bacon.

Moon, L., & Scorpio, C.M. (1984). When word recognition is OK—almost! *The Reading Teacher, 37*, 825-827.

Samuels, S.J. (1988). Decoding and automaticity: Helping poor readers become automatic at word recognition. *The Reading Teacher, 41*, 756-761.

Taylor, B.M., & Nosbush, L. (1983). Oral reading for meaning: A technique for improving word identification skills. *The Reading Teacher, 37*, 234-237.

Trachtenburg, P., & Ferruggia, A. (1989). Big Books from little voices: Reaching high-risk beginners. *The Reading Teacher, 42*, 284-289.

White, T.G., Sowell, J., & Yanagihara, A. (1989). Teaching elementary students to use word-part clues. *The Reading Teacher, 42*, 302-309.

Wiesendanger, K.D., & Bader, L.A. (1987). Teaching easily confused words: Timing makes the difference. *The Reading Teacher, 41*, 328-332.

This activity, which I use daily with my first graders, promotes oral communication and increases reading vocabulary—and it's also fun.

Before we begin a reading group, each child collects his or her own set of word cards and uses them to create a sentence to share with the group. All are very attentive during this activity, and they are always interested in hearing one another's sentences. After each child reads a sentence from the cards, he or she requests a new word to add to the collection.

When a child tells me the new word she or he would like to add, I write it in large letters on a small card and then we discuss it. The child may choose any word at all. Once we've talked about the word, the new card is placed with the others in a large envelope the child has decorated. The youngsters may use the cards any time during the day for writing stories, reading to their classmates, or constructing sentences for spelling or handwriting practice.

As the year goes on, the card collections grow—and so do the children's vocabularies. No matter what their words are, the children recognize them by sight each time. It may be that because these words are important to the children, they are easily remembered.

As an undergraduate, I read *Teacher*, Sylvia Ashton-Warner's story of her work with Maori children in New Zealand. From this I borrowed the idea of The Key Vocabulary and adapted it as A Word a Day. Although I use a basal reading series, I feel that the children's daily words give them a bonus by letting them use their own special words and phrases.

A Word a Day

Robin Shumaker
Ligonier, Pennsylvania
November 1988

The *Magic E* game provides an interesting way for small groups of students (such as reading groups) to practice decoding skills. The game is simple to prepare and easy to store.

The materials needed are oaktag paper, a colored pen, and a lunch-size paper bag. Cut from the oaktag 40 rectangles 1" x 3" (or 3 cm x 8 cm). On 20 of these cards write words—such as *kit, pan,* and *shin*—that can be changed into other words with the addition of a final *e*. On 10 cards write words that do not form a new word by adding *e*, such as *ham, stem,* and *slip*. On the remaining 10 cards write *magic e*. Place all the cards in the lunch bag and shake to mix.

To play, each child in turn draws a card from the bag and sounds out the word. If the child is successful, he or she

Bag the Magic E

Marilyn Marston
Wayne, Pennsylvania
January 1989

keeps the card until the game is over. If the player is unable to say the word, it goes back into the bag. When a *magic e* card is drawn it may be added to a previous word card to form a real word or saved to play on future turns. For example, if the word *shin* is drawn on the first turn and a *magic e* on the next, they may be combined to make *shine*. Occasionally a child attempts to attach a *magic e* to a card that will not form a new word, and this gives students practice in discriminating between real and nonsense words.

Play continues until a time limit is reached or until all the cards are used. To score, count each word-*magic e* combination as 5 points and other words as 1 point; unused *magic e* cards do not count. The winner is the high scorer.

The bags may be labeled and decorated and can be folded with the cards inside to store for future use.

Children ask to play again and again. With this activity, success is in the bag!

Spicing Up Vocabulary Study and Review

Judith L. Martin
Waco, Texas
(now San Antonio, Texas)
October 1984

Memory experts recommend attaching some visual image—even a crazy one—to an item you want to remember. If you're making flashcards to teach vocabulary from a story, why not help your students a bit by giving them a shape that suggests the story topic or a symbol from the story without being a dead giveaway of the word? For example, make bone-shaped flashcards for words from a story about a dog. Design fish-shaped flashcards for a story on fishing. Cut out lemon-shaped flashcards for a story like Frank Asch's "Good Lemonade" (from Houghton Mifflin's *Skylights* 2-1 reader, 1981).

Almost every story has a good symbol embedded in it. Using these symbols helps children remember vocabulary and connect written with spoken words. And *you* won't forget which flashcards belong with a particular story.

Where There's a Word, There's a Vowel

Jennie Jennings DeGenaro
Highland Springs, Virginia
December 1987

Children enjoy the discovery method of learning and the "ah ha" feeling they get when they find something out without being told. Here's an activity that teaches students there must be a vowel in every word. Use it with small groups of four to six children.

The materials needed are cardboard, plastic, or wooden letters (all 26). Chalkboard and chalk will be needed later, along with a child's reader.

Place on a table all the letters except the vowels. Ask the children if they can make a word with the letters. When they see 21 letters, they will be certain they'll be able to do so. After a few minutes, they will start to ask for the vowels. This will be the moment of truth when they realize they cannot make a word without a vowel. Place the vowels on the table. When a child makes a word, write it on the board. When the children have made all the words they can, have them pronounce each one.

The next day, write a short sentence on the board. Omit the vowels and draw a straight line where the vowels should be. Ask the students to figure out the sentence and name the vowels that are missing. Let a child go to the board and fill in the spaces with the correct vowels. Sentences such as "The cat is fat" are challenging for students reading at a first grade level; older poor readers may be ready to attempt "George Washington slept here."

To extend the activity to include the auditory channel, attempt to say words such as "cat" or "drum" without pronouncing the vowels. Let the children help figure out that without a vowel, "words" cannot be spoken clearly.

To conclude the activity, have the students copy a page from their reader. Ask them to omit the vowels and draw a line where each vowel should be. They can then exchange papers and fill in the blanks on their partner's sheets. Students can check their own work by consulting the book to determine whether their responses are correct.

To ensure concept mastery, repeat all these steps after a week or so.

Action Phonics

Patricia M. Cunningham
Winston-Salem, North Carolina
November 1987

What to do about phonics is a constant and emotional topic of debate among parents and teachers of young children. On the one hand, we know that children who learn letter-sound relationships early get off to a better start in reading. On the other hand, we know that letter sounds are difficult for young children to learn and that children who have had little experience with books or are immature can be taught the sounds but do not remember them. We need some new approaches.

Action phonics is an alternative teaching strategy that many teachers of young children find both effective and enjoyable. Action phonics is just what its name implies: children learn actions for initial consonant, digraph, and blend relationships.

Imagine that we are in a kindergarten or first grade classroom. The teacher puts on some marching music, and the children march around the room. Rhythm sticks and other instruments can be used if available. After the children have marched, the teacher shows them a large card on which the word *march* is printed. On the other side of the card, a capital and small letter *m* are clearly printed. The children learn that the printed word is the way we write "march" and that the first letter of march is *m*. To help them remember the letter *m* and its sound at the beginning of a word, the children are told that they should march when the letter *m* is shown.

One or two initial consonants can be introduced each week. Before a new consonant is introduced, all the old consonants should be reviewed by having the whole class do the corresponding action when the teacher shows each letter. The teacher should make comments like "Good, you were all jumping because I showed the letter *j* and *j* is our jumping letter."

Another fun review activity is to give each child in the class a card with a letter on it. A child does the action for the letter and then calls on another child to guess what letter she or he has. If the child called on guesses correctly, that child gets to do the next action and call on someone else to guess. Similar to this is "Follow the Letter Leader." One child picks a letter card and does the corresponding action. Everyone else follows the leader in the same action. The leader then picks another card and the game continues. Young children love these games, and teachers can use them to teach phonics while having a physical education class.

Of course, many actions are possible for each letter. It is important to choose an action that is familiar to the children and that they call by the name you are using. Here is a list of action words many teachers have used. The action for *s* is often used to end the game. Children say, "That's not an action at all," but they remember what sound *s* stands for when it begins a word.

b bounce	g gallop
c catch	h hop, hum
d dance	j jump
f fall	k kick

l lick, laugh	t talk
m march	v vacuum
n nod	w walk, wiggle
p paint	y yawn
r run	z zip
s sit	

The digraphs can be taught in the same way. Some teachers like to teach digraphs only after all the consonants have been taught. Others like to teach /sh/ following /s/, /th/ following /t/, etc., so that children learn from the beginning that *h* is a "magician"—a letter that can completely change the sound of the letter preceding it. Here are actions commonly used for the digraphs:

ch cheer
sh shiver, shout
th think
wh whistle (children who can't whistle like to try)

Whether teachers should use actions for the blends depends to a great extent on the children. Some children seem to infer the sound of blends once they know the sounds of the consonants; others have great difficulty distinguishing the *l* blends from the *r* blends and confuse the *s* blends. Many first grade teachers find action phonics a fun way to teach blends if the children have learned the consonants in kindergarten. Teachers of remedial readers in grades two and three report that actions also help these children learn blends. Here are some examples:

br breathe (deeply)	sw swallow, swim
bl blow, blink	sk skate, skip
cr crawl, cry	sl sleep
cl climb	sm smile
dr drive	sp spin
fl fly	st stand
fr frown	tr track
gr grab	tw twist
pl plant	

Teachers who have used action phonics to help children learn the common letter-sound relationships report that children beg to do the activity and appear to learn the actions that go with the letters naturally and effortlessly. Furthermore, teachers report that they can almost see the children's bodies move into action when they try to read or spell a word.

When a child needs help, a teacher can say, "What action do we do for *p*?" This does not isolate the sound and makes more sense to children than the more usual question "What sound does the *p* make?"

One teacher explained the success of action phonics in her classroom simply and directly: "They are always in motion anyway. They cannot sit quietly and listen. They just naturally move some part of their bodies. Now they all move together purposefully."

Seven Strategies for Teaching Context Clues

Joan W. Fuqua
University, Alabama
(now Valdosta, Georgia)
February 1985

Don't assume students know how to apply context clues when attacking unknown words; methods of interpreting these clues should be carefully taught. Context clues can be words, phrases, passages, pictures, or graphs that help readers make correct guesses when dealing with unknown words. The following seven strategies help teach students how to use context clues.

Picture clues. Begin teaching children about picture clues as early as kindergarten. Display large pictures and let the students interpret them, guiding them with your questions. A story can be told to complement the picture. In another activity, purposely miscall items depicted and wait for students to correct the errors. In later elementary grades, ask students to look at illustrations in books and describe what they see. Students will then form mental images to use in predicting story content.

Filling in blanks. Prepare fill-in-the-blank sentences in which the correct choice for the blank is obvious from the rest of the sentence. For example:

- The fire is very _____ [cold, wet, hot].
- Joan has put on her socks and _____ [shoes, glove, scarf].

In this last sentence, all the answers could be correct, but you would point out that socks with shoes go more often than with gloves or a scarf.

Listening. Rhymes provide a good way to begin teaching how to pick up context clues by listening. Start with a two-line rhyme such as "John caught the high ball because he is... [tall]." This prepares students to listen to a short story and supply omitted words. Read a story once through and then reread, omitting words and phrases for students to provide. The books *Awful Alexander* by Judith Choate and *One Fine Day* by Nonny Hogrogian contain excellent stories with words and phrases that are repeated often.

12

Game playing. Prepare a game by cutting pictures and corresponding text apart, mounting them individually on sturdy paper, and laminating them. Students then match the picture with the correct text. You can also have students construct sentences from word cards. Cut old chart stories into words and phrases, and let students reconstruct the story. (Teachers in the upper grades should use more advanced word lists.) To vary the activity, students can work in small groups to form sentences and stories.

Expanded reading. Expanded reading activities introduce unfamiliar vocabulary before reading begins. After introducing a story theme, ask students to anticipate what words might be in the story. A picture of a construction site might suggest words such as *building, construct,* and *foundation.* After developing a word list with the students, write sentences giving special emphasis to the words on the list. To set off these new words, underline them, place them in quotation marks, or write them in colored chalk.

Cloze procedure. The cloze procedure checks both content knowledge and syntax skills. To construct a cloze exercise, use a passage of about 100 words. Leave the first sentence intact, and delete every *n*th word (most delete every fifth word). Students must supply the missing word or a synonym for it.

Teaching idioms. Make a list of familiar sayings such as "piece of cake" and "green thumb" and teach their meanings. To clarify what the idioms mean, have students illustrate them.

As students learn how to use context clues, they acquire another aid to determine word meanings, which leads to greater reading fluency.

Children with severely limited sight vocabularies can rarely read more than the first two preprimers of basal reader series. If they must repeat grades, they often end up reading the same books year after year. A first step toward building such students' sight vocabularies is to assess their knowledge of high-frequency words. Beginning with a preprimer list, I determine which words the children know at that and at each successive level. Then we work on the words that most of the students do not know.

I feel that these students are most interested in reading about things close to home, so I find logos used by local businesses and attach them to cards. I use these cards to help pro-

Use Commercial Logos to Teach Basic Sight Words

Leslie Anne Perry
*Oxford, Mississippi (now Boone, North Carolina)
October 1984*

vide a context to teach related words. The children usually recognize the logos immediately, so they are not burdened with having to learn "extra" words.

Besides using the logos, I use the children's names to create sentences such as "Tracy went to McDonald's" and "Ronnie got three blue hats at TG&Y." Children are particularly motivated to participate when sentences and stories contain their names.

When students master a target word (as indicated by their ability to identify quickly and accurately a word from a word card on three separate occasions), I let them place the word in their word banks. In addition, I duplicate each story or list of sentences that they read so they can put copies in their individual notebooks for later reading. As they accumulate more and more words and stories that they can read, the students experience a (for them) rare sense of accomplishment.

By using something already familiar to the children (logos and their own names), I find they are able to learn a large number of basic sight words. As a result, these students actually begin to enjoy reading.

Practicing High-Frequency Words with Rebus Stories

Mary W. Olson
San Marcos, Texas
(now Greensboro, North Carolina)
April 1985

Reading teachers should take advantage of the high degree of motivation and variation associated with art activities. Giving children time to draw not only encourages them to exercise their artistic and creative abilities, it can liven up their reading and language arts practice.

Using rebus stories provides beginning readers with practice in reading high-frequency words as well as with opportunities to determine and illustrate the content words in a story.

1. Create a rebus story using words from a high-frequency word list, but don't draw the pictures (which usually represent the nouns in the story).

2. Type the story, triple spacing between lines so that ample space remains for the rebus pictures.

3. Have the children create the stories by drawing whatever they choose in the blank spaces.

4. Have each child read his/her story to a classmate.

5. Compile a book of the children's rebus stories for the class library.

This activity allows children to work with function words and discover how these words support and frame the

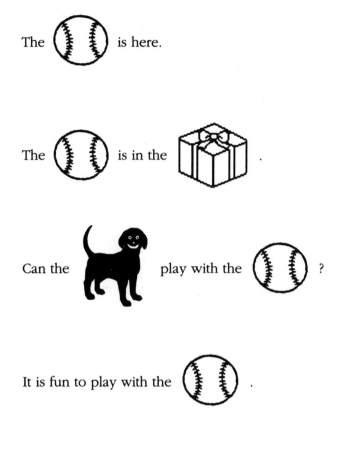

The ⚾ is here.

The ⚾ is in the 🎁 .

Can the 🐕 play with the ⚾ ?

It is fun to play with the ⚾ .

---

ideas and concepts language users wish to convey. It also provides practice reading the high-frequency words beginning readers must master.

Many children have trouble memorizing sight words at the beginning of formal reading instruction, so learning to read can be very slow and sometimes frustrating for them. Sticker books can be a successful addition to reading instruction for all beginning readers, especially those who need a lot of sight-word practice and extra motivation.

Sticker books use a predictable language pattern along with picture clues from stickers (these can be donated at the

Sticker-Book Sight Words

Patsy G. Higdon
Arden, North Carolina
December 1987

beginning of the year by parents). Each book consists of about eight pages with a sticker on each page and a sentence written about the sticker.

The books follow a specific theme and use sight words selected by the teacher. A typical book entitled *Fruit* may read: "I can smell a banana. I can smell an apple. I can smell a pineapple. I can smell a peach. I can smell a grape." A sticker of each type of fruit would appear on the appropriate page; smelly stickers add an extra sensory experience. Other sentence patterns that can be used to teach sight words include these:

- This is _____.
- I see a _____.
- This is number _____.
- I like to eat _____.

Sticker books are excellent for individual tutoring with students who are having trouble understanding how to use context clues. The text can be written in advance and the stickers left on a table in front of the student. The student can read the predictable sentence, stopping at the unknown word. By using the picture clue from the stickers along with knowledge of letter sounds and the theme of the book, the student should be able to figure out the word and which sticker belongs with it.

These special teacher- or student-made books can help teach concepts as well as sight words. Other titles I have used include *Shapes, Money, Toys, Food, Numbers, Insects, Dinosaurs, Flowers, Holidays,* and *Colors*.

Children have instant whole-book reading success with sticker books. They feel very confident reading them with minimum instruction. The potential for these books is limited only by what kind of stickers you can find.

Big Books: Resource Centers for Skills and Activities

Sylvia Zdaniak
Montreal, Quebec
March 1984

Big Books—oversize versions of popular stories or poems—that are made and illustrated by teachers and children are a marvelous tool for teaching beginning readers or remedial students in grades two to four. Each Big Book can also become a resource kit with activities for independent learning and group practice.

First, list key words from the story on the last page, facing the back cover. Ten words are adequate for beginning readers. Second, fit the inside of the back cover with pockets to hold a variety of games and activities for that story. Mark each pocket with a symbol or color code. Mark the pocket's contents with the same symbol or color. Write simple directions on the pockets, geared to the children's reading levels.

Here are some general hints:

- Set aside a large area for using the Big Books.
- Make specific rules for their use (how many children at a time may use the book; activity cards must be replaced in their pockets; etc.).
- Laminate the activity cards for durability.
- Make activities self-correcting by putting answers on the back of the cards, including an answer key in the pocket, or giving an answer key to children when they complete an activity.
- Put checklists (children's names and the activities) on the back of the word list or the inside back cover (see Figure).
- Encourage children to create their own Big Books; keep materials available.

Sample Checklist for Two Grades

| | | | | Activities | | | | |
The Very Hungry Caterpillar	1	2	3	4	5	6	7	8
Grade one	x		x	x	x	x		
Sue								
John								
Lee								
Grade three		x			x		x	x
May								
Nina								
Paul								

Children do the activities designated for their grade level, as shown by the *x*.

Here are eight activities based on the theme and vocabulary of *The Very Hungry Caterpillar* by Eric Carle, which uses two predictable sequences (the days of the week and numbers). In each activity, "Instructions" refers to the instructions written on pockets in *The Very Hungry Caterpillar* Big Book.

Word Matching (K-2)

Materials. Big Book with several copies of a word list; the same words printed on cards. (Words to be included are *egg, caterpillar, hungry, one, two, three, four, five, Sunday, Monday, Tuesday, Wednesday, Thursday, Friday,* and *Saturday.*)

Instructions. "Match the word on each card to the words on the word list."

Procedure. The children match word cards to the word list. The words may then be read to another student or to the teacher.

Alphabetizing (grades 2-4)

Materials. Word cards (as in previous activity).

Instructions. "Put these word cards in alphabetical order."

Procedure. The children put the cards in alphabetical order. The teacher or a peer can check them.

Tracing and Copying Words (K-2)

Materials. Plastic-covered word cards; washable felt marker or grease pencil; lined paper; children's personal word banks; pencils.

Instructions. "Trace the words on the cards; copy the words into your word bank."

Procedure. Children trace the words on the cards (laminated cards can be washed or rubbed clean) or copy them on paper.

Match Pictures to Words (K-2)

Materials. Pictures to illustrate words; Big Book with word list.

Instructions. "Match these pictures to the words on the word list."

Procedure. The children match picture cards to the words on the word list.

Sequencing and Retelling the Story (K-4)

Materials. Picture cards as in previous activity; an additional card depicting what was eaten on Saturday; tape recorder (optional).

Instructions. "Put these picture cards in order to help you tell the story. Tell the story to a friend using these pictures."

Procedure. Children put the picture cards into correct sequence and retell the story to the teacher, another student, or onto a tape.

Drawing (K-2)

Materials. Word cards from first activity, excluding *hungry* and the days of the week; felt markers, crayons, or colored pencils; drawing paper or small scrapbooks (made by the teacher).

Instructions. "Print the words on the word cards in your scrapbook. Draw pictures to show what the words mean."

Procedure. Children draw pictures of what is on each word card.

Sentence Building (grades 2-4)

Materials. Sentences from the text, each printed on different colored paper or in different colored ink, cut into individual words and placed in an envelope of matching color.

Instructions. "Each envelope has words that will make a sentence when they are put in the right order. Make sentences and check them by looking in the Big Book."

Procedure. Children put the words together to form sentences.

Fluency and Reinforcement (grades 2-4)

Materials. Any version of the book; tape recording of story; tape recorder.

Instructions. "Listen to the story on the tape. Follow the story in the book. Read along with the tape."

Procedure. Children listen to the story while following the print in the text.

Don Holdaway's *The Foundations of Literacy* (Ashton Scholastic, 1979) describes more ideas for using Big Books to foster the natural development of reading skills.

Advertising Adds Interest

Sheila K. Berenson-Hartshorne
Wichita, Kansas
March 1985

Some national advertising—which children find interesting, absorbing, and clever—can be used by classroom teachers as a tool for teaching word recognition, vocabulary, grammar, and comprehension, as well as consumer savvy, poetry, and creative writing. Since students are familiar with many ads, you can use them to develop a language experience program without much extra effort.

Word recognition. Youngsters who cannot read can recognize Smurfs and Care Bears and remember slogans. Capitalize on such familiarity by having individual students hold large cards with portions of well-known slogans. Have students arrange themselves in correct order so the class can recite the slogan and then scramble themselves so the class can try out a new mix of words. Individualize the activity using index cards to make different sets of slogan cards. Create an activity corner with children supplying new slogans daily.

Once the words in a jingle or slogan are learned, substitute new vocabulary words. "The incredible, edible egg" can become "the impossible, detestable egg," and finally "the delectable, desirable carrot." The more absurd the substitutions, the more students get to practice decoding skills.

Letter mazes are easily adapted to a reading activity. Write an ad jingle along a path in a maze; students must read the jingle, following the words to the finish. Incorrect words placed at strategic turns force readers to attend to the reading tasks.

Repeated exposure to words reinforces word recognition. Use this recognition to stress word attack skills in fill-in-the-blank activities, like "Coke is ____ [at, it, ate]." Students then support their answer using rules of language and reasoning.

Vocabulary and grammar. The language used in advertisements does not always adhere to grammar rules; therefore, ads may be used as a springboard to further vocabulary and grammar lessons. Have older students search a chapter in the grammar book to prove why the wording is incorrect.

For a vocabulary activity, underline key words in a slogan. Have students find the exact meaning of the underlined words and also an antonym and synonym for each. Words chosen may be as elementary as "Doing what we do *best*," or as complex as "Keeping our *communications* the best in the world." In this activity, the dictionary becomes a friend rather than a foe.

Reading comprehension. Familiar commercial tunes and slogans convey a message, but exactly what is that message? What does the advertiser want consumers to infer from a slogan like "We will sell no wine before its time"? Students practice inference skills when they analyze the many different meanings in advertising slogans. They can study metaphors used, persuasion techniques employed, and ideas espoused.

Consumer education. Make your students aware of the purpose of advertising. Teach kindergartners that the commercials on Saturday morning are trying to sell something, and that maybe they don't really need what is being sold. Older children can examine the total game plan of advertisers, looking at the persuasion techniques with a critical perspective.

Poetry and creative writing. Well-known advertisements can be used as topics for creative writing. Introduce rhyme and meter by referring to a popular jingle. If you choose a jingle for a fast-food chain, for example, you can have students write about food or invent their own fast-food jingle. For creative writing have the class design a fast-food restaurant and write an essay using their ideas.

Adding familiar advertising to a reading program may lead to more interest and liveliness among your students, and you will all enjoy the flexibility and break from routine in the lessons.

"Gee, reading is really fun!" exclaimed Joe, age five, as he proudly reviewed the story he had just reconstructed. He had organized (arranged words logically) and read a language experience WRAM (writing, reading, and manipulating) chart story written by his reading group.

In my kindergarten classroom, the WRAM language experience chart integrates reading readiness skills with the writing process through a kinesthetic approach.

A WRAM chart consists of a sheet of oaktag paper 24" x 36" (60 cm x 90 cm) with a brief story or event (usually four or five sentences) that the students have dictated and illustrated. The bottom 5" of the chart are folded up and stapled on each side to form a pocket for storing word cards. The top of the chart is attached to a coat hanger by folding over and stapling. The chart can then be hung along with previously constructed WRAM charts so it is always available for reinforcement and review activities.

This is the procedure for developing and using a WRAM chart.

Day 1. The children in a reading group dictate a brief story which I print directly on a WRAM chart. (Inspiration can come from a current social studies or science unit, word banks, the season, a visitor, etc.) The authors then sign their names on the pocket at the bottom of the chart. Later a student illustrates the story at the top.

Before the group meets again, I code the WRAM chart. For example, I would mark the "Brown Rabbits" story with a large brown "5" on the bottom of the chart, indicating that this is the fifth chart story written by the group. I also mark individual word cards for the story, coding each card along with the chart. This enables students to pocket the cards correctly if more than one chart is being used.

Day 2. Now we discuss and reread the chart story. Word cards are divided among the children and the story is reconstructed using a pocket chart (hung from the chalkboard

WRAM—Writing, Reading, and Manipulating

Rosalyn Layton
Babson Park, Florida
December 1988

next to the WRAM chart). Various manipulation activities may follow:

- Have students highlight selected words with highlighter pens.
- Have students match the word card to the word in the story.
- Remove a word from the story and then have children read the story silently and identify the missing word.
- Introduce the "find and point" game—children use a yardstick to point to naming words, words beginning with a certain letter or with a capital letter, rhyming words, etc.

Day 3. Today we briefly review the WRAM chart. Then I give each student a copy of the story to illustrate and take home. One extra copy is illustrated as a class book, to be reread and enjoyed at leisure. (Photograph albums with single plastic pages are perfect for creating these books, since stories may be inserted as they are written. Students say these feel like "real books.") This class book is always available at the reading or writing center.

Subsequent days. The WRAM chart is placed in the reading center. To use it, children usually place the chart on the floor and then reconstruct the story to the right of the chart. Alone or with their "study buddy," students read the story aloud to an older student, a volunteer, or me.

When the WRAM storage rod becomes crowded with charts, I send several home with lucky students to be shared, reread, and reconstructed for family and friends.

It's no wonder Joe thought reading was really fun! It was fun because he had helped write the story, and it had his name on it as an author. Also, it was easy to use—after all, he had reread it, manipulated it, and organized the word cards into an order that made sense. Finally, it was fun because he could share his reading and composition skills with his family and friends.

First-Year Group Diary

Carla Fox
Salem, Connecticut
November 1988

I have found that a daily class diary helps accomplish my goals of encouraging awareness of the nature and purpose of print and strengthening the reading-writing connection with my first graders. Each year I fashion the diary like a commercially prepared Big Book, using large sheets of oaktag paper (for durability) and notebook rings, so we can add pages as needed. The class titles the book something like *All about Us* and adds class photographs on the cover.

During the first month of school, we begin a routine that is faithfully continued each school day. The last moments of the day are spent sitting as a group, reviewing the day's events. After the date is written in the diary, we have a "moment of thinking." Then we discuss favorite and maybe not-so-favorite activities that occurred during the day. One child is called on to summarize an event he or she would like to have recorded in the book. As it is spoken, I write the child's idea in the diary. Depending on time and need, the sentence can be a springboard for a brief language lesson.

As the year progresses the children become adept at using the diary format to express their thoughts and ideas. The group writing activity often leads to an independent writing activity in which children write in their own "weekly diaries."

This activity has many benefits. It helps the children discover that what they say can be written and that what is written can be read. Creative expression is encouraged. Emphasis is placed on sharing and consideration of others' thoughts and feelings. The diary provides a vehicle for class communication. It helps each child evaluate the day's activities and provides closure to the school day. The class has many answers when Mom and Dad ask, "What did you do in school today?"

Occasionally, we read the book and reminisce about what happened way back when. At the end of the school year, I present each child with a small-size copy of our classroom daily diary. The book is a convenient way to remember the "greatest hits" of the school year. The daily diary is also a great conversation starter at open houses and during parent-teacher conferences.

Chapter 2

Reading Orally, Reading Fluently

Although reading fluency was once considered to be simply smooth and expressive oral reading, it has now been further defined to include accurate and fast word recognition (Samuels, 1979). This more complete definition is compatible with the theory of automaticity (LaBerge & Samuels, 1974), which argues that automatic decoding of words removes the need for readers to direct attention to decoding and allows them to focus on understanding the text and thus engage higher order comprehension skills. Samuels urges instruction that gives children opportunities to reread short passages until they achieve a satisfactory degree of fluency. He argues that with each rereading the number of errors decreases as the rate increases, and that gradually children will require fewer rereadings of new passages before reaching fluency and—according to automaticity theory—comprehension.

Carver and Hoffman (1981), Dowhower (1987), Gonzales and Elijah (1975), and Rasinski (1989) all agree that repeated reading can improve reading fluency, increase comprehension, and facilitate reading with meaningful phrasing. Variations of repeated reading include using predictable books, choral reading, paired reading, and echo reading. Listening to teachers read aloud provides a model of fluent reading for children. Listening to taped readings and then practicing reading the same passage orally is also helpful to poor readers (Laffey & Kelly, 1981).

Reading fluency is also seen as "smoothness in constructing meaning from text using all aspects of the reading process, not just those relating to words" (Duffy & Roehler, 1989, p. 120). In other words, fluent readers combine word-recognition strategies, topical knowledge, comprehension strategies, and metacognitive strategies to understand the text as well as to recognize and repair comprehension difficulties. Fluency is also linked to the meaningfulness a text holds for particular readers. An important note is that readers seem to read with much more success in terms of oral reading errors and comprehension when texts are interesting and meaningful to them.

Oral reading practice may contribute to reading fluency; by the same token, reading fluency probably contributes to expressive oral reading. Oral reading must be used carefully, however, if it is to benefit students. Certainly, mindless round-robin reading practice is not recommended. However, oral reading provides a way of evaluating students' reading ability. Teachers can consider speed and accuracy of word recognition and comprehension as suggested by children's pronunciation, use of expression, phrasing, pauses, and intonation. When evaluation is the purpose, students reading orally should have privacy with the teacher, not an audience of peers. Oral reading also has purposes other than evaluation. Students can read aloud to share a funny or exciting part of a text; if the teacher wants to highlight expressive language, poetry can be read aloud; or if oral interpretation of a text is the emphasis, oral reading of plays, poems, or dialogue will help students improve the rhythm, intonation, and phrasing of their delivery of text. It is important to remember that oral reading of new text without practice requires readers to attend to performance rather than meaning. If the focus is on meaning, students might read aloud only those parts of the text that pertain to the question under discussion.

All the activities in this chapter are grounded in current notions of reading fluency and the benefits of oral reading. As always, however, teachers will want to choose carefully among them, taking into account needs, available materials, and classroom circumstances.

References

Carver, R.P., & Hoffman, J.V. (1981). The effect of practice through repeated reading on gain in reading ability using a computer-based instructional system. *Reading Research Quarterly, 16,* 374-390.

Dowhower, S.L. (1987). Effects of repeated reading on second grade transitional readers' fluency and comprehension. *Reading Research Quarterly, 22,* 389-406.

Duffy, G.G., & Roehler, L.R. (1989). *Improving classroom reading instruction* (2nd ed.). New York: Random House.

Gonzales, P.C., & Elijah, D.V. (1975). Rereading: Effect on error patterns and performance levels on the IRI. *The Reading Teacher, 28,* 647-652.

LaBerge, D., & Samuels, S.J. (1974). Toward a theory of automatic information processing in reading. *Cognitive Psychology, 6,* 293-323.

Laffey, J.L., & Kelly, D. (1981). Repeated reading of taped literature: Does it make a difference? In G.H. McNinch (Ed.), *Comprehension process and product: First Yearbook of the American Reading Forum* (pp. 80-82). Athens, GA: American Reading Forum.

Rasinski, T.V. (1989). Fluency for everyone: Incorporating fluency instruction in the classroom. *The Reading Teacher, 42,* 690-693.

Samuels, S.J. (1979). The method of repeated readings. *The Reading Teacher, 32,* 403-408.

Further Reading

Allington, R.L. (1977). If they don't read much, how they ever gonna get good? *Journal of Reading, 21*, 57-61.

Allington, R.L. (1983). Fluency: The neglected reading goal. *The Reading Teacher, 36*, 556-561.

Allington, R.L. (1984). Oral reading. In P.D. Pearson (Ed.), *Handbook of reading research* (Vol. 1, pp. 829-864). White Plains, NY: Longman.

Chomsky, C. (1976). After decoding, what? *Language Arts, 53*, 374-390.

Dowhower, S.L. (1989). Repeated reading: Research into practice. *The Reading Teacher, 42*, 502-507.

Lobbo, L.D., & Teale, W.H. (1990). Cross-age reading: A strategy for helping poor readers. *The Reading Teacher, 43*, 362-369.

Miccinati, J.L. (1985). Using prosodic cues to teach oral reading fluency. *The Reading Teacher, 39*, 206-213.

Wood, K.D. (1983). A variation on an old theme: 4-way oral reading. *The Reading Teacher, 37*, 38-43.

Using Multipaired Simultaneous Oral Reading

Virginia L. Poe
Lafayette, Louisiana
November 1986

In elementary school it is fairly common for students to work in pairs, and occasionally one student may read orally to his or her partner. Applying this procedure simultaneously with all the pairs in a reading group does not seem to be prevalent. However, this technique should be considered when classroom teachers are struggling to find time to develop the oral reading skills of upper-elementary children.

I observed a class using multipaired simultaneous oral reading in an elementary school in Scott, Louisiana. A fourth grade language arts class was divided into two relatively homogeneous reading groups. While one group completed individual assignments, the 14 children in the other group simultaneously read a story from their basal reader to their partners. There were never more than seven individuals reading orally at one time. The teacher monitored the pairs and assisted as needed. Before the oral reading, each child had completed a vocabulary study and had read the entire story silently.

Although the classroom was noisy when the process began, as each pair completed the oral reading and started the comprehension-check worksheets, the classroom gradually got quiet. None of the children—including those working on individual assignments—appeared to be disturbed by temporarily heightened classroom noise. The benefits of providing time for oral reading and fostering children's ability to concentrate under less than ideal conditions seemed to outweigh the minor disruption of several voices talking at once.

These fourth grade children appeared to take their tasks seriously and to enjoy assuming some responsibility for their own learning. It was apparent that because these children read in pairs, they did not experience the emotional stress often associated with reading aloud before an entire group. Other indications of this technique's success were the large number of children who participated in the subsequent class discussions, the high quality of that participation, and the good scores on the comprehension-check worksheets.

Steps for using multipaired simultaneous oral reading, as developed from this observation and conversation with other teachers, follow.

1. Have children choose different partners each time so that no one becomes dependent on one particular peer. If a pair does not work well, ask the children to change partners.

2. Let the pairs set their own rules as to how much each child will read—one page, one paragraph, two paragraphs, two pages, or whatever—before switching over to the second reader.

3. Allow children to read the story to their partners at their own speed.

4. Monitor constantly and suggest tactics such as alternating the reading more frequently if one child is a more halting reader than the other.

5. When a pair finishes oral reading, give each child a comprehension worksheet (provided with the basal reader series or teacher-made) to complete individually.

6. After everyone has completed the paired oral reading and the comprehension worksheet, lead a group discussion of the story.

Multipaired simultaneous oral reading can help upper-elementary teachers find oral reading time for their students daily, biweekly, or triweekly, depending on group need. This activity can provide an enjoyable way for children to gain experience in reading for an audience without the added strain of reading before a large group. This process will also allow time for oral practice of newly learned vocabulary words and for assessing comprehension.

Repeated Readings— Naturally

Timothy V. Rasinski
Katherine Rasinski
Athens, Georgia (now Kent, Ohio)
November 1986

Repeated reading is a practice technique that allows readers to become fluent. The theory behind the method is straightforward: practice in reading targeted passages will lead to generalized gains in fluency and comprehension.

One variant of repeated reading is used successfully in many schools and homes. It maintains the technique's behavioristic basis (practicing a skill until it becomes automatic) and at the same time nurtures equally important but more subtle ideals. Children love stories, and they love to be read to, often asking that a book be read over and over again. This is repeated reading—naturally.

For example, four-year-old Emily insists on being read to each day. Often she asks to hear her favorite book several times a day. The format of her current favorite is predictable. At first she read along with the adult who was reading to her. After several readings she could read more and more of it by herself. Because of the repeated exposure, she can now read the book with expression. She pauses at the correct points and, with appropriate emphasis, embeds anger or love or amusement in her voice at just the right places. She reads it every day.

Michael, a first grader who took 8 weeks at school to read the 72 pages and 32 words of the basal reader chosen for him by someone else, reads and rereads his own books at home with much greater facility. Every night before bed he insists on reading the book he has chosen from the library; many of his library choices are at a higher level than one would expect from a first grader so early in the year. His first attempts are often halting and stilted, yet after a few days of listening to the book and reading it himself, he can read it fluently, with confidence, expression, and joy. His quest to learn more about a topic and his love of stories empower him to overcome difficulties in word identification.

Several schools have opted for this natural approach to repeated readings. In one first grade classroom the teacher reads to the children not once, but several times a day. Although many types of stories are included, children often ask to hear their favorites repeatedly. Books the teacher has read aloud, as well as others, are placed conveniently around the room. The children take these books and try to read them alone or with a group of friends, or ask the teacher, aide, or an older student to read the book to them.

The children often write and publish their own books, using favorite books as models. Their new books are then the objects of more repeated readings. At other times the children act out books they have read over and over, using the text as a script and a guide.

The teacher regularly involves the students in shared composition and reading. Students write short poems or chant a poem that has been written on chart paper. Throughout the week they return to the charts, chant the rhyme to themselves, and move on to other activities. Group activities are often initiated with a choral chant of the week's poems.

All of these activities are repeated readings. However, unlike many behavioristic applications, they employ a different set of priorities. Natural repeated reading uses whole stories. It is guided by the students' own interests and purposes, their need for socialization and audience, and their intense desire to read. The repeated readings take a variety of forms and occur in a variety of contexts. However, the basic understanding that defines and underlies the method—namely that repeated reading leads to fluent, automatic, and attention-free reading—remains. Indeed, the variety of form and context and the control given to the students add to the power of repeated reading.

The Reading Pals Program

Daniel J. Shoreman
Wakefield, Massachusetts
December 1986

One of the highlights of the reading year at our school is the "Reading Pals" program. First grade students are paired with fifth grade students as Reading Pals for one period each week. During this period the partners read a primary-level storybook together.

The process begins with a fifth grade session during which the goals of the program are discussed. These goals are to help the first graders enjoy reading and to improve their reading skills. Students are then asked to brainstorm ideas on how to accomplish these goals. With the results of this discussion in mind, fifth graders are presented with the following procedure for the Reading Pals sessions.

Planning the Lesson

1. Choose a primary-level storybook and have it approved by your teacher.
2. Read the book from cover to cover.
3. Select 6 to 12 vocabulary words that you think may be difficult for a first grader to read or understand.
4. Prepare a flashcard for each word. Print the word neatly on the front. On the back, use the word in a good sentence.
5. Write six comprehension questions. At least one question must ask *why?*
6. Show the book, flashcards, and questions to your teacher for suggestions.

Teaching the Lesson

1. Show the book to your first grade Reading Pal. Read the title and look at the illustrations. Ask your students to predict what the story will be about.
2. Present each flashcard. Read the word first. Then use the sentence to help your Reading Pal discover the word's meaning.
3. Take turns reading the book orally. Enjoy the illustrations as you read.
4. Discuss the comprehension questions. Encourage your Reading Pal to look back in the story to find the answers.
5. Present the reader with a certificate as a reward for a job well done.
6. Offer the book to your Reading Pal to take home until next week's lesson.

The benefits of this program are many. The fifth graders not only serve as positive reading role models, but they also gain positive feelings about reading themselves. Even fifth graders reading below grade level are able to participate in this program and are thereby placed in a reading leadership position. As "teachers," they have the opportunity to succeed in an area that is often frustrating for them. The first graders are motivated to read for enjoyment in a structured setting. Their Reading Pals set an example of reading as an important and enjoyable experience. The certificate presented at the lesson's end concludes the experience with a tangible reward to share with parents and friends. Many specific reading skills—such as decoding, vocabulary, and comprehension—are reinforced for both age groups. In addition, the students are placed in a situation where an awareness of the reading process can be nurtured and internalized.

Some Tips for Using Big Books

Dorothy S. Strickland
New York, New York (now New Brunswick, New Jersey)
May 1988

The use of enlarged texts for shared reading activities has become increasingly popular among teachers of young children. Largely inspired by the work of Don Holdaway, many teachers are using these Big Books to help children develop concepts about print and understandings about the reading process.

Although most teachers are aware that children enjoy and benefit from experiences with Big Books, many are unaware of the potential range of these experiences or fail to see how these activities tie into their curriculum objectives. The chart on the next two pages describes the wide range of reading concepts that may be explored with Big Books. The activities are organized for best use before, during, or after the reading; some should be used only after repeated readings. Each is tied to an objective commonly found in curriculum guides for reading instruction.

Activities to Be Used with Big Books

What the Teacher Does	What the Child Does	Objective
Before Reading		
Stimulates discussion about relevant content and concepts in text.	Talks and listens to others talk about relevant content and concepts.	To focus listening and speaking on vocabulary and ideas about to be met in print; to activate background knowledge related to text.
Reads aloud title and author; uses words *title* and *author* and briefly explains what they mean.	Notes what the words on the book cover represent.	To build vocabulary and understanding of the concepts *title, author, authorship*.
Asks children what they think the story might be about based on title and cover, or thinks aloud about what the story might be about.	Uses clues from title and cover together with background knowledge to formulate predictions about the story, or observes teacher model the above.	To use clues from text and background knowledge to draw inferences and formulate predictions.
Shows pleasure and interest in anticipation of reading.	Observes as teacher models interest in and eagerness about reading.	To build positive attitudes toward books and reading.
During Reading (teacher reads aloud)		
Gives lively reading; displays interest and delight in language and storyline.	Observes teacher evoke meaningful language from print.	To understand that print carries meaning.
Tracks print with hand or pointer.	Follows movement of hand or pointer.	To match speech to print; to indicate directionality of print.
Thinks aloud about her/his understanding of certain aspects of the story (self-query, making predictions, drawing conclusions, etc.).	Observes as teacher monitors her/his own understanding.	To develop an understanding of the reading process as thinking with text.
Hesitates at predictable parts in the text; allows children to fill in words or phrases.	Fills in likely words at pauses.	To use semantic and syntactic clues to determine what makes sense.
At appropriate parts in a story, queries children about what might happen next.	Makes predictions about what might happen next in the story.	To use storyline to predict possible events and outcomes.

What the Teacher Does	What the Child Does	Objective
After Reading		
Guides discussion about key ideas in the text; helps children relate key concepts.	Participates in discussion of important ideas in the text.	To reflect on the reading; to apply and personalize key ideas in a text.
Asks children to recall important or favorite parts; finds corresponding part of the text (perhaps with help of children) and rereads.	Recalls and describes specific events and parts of text.	To use print to support and confirm discussion.
Guides group rereading of all or specific parts of text for reinforcement.	Joins in the reading at parts where he or she feels confident.	To develop fluency and confidence through group reading.
Uses cloze activities to involve children in meaningful prediction of words; gives praise for all contextually plausible offerings; discusses responses with children.	Fills in appropriate words for a given slot.	To use semantic and syntactic clues to determine what words fit in a slot and why.
After Repeated Readings		
Focuses children's attention on distinctive features and patterns in the text (repeated words, repeated letters and consonant clusters, punctuation marks, etc.); uses letter names and correct terminology to discuss these features; extends discussion to developmentally appropriate level.	Notes distinctive features and patterns pointed out by teacher and attempts to find others on her/his own.	To analyze a known text for distinctive features and patterns; to develop an understanding of the elements of decoding within a meaningful context.
Makes books and charts available for independent reading.	Selects books and charts for independent reading and reads them at own pace.	To increase confidence and understanding of the reading process by practicing it independently.

Big Books and Recorded Books: A Great Combination

Betty J. Erickson
Woodbridge, Virginia
December 1988

I am a reading teacher working in a pull-out program with small groups of first, second, and third graders who are considered to be at risk in reading. I'm a mature teacher (a gentle way of saying I'm old) but I keep up with reading research and continue to take classes to keep me up to date. Some of the "new" ideas and trends come across as déjà vu, but when you rethink them in light of a career full of experiences, exciting things can happen.

I am particularly delighted with the quality of the new Big Books that have become a daily and vital part of our whole language program. Children's responses to these books are exciting. Third graders are as eager as younger children to read along with the Big Books. The content of these books is child-centered, the vocabulary unstilted and freshly appealing. Readers get caught up in the rhyme and cadence. Children readily focus on the large print and colorful pictures as they learn story grammar and broaden their understanding of language and context.

To go along with Big Books, I make additional materials to help children become more involved in reading by using various senses. These multisensory materials include electric boards, puzzles, and vocabulary games.

I also make recorded books. I start by selecting some really good stories that I know children enjoy—stories that are above my students' reading level. I type these stories in appropriate-sized print, carefully chunking the phrases to make the print easier to follow. Then I record the story slowly, reading clearly and with careful phrasing.

One of the first things to remember with this method is to select literature that you truly like. It must grab the children's attention while providing a challenge. Language development is crucial for children who have difficulty in learning to read, so give them real literature rather than stories with watered-down, "controlled" vocabulary.

Initially, read the entire story to the children and then give them a recorded passage to listen to as they reread the text. After they read the passage three times, they should read it to a peer. Children enjoy this procedure for the first week or two. After two weeks, some children may begin to resist. After the first reading, pairs of eyes may come away from the print and scan the room. When this happens in my classroom, I search for ways to keep excitement alive. For example, rather than record the passage once and have the child at the controls rewind the tape so that it can be heard three times, I make three recordings on the tape to eliminate the necessity of rewinding. (Every time the tape stops, concentration is lost.) Although the first reading has to be done very slowly and

34

deliberately and with the best inflection possible at that slow pace, the second can move a bit more rapidly. The third reading should move at "normal" rate for reading a story. Readings at varying rates help to hold the children's interest. Children may read aloud with the tape without disturbing anyone if they wear headsets.

I also vary the way the recorded readings are used. Sometimes children listen to part of the story in a "live" oral reading, then continue on a tape to find out what will happen next. Sometimes they begin with the recorded reading, write or discuss their predictions, and continue with the recorded reading the next day. Sometimes they illustrate the stories before they see the illustrator's pictures, then compare the way they see the characters with the artist's conceptions. Finally, they may assume the parts of the characters in a recorded story and create a play to record themselves.

One part that is never excluded is rereading to a peer after listening to the recorded reading. Children choose from the passage the parts they wish to read. Sometimes passages lend themselves to dialogue, with the children reading various characters' parts. Sometimes they each read different passages, or each partner may select the same passage. Children may even choose a passage to record and then play it back to listen to themselves.

Our routine is lively and varied, but it follows a basic pattern: we share new and familiar Big Books, possibly dramatizing the story or singing along with a Big Book. We discuss previously read stories or the content of some of the children's own writings. As a part of the session with Big Books, children observe word meanings and patterns, punctuation, and decoding strategies within the context of a story. We keep a world map handy as many of the stories come from different countries; even the very young can understand why some writers write about the sea and others about the cold when they locate authors' home countries on the map.

Following a group session with Big Books, children head for the skills center, don a headset, and follow along with the recorded reading. This takes 10 to 20 minutes, depending on the readers' ages. Children are asked to read the passage with the tape, running their fingers beneath the words if they choose. Following the reading, children select any spot in the room and read to a partner of their choice.

After reading to a peer, children engage in small-group and independent activities such as writing on paper or at the computer, painting, working with the multisensory materials, or writing or reading a good book or magazine.

Working with recorded books supports auditory as well as visual learners, and it is compatible with the theory behind the Big Books—we learn to read by reading. I like what I see happening to children in our whole language classroom, and I highly recommend this combination of Big Books and recorded books to motivate and guide children in a reading program that is rich in language, gentle, but relentless in urging them to be the best readers they can possibly be. This powerful combination provides definite structure but grants freedom of choice within that structure.

Grades One and Two Love Readers Theatre

Sharon Bennett
Kim (Beatty) Wisz
Rockford, Michigan
January 1988

We wanted to give our first and second graders opportunities to practice reading aloud so they could develop fluency and comprehension, but the usual methods weren't working too well. Round-robin reading, for example, is painfully slow and needlessly stressful. And while repeated readings of the same story are supposed to be effective, when we tried having children do repeated readings of basal stories, they showed a distinct lack of motivation. The solution came when we noticed the excitement generated whenever the children came to a selection that was designated "play."

While we were looking for ways to encourage oral reading, we learned about Readers Theatre whereby a favorite story, like *Ira Sleeps Over* by Bernard Waber, can be turned into a script. Since the children act with just their voices, this seemed a logical way to expand on the excitement of the play format without the hassle of costumes, props, and scenery.

The children were familiar with and delighted by *Ira Sleeps Over*. The members of one reading group eagerly volunteered to read their favorite parts over and over. Other children became excited about the script, and soon representatives from every reading group were blended together by choice, not ability.

When the children, after sufficient practice, presented their Readers Theatre to their classmates, they were met with an overwhelmingly positive response. Their self-esteem improved, and they felt encouraged to practice, rehearse, and perform additional scripts. The result was a significant improvement in their enthusiasm, fluency, expression, and oral language.

Oral reading is often drudgery for teachers and students because most practice is connected with basal readers and content area textbooks. SAY IT RIGHT! allows students to see that reading aloud can be more than simply reading from their textbooks.

Divide the children into small groups and place face down in front of each group a set of sentence strips and a separate set of expression strips (see Figure). The first child draws one slip from each pile and reads the sentence silently and then orally for initial practice. Then the student rereads the sentence with expression as indicated by the expression strip. Students take turns for the time allotted by the teacher. Other students in the group can help with unknown or unfamiliar words.

SAY IT RIGHT!

Mary E. Person
Minot, North Dakota
February 1990

Sample Expressions and Sentences

Expression Strips

Fear	Panic	Joy
Love	Excitement	Anger
Hate	Child's voice	Old person's voice

Sentence Strips

1. The queen said, "Let them eat cake."
2. "We will learn to read well orally," said Jean. "It is not so easy to read smoothly."
3. The handsome prince said, "I will kill the dragon and win the hand of the fair princess."
4. The coach said, "I am a strong person, but _____ is stronger and smarter."
5. The lightning flashed! Dracula said, "The castle is cold tonight, my dear. I think we need a fire."
6. Betty said, "I am afraid of the dark."
7. Dr. Frankenstein's monster said, "Don't be afraid. I won't hurt you."
8. The burglar said, "Your money or your life."
9. The girl said, "I like you very much, John."
10. Cinderella said, "Please turn the pumpkin into a coach, dear fairy godmother."
11. The night was dark and windy. The night watchman said, "How about another cup of coffee, Tom, before I make my rounds."
12. Snow White said, "I hope that the seven dwarfs will be home soon. They are very late tonight."
13. The king said, "It is a cold day. Bring my fur robe."

(continued next page)

14. The mother said, "You are the smartest and nicest child in the whole world."
15. Superman said, "I must save the world from the evil Captain Crazy. He wants to destroy New York City."
16. Wonder Woman said, "That girl is driving too fast. I must try to stop her before she drives off that bridge."
17. The young man said, "The play is performed tonight. I hope you will like it."
18. The teacher said, "Children, you must finish this homework tonight. There will be a test tomorrow."
19. Popeye said, "Olive Oyl is my girl. I will buy her some flowers."
20. The little girl said, "My favorite animal is a kitten. But they can scratch and hurt you."
21. Tom said, "My dog, Rex, is in his doghouse. He is small, but he is a fighter."
22. Dr. Cliff Huxtable said, "Go upstairs and get your homework done right now."

_____

As the game progresses, students may make a second choice from the expression strips when the expression simply does not fit the sentence. As a variation, students may read a single sentence in several acceptable ways, or they may want to use one expression for all the sentences. Teachers can also extend what students are learning about oral expression by having students rehearse portions of trade books to read orally to the class.

Chapter 3

Developing Vocabulary

Vocabulary development refers to the acquisition of the meanings of words and concepts, and success in this area is strongly related to success in school. Understanding both spoken and written language is dependent upon understanding the words. The more words children can understand and produce, the greater the likelihood they will become skilled readers, since readers must be able to combine strings of words in order to re-create the author's intended message.

The number of words that students acquire and the knowledge related to those words grow with age and experience. During their first 18 years, students' rate of vocabulary acquisition is truly astounding; by that age, students often have vocabularies of 40,000 to 50,000 words.

The importance of developing children's vocabulary would be difficult to overestimate, and educators are therefore rightly concerned about finding effective ways to teach vocabulary terms. Graves (1987) points out that learning vocabulary includes "learning new meanings for known words, learning new words representing known concepts, learning new words representing new concepts, clarifying and enriching the meanings of known words, and moving words from receptive to expressive vocabularies" (p. 167).

It is not the words themselves that are so critical, however, but the meanings the words convey. Words are simply labels for concepts that are constantly being changed, modified, categorized, or created as new information is encountered. According to researchers, all the experiences and knowledge people have are stored in the brain in cognitive categories called "schemata" (Rumelhart, 1980). These schemata are constantly being refined, expanded, or restructured, because as we experience new ideas, events, or words, we try to relate the new information to existing schemata. We do this by adding the new information to an appropriate schema, refining the information we already have stored in the schema, or restructuring the schema so that the new information makes sense. Vocabulary knowledge is believed to develop by connecting new information with the old information surrounding a known word or concept. Certainly when students learn a new term, they usually link that term with their knowledge of the world.

Whether vocabulary is best taught and learned through direct instruction of word meanings or acquired through contextual analysis during reading is a matter of debate; both approaches have their merits. When planning direct vocabulary instruction, it is important to remember that vocabulary development is an associative task. Several strategies build on schema theory. Semantic mapping and semantic feature analysis are techniques that help students build categories and associations to remember new concepts or terms (Johnson & Pearson, 1984). The key-word method, which involves visual or verbal elaborations as mnemonic devices to build associations, is also effective (Pressley, Levin, & McDaniel, 1987), as is instruction in new vocabulary prior to reading (Jenkins, Stein, & Wysocki, 1984).

Children can also learn new vocabulary when they listen to stories (Elley, 1989) or read books. In this case, the meanings of the words encountered are revealed by the context in which they appear. Obviously the more words students meet, the more word meanings they are apt to master; teachers should therefore create an environment that encourages wide reading. Teachers can also provide instruction about the different ways writers use language to define words so that students can infer meanings.

In sum, vocabulary development and increased understanding of concepts are closely related and may be nurtured by direct vocabulary instruction and extensive exposure to language through listening to and reading books. The teaching ideas and strategies in this chapter can help children build extensive vocabularies.

References

Elley, W.B. (1989). Vocabulary acquisition from listening to stories. *Reading Research Quarterly, 24*, 174-187.

Graves, M. (1987). The roles of instruction in fostering vocabulary development. In M.G. McKeown & M.E. Curtis (Eds.), *The nature of vocabulary acquisition*. Hillsdale, NJ: Erlbaum.

Jenkins, J., Stein, M., & Wysocki, K. (1984). Learning vocabulary through reading. *American Educational Research Journal, 21*, 767-787.

Johnson, D.D., & Pearson, P.D. (1984). *Teaching reading vocabulary*. Orlando, FL: Holt, Rinehart & Winston.

Pressley, M., Levin, J.R., & McDaniel, M.A. (1987). Remembering versus inferring what a word means: Mnemonic and contextual approaches. In M.G. McKeown & M.E. Curtis (Eds.), *The nature of vocabulary acquisition*. Hillsdale, NJ: Erlbaum.

Rumelhart, D.E. (1980). Schemata: The building blocks of cognition. In R.J. Spiro, B.C. Bruce, & W.F. Brewer (Eds.), *Theoretical issues in reading comprehension* (pp. 33-58). Hillsdale, NJ: Erlbaum.

Further Reading

Bromley, K.D. (1984). Teaching idioms. *The Reading Teacher, 38*, 272-276.

Duffelmeyer, F.A. (1985). Teaching word meaning from an experience base. *The Reading Teacher, 38*, 6-11.

Jiganti, M.A., & Tindall, M.A. (1986). An interactive approach to teaching vocabulary. *The Reading Teacher, 39*, 444-448.

Johnson, D.D., Pittelman, S.D., & Heimlich, J.E. (1986). Semantic mapping. *The Reading Teacher, 39*, 778-783.

Just, M.A., & Carpenter, P.A. (1987). *The psychology of reading and language comprehension.* Needham Heights, MA: Allyn & Bacon.

Konopak, B.C., & Williams, N.L. (1988). Using the keyword method to help young readers learn content material. *The Reading Teacher, 41*, 682-687.

Marzano, R.J. (1984). A cluster approach to vocabulary instruction: A new direction from the research literature. *The Reading Teacher, 38*, 168-173.

McKeown, M.G., & Curtis, M.E. (Eds.). (1987). *The nature of vocabulary acquisition.* Hillsdale, NJ: Erlbaum.

Schwartz, R.M., & Raphael, T.E. (1985). Concept of definition: A key to improving students' vocabulary. *The Reading Teacher, 39*, 198-205.

Smith, C.B. (1988). Building a better vocabulary. *The Reading Teacher, 42*, 238.

Stahl, S.A., & Vancil, S.J. (1986). Discussion is what makes semantic maps work in vocabulary instruction. *The Reading Teacher, 40*, 62-69.

Swisher, K. (1984). Increasing word power through spelling activities. *The Reading Teacher, 37*, 706-711.

Wixson, K.K. (1986). Vocabulary instruction and children's comprehension of basal stories. *Reading Research Quarterly, 21*, 317-329.

Show and Tell— Alive and Well

Karen Laner
Evanston, Illinois
April 1986

Show-and-tell time can be valuable in teaching and reinforcing vocabulary. Each Wednesday I give the six-, seven-, and eight-year-olds in my class a word to explore for the next week's show and tell. Children may volunteer to find and bring to class an object, a picture, or some other representation of the word. I encourage the children to use a dictionary or to question adults or their peers to find out about the show-and-tell word.

On the next Tuesday morning, the whole class discusses the various meanings the children have discovered for the target word. Then volunteers take turns giving speeches about how the objects they've brought in relate to the word, and the children ask and answer questions.

Many words can be hits with students; favorites include *flexible, perplexing, ludicrous,* and *consumable.* Occasionally a child will misunderstand a word, like the day one boy proudly showed a picture of a mouse and its newborn babies to illustrate the meaning of *pregnant.* I congratulated him on his creativity and gently explained that the word for that day was *fragrant!*

The success of this activity comes when the children use the vocabulary they have learned in their everyday conversation. I reinforce the word in casual conversations several times during the week. The children are proud to know such "big words" and often use them in a variety of classroom activities. In addition, the activity provides the children with positive experiences speaking in front of a group.

Humorous Homonyms: Using Visual Clues to Teach Sound-Alike Words

M. Dianne Bergenske
Mineral Point, Wisconsin
March 1987

Homonyms are age-old spelling and comprehension demons. One way to teach them successfully is to tie a picture that illustrates the word's meaning to its particular spelling. This is most effective when the picture is drawn as part of the letter or letters that differentiate a pair of homonyms.

It is imperative that the picture be tied conceptually to the meaning of the word. This strengthens the visual clue association. It is also important that the picture not mask or obliterate the letter, but be as simple as possible and let the letter show through. Using heavy lines for letters and fine ones for the drawings, as well as using different colors, can contribute to the picture's effectiveness. (See the Figure for some examples.)

Students bring different modality strengths to learning, including visual, aural, and tactile. Because this visual method is easily understood, it helps children who need to strengthen the links between the spelling and the meaning of words that are indistinguishable aurally.

Homonym Pictures

1. Letters that appear in one word but not the other.

tow
toe

2. The place of the letter in the word.

tail
tale

3. The juxtaposition of two letters in one of the words, if the same letters are in both words.

bear
bare

An unusual and interesting way to enrich students' word power is through the study of surnames. Identifying the source of a surname can increase interest in as well as expand vocabulary.

Introduce some background on surnames to help pique curiosity. Explain that after the population of early communities increased, surnames, or family names, became necessary. Although some cultures do not use surnames, Western cultures began using them some time during the middle of the 12th century. Surnames developed from several sources, including location, relationships, occupation or office, and nicknames derived from physical or personal characteristics.

On the next page are some examples of surnames developed from different sources.

What's in a Surname?

Harry B. Miller
Cindy Thompson
Monroe, Louisiana
December 1984

- **Location:** Echols (Scottish name meaning dweller near the church); Romero (Spanish name meaning one who travels); Brook; Stone; Hill.
- **Relationship:** Jackson (son of Jack in English); Adamczyk (son of Adam in Polish); MacAdam (son of Adam in Scottish); Cohen (priestly family in Hebrew).
- **Occupations:** Sawyer (one who works sawing wood); Mason (bricklayer); Boulanger (French for baker); Cooper (barrel maker); Berger (derived from the French for shepherd).
- **Nicknames:** Bruno (brown, Italian); Reid (red hair, Irish); Rosen (rose, Yiddish); Stalin (steel, Russian); Young; Armstrong; Savage.

Here are some activities to help expand students' vocabularies.

Name match. The object of this game is to match the surname with its classification (location, relationship, occupation, nickname). Divide the class into two groups. Print the four classifications on large strips of paper and attach them to a bulletin board. Print surnames on smaller pieces of paper and place these face down on a table. Each group takes turns drawing a name to classify by placing it under the correct heading. If one group fails to place the name correctly, the card is returned to the bottom of the stack. Points are earned for correct classifications, with extra points added for giving the meaning. For example, "Weiss" should be placed under the classification "Nickname" and extra credit earned if the student knows that it means white.

Surname origin. Instruct your students to use reference materials from the school or public library to discover facts about their surnames. (A number of good reference books about surnames, including Rudolph and Marney Wagner's *The Story of Family Names* and Elsdon Smith's *Treasury of Name Lore*, are available.) Students may also be assigned to find information about three of their neighbors' last names. The students' findings should be displayed on attractive posters.

Choose a name. Ask your students to pretend that no one in the class has a surname. Each student must choose an appropriate surname based on one or more of the four categories described. Students then share their "fitting surname" with the class. Watch for the fun and laughter.

Word Maps and Student Involvement

Frederick A. Duffelmeyer
Ames, Iowa
May 1988

As students progress from one grade to the next, they are exposed to an increasing number of new concepts in their reading material. While some new concepts do not need to be taught (either because they are not particularly useful or because they are readily learned independently), others that are useful and not easily learned merit instructional attention.

A word map can be developed to teach new concepts in several ways. Basically, a word map is a visual representation of a definition. It shows the general class a concept belongs to, what properties or characteristics it has, and several familiar examples. A word map for *rodent* is shown in the Figure. Note that the map's clusters are made graphically different so that the groupings are easily distinguishable. This is easy to do on the chalkboard while the map is being developed. (It helps to have your map planned ahead.)

The logical sequence for presenting the components of a word is (1) target concept, (2) general class, (3) properties or characteristics, and (4) familiar examples; dictionary definitions typically follow this pattern. For the *rodent* word map, the application of that sequence would result in something like the following conversation, with the teacher filling in the map as she or he names the components.

Word Map of *Rodent*

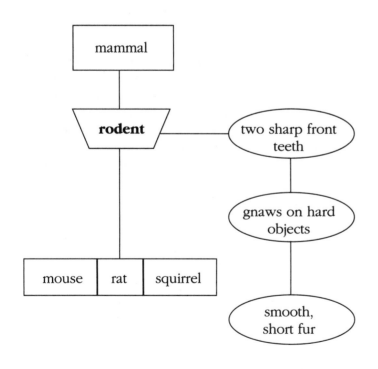

Teacher: This word is *rodent*. A rodent is a type of *mammal*. A rodent has *two sharp front teeth*; likes to *gnaw on hard objects*; and has *smooth, short fur*. Some examples of a rodent are a *mouse*, a *rat*, and a *squirrel*. Can you think of any other examples?

Student: Hamster.

Student: Prairie dogs.

An alternative sequence with a little less presentation and a little more elicitation is (1) familiar examples, (2) properties or characteristics, (3) more familiar examples, (4) target concept, and (5) general class. Use of this sequence would result in something like the following, with the teacher developing the word map on the chalkboard as the appropriate words occur in the discussion.

Teacher: What do a *mouse*, a *rat*, and a *squirrel* have in common?

Student: They both have *two sharp front teeth*.

Student: They like to *gnaw on things*.

Student: They have *smooth fur*.

Teacher: Can you think of any other animals that have these same characteristics?

Student: Hamsters.

Student: Prairie dogs.

Teacher: All of the animals we've named are examples of *rodents*, and a rodent is a type of *mammal*.

The modified sequence is appropriate whenever the teacher can envision examples that the students would be familiar with. If the target concept label is not familiar, the students cannot generate properties or characteristics after the teacher gives the opening examples. (This happens only infrequently.)

The modified sequence leads to more student involvement, and the feedback received from teachers who have implemented it has been very positive.

Rote memorization of vocabulary definitions and root words can be tedious, and things learned that way are often quickly forgotten. Study etymology instead! In this type of instruction students use existing vocabularies, which makes it easier for them to incorporate new words into their vocabularies. It also helps students discover a structure to their language that makes sense to them.

To begin an etymology unit, I list 15 to 20 affixes on the board (for example, *aud, bio, cide, homo,* and *omni*). Students copy these affixes, leaving lines between them. They are given time to brainstorm and list words that they already know that contain these affixes. Next, we discuss their lists, adding words they had not originally thought of. After examining the lists and looking for connections in meanings, I ask students to guess at the meaning of each affix. Their guesses are very often accurate. Toward the end of the class, I review the correct meanings and add some words of interest that have not been mentioned. For homework, students use a dictionary to find new words that contain the affixes and prepare to discuss their words and meanings in class. Often competition for the best words develops, as does curiosity about meanings and how they have changed and stretched over the years. Words that are already familiar trigger recall of the meaning of new words.

Through discussions, worksheets, writing assignments, and tests, the students have opportunities to use the words creatively and intelligently. For example, they may be asked to *eulogize a philanthropic Russophobe*, or to write an *autobiography* using ten of their new words; they may be asked to create names for new products or new phobias with the roots they have learned. This method fosters an interest in vocabulary that is difficult to achieve through other methods.

Familiarity Breeds Vocabulary

Frances Maria Sodana
Havertown, Pennsylvania
February 1985

While searching for an activity that would ensure meaningful learning from vocabulary instruction, I tried to recall words I learned suddenly—but for a lifetime—in elementary school. One instance immediately came to mind. Seemingly for lack of anything else to do, a substitute teacher of my third grade class initiated an activity that can be easily adapted to fulfill the conditions for meaningful vocabulary instruction (described by Thelen in the April 1986 *Journal of Reading*): organizing the words to be learned, relating them to

Round-Robin Vocabulary

Donna Kotting
Fulton, Maryland
March 1987

the learner's existing vocabulary, and ensuring the learner's active involvement. The substitute had just completed a well-organized science lesson on snakes and reptiles in which she had explained many new terms, and had 20 minutes left. She asked us to sit in a circle and start a round-robin story in which one person would begin, stop dramatically, and let the next person continue.

The first person began a story about a haunted house. As the story developed, we started to include the concepts we had just discussed in the science lesson. The haunted house was soon populated with all kinds of creatures, snakelike and otherwise. The last third grader to speak began to warn ominously that the "viper would be coming in one week...the viper would be coming tomorrow...the viper is *here!*" After building the threat to a climax, the student proudly ended with "Hi! I'm the vindow viper! I've come to vipe your vindows!" I never forgot the meaning of "viper" after that.

Teachers can plan the prior instruction of vocabulary terms and then begin the round-robin story activity by telling the children to use one of the new terms before passing the story to the next person. To help students on a lower level participate fully, let students use any of the words, even if some are repeated. More advanced students like to use several words, often getting applause for cleverly combining two or three in the same sentence. If you want to ensure that all words are used at least once, challenge yourself or students to use all leftover words in a few sentences.

This activity is successful with remedial and advanced reading students at many levels. The creativity allowed in adding mystery, humor, and adventure does much to encourage students in their active learning roles.

Multiple Meanings and Science Reading

Jeffrey Lehman
Robert Wright
Gainesville, Florida
October 1983

During a science lesson, an elementary student confidently defined *gas* as "something that is put into cars." The answer was consistent with his everyday experiences; he was not aware of the different meaning of the word *gas* in science.

Elementary science textbooks contain many common words that have special meanings. To help students comprehend science material, use this vocabulary exercise to highlight multiple uses of common words. By completing the exercise, children not only learn new vocabulary in an enjoyable way, they also learn something about different careers and the importance of context. The Figure shows a very easy approach that can be planned quickly and executed on either the chalk-board or a handout sheet.

Start by noting specialized vocabulary before students read their science text. Then construct a "Words in Context Vocabulary Exercise" with those words. In class, students discuss what each word means to people in different occupations. For example, when students explain what the word *charge* means to a lawyer, a storekeeper, or an auto mechanic, they soon realize that context is important for many words.

We have used this procedure to increase science comprehension, but teachers in other areas should find the exercise equally useful.

Words in Context Vocabulary Exercise

Directions: Describe what each of the following words means to the people indicated.

1. What does the word *conductor* mean to:
   a train passenger?
   a musician?
   an electrician?

2. What does the word *model* mean to:
   an architect?
   a clothing merchant?
   a chemist?

3. What does the word *volume* mean to:
   a librarian?
   a pharmacist?
   a guitar player?

4. What does the word *force* mean to:
   a meteorologist?
   a military officer?
   a baseball player?

5. What does the word *charge* mean to:
   a lawyer?
   an automobile mechanic?
   a store owner?

6. What does the word *scales* mean to:
   a fisherman?
   a physicist?
   a teacher?

A Semantic Mapping Lesson Plan

Susan D. Pittelman
Madison, Wisconsin

Kathy M. Levin
Dale D. Johnson
November 1986

Semantic mapping is a categorical structuring of information in graphic form. It is an individualized content approach in that students are required to relate new words to their own experiences and prior knowledge. A completed semantic map provides teachers with information about what the students know and reveals anchor points upon which new concepts can be introduced. (The Figure is a map from a vocabulary lesson developed for the topic "Water.")

Objectives

- Students will brainstorm words related to a specific topic.
- Students will demonstrate an understanding of the target vocabulary.

Materials

- List of target words you want to introduce and their definitions.
- One blank map for each student.
- Pencil for each student.
- Chalkboard and chalk (or transparency, overhead projector, and AV pen).

Procedure

1. Explain the purpose of the lesson (to learn new words).
2. Review procedures for semantic mapping. Draw a blank map on the chalkboard.
3. Distribute blank maps to students.
4. Introduce the topic, write it in a circle on the chalkboard, and have the students write the topic in the circle on their maps. Tell the students that as they brainstorm words for the topic, you will have some words that you want to introduce and that whenever you write one of these words on the board, you are going to put a star by it. Tell the students that they should copy the starred words on their maps.
5. Elicit words from students and write them in related groupings on the map on the chalkboard. Tell the students that if they really like a word, they can add it to their maps.
6. After three or four words are listed in a group, discuss an appropriate category label and write it above that list of words.

Semantic Map

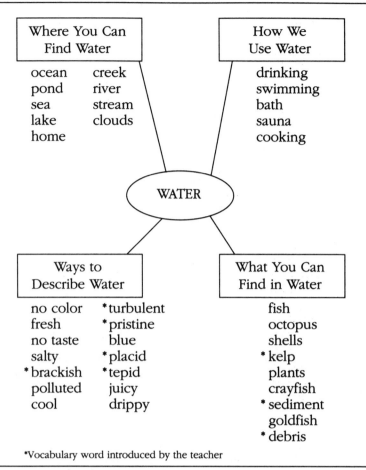

Where You Can Find Water	How We Use Water
ocean creek pond river sea stream lake clouds home	drinking swimming bath sauna cooking

WATER

Ways to Describe Water	What You Can Find in Water
no color *turbulent fresh *pristine no taste blue salty *placid *brackish *tepid polluted juicy cool drippy	fish octopus shells *kelp plants crayfish *sediment goldfish *debris

*Vocabulary word introduced by the teacher

Wisconsin Center for Education Research

7. Present a target vocabulary word. If the target word fits into an existing category, add the word to that list. If the target word does not fit into an existing category, suggest an appropriate category label and write it on the board. Have students brainstorm two to four related words, and then add the target word to that list. Pronounce the target word and have the students repeat it. Then discuss its definition. Try to relate the target word to another word on the map. Remind students to copy the category label and target word on their maps.

8. Continue brainstorming a few more words.

9. Add each remaining target word, following the procedure in steps 7 and 8. (You may add the last few target words in each category without having students brainstorm additional words in between.)

10. Allow students two to three minutes to add words or categories to their maps independently.

11. Ask students to share their new words or categories and add them to the map on the board.

12. Review each target vocabulary word. Use as many of the following techniques as time permits:
   - *Cross-category comparison and questions to clarify word meanings.* Ask questions that cause students to apply the target words. In the questions, relate words in one category to those in another (e.g., Would you find garbage in *pristine* water? Is seaweed considered *debris*?).
   - *Synonyms for target words.* Let students suggest words that have a similar meaning.
   - *Antonyms for target words.* Let students suggest words that have an opposite meaning.
   - *Sentences.* Have students use the target words in sentences.

(This semantic mapping lesson plan has been slightly modified from *An Investigation of Two Instructional Settings in the Use of Semantic Mapping with Poor Readers*, by Susan D. Pittelman, Kathy M. Levin, and Dale D. Johnson, Program Report 85-4, Wisconsin Center for Education Research, University of Wisconsin, Madison, Wisconsin.)

Mobile Making

Aurelie Miller
West Islip, New York
December 1986

Using concrete materials to create graphic representations of ideas is the perfect way to keep children's attention on a learning task. Mobile making for children in grades three through six provides both recreation and reinforcement, contributing to vocabulary development and other comprehension skills.

My third graders, who were studying clouds, began by gluing cotton balls to oaktag to fashion their own cloud. Descending from this puffy cloud were long pipe cleaners, each with an oaktag square on which students wrote the names of the four types of clouds (cirrus, cumulus, stratus, cumulo-nimbus). After this vocabulary practice, the children hung individual descriptive phrases from the squares, attached with pipe cleaners of varying lengths to ensure visibility. The children were so excited about writing information in this manner that they asked if they could write on both sides of the oaktag so the words could be seen from both sides.

For follow-up, we drew a semantic map of the information on clouds and made a cloze comprehension story frame from the map. This provided an opportunity to evaluate the effectiveness of the original activity in building vocabulary.

Mobile making can be adapted to various activities where categorization skills and vocabulary are emphasized. The sky's the limit!

The Dictionary Game

Scott Koeze
Grafton, Vermont
April 1990

This is a game I developed for my Chapter 1 students to teach them a number of skills. It is played in groups of two to five children, who sit in a circle. To begin, one person selects a word that everyone knows. The person to the left gives a word that she or he predicts will appear in the dictionary definition of the chosen word. (Articles or prepositions are not allowed.) Play continues around the circle. A player cannot predict a word that a previous player has chosen. The person who selected the original word predicts last and then looks the word up in the dictionary and reads the definition. A point is awarded to each player who made a correct prediction. After each round, the dictionary is passed to the left, and that player selects a new word.

Suppose, for example, the word *dinosaur* is selected. The first player predicts *reptile* will appear in the definition; the second player predicts *brontosaurus*; the third, *extinct*; the last player, who chose the word *dinosaur*, predicts *animal*. He or she then looks up *dinosaur* and reads the definition. The words *reptile* and *extinct* are in the definition, so players one and three score a point. (If the player had predicted *extinction*, that would count as a correct guess because it is a form of a word in the definition.) I explain to students that just because their words do not appear in the definition does not mean they are not good guesses. Word definition is not exact; another dictionary might include their words in its definition. On the other hand, I explain when necessary that some guesses are clearly inaccurate.

This game can be adapted for whole-class use. Instead of taking turns making predictions, each student writes down a guess on a piece of paper. Thus, more than one player may predict the same word. A few volunteers may read their words. Then the definition is read, and a point is awarded for each correct prediction. The teacher can select the word each time, or students can take turns choosing words.

The Dictionary Game leads students to grasp what it means to define something and so to think about the essential meanings of specific words. It also develops dictionary and reading skills. And it is easy to implement because children love to play it.

The Expert's Tic-Tac-Toe

Caroline McKinney
*Lafayette, Colorado
April 1990*

One of the best ways to build self-esteem in low-level readers is to give them opportunities to be experts in their own chosen areas of interest. Such opportunities can be provided through the use of a special form of tic-tac-toe.

In the back of their writing journals, students keep an ongoing list of topics about which they know a great deal. The topic may be based on a personal experience, such as a trip to the emergency room, or it may involve a hobby or words they have gathered from their reading. Several times during the semester, the students develop vocabulary cards from these lists of topics. At first, the students write these words with invented spellings; later in the year they can edit them. When the students feel confident enough to teach and share these words with a friend, it is time to bring out the tic-tac-toe games.

The teacher and the student should determine together when the student knows a group of words well enough to play the game. There are many good ways to do this, so it's not difficult to find a method that is appropriate for each student. Some suggested methods are (1) a cloze passage devised by the teacher based on the child's word list, (2) a conference during which the student uses the words to develop questions, (3) a story written with the words from the list, or (4) sentence strips created by the student and teacher. It is important to note that this game is part of a process of learning vocabulary, and correct recognition of words is not always possible. However, with young students or low-level readers, some important concepts can be explored. For example, the child may not recognize the entire word, but he or she may remember that the word begins with a particular sound or letter. That knowledge also needs to be recognized and applauded.

Playing the Game

At the beginning of the school year, the students each design a tic-tac-toe board by cutting a square out of construction paper (approximately 12" x 12") and gluing thin strips of black paper on it to form the lines. The board is then laminated. Students tape a self-sealing plastic bag on the back to hold the vocabulary cards and make the Xs and Os from construction paper. Then they switch game boards with other students so they will be playing with unfamiliar vocabulary.

54

The vocabulary cards are placed face down between the players, who take turns picking cards and reading them. If the student correctly identifies the word, then he or she may place an X or O on the board. If the student doesn't recognize the word, the turn passes to the other child. By seeing these words over and over, the students become familiar with them. This activity can be repeated often with different classmates. The games may also be sent home periodically for parents to play with the child.

Once a child feels confident about knowing the words, he or she is ready to put up a banner. In our classroom, we hang up colorful construction paper banners with the vocabulary words written on them and a heading that proclaims, "[Student's name] is an expert about [topic]." This provides the student with an opportunity to show off a little.

This activity has been successful with my reading groups, and it can be adapted for any classroom or subject area. It can be utilized at any grade level, although it may be most successful with second and third graders. Older students

Banners for the Classroom

Third Grader	Second Grader
Michael is an expert about	Sarah is an expert about
Football	Skiing
player	snow
pads	hill
jersey	pole
stadium	boot
helmet	cold
uniform	lift
goal	ticket
flag	jacket
coach	ski
game	ice
tackle	trees
fumble	gloves

might develop word lists about topics such as authors, characters, illustrators, historical figures, scientific terms, or foreign language vocabulary. A final value of the game is that it is easy, flexible, and cheap!

The Affixionary: Personalizing Prefixes and Suffixes

Thomas Lindsay
*Melrose Park
(now Franklin Park), Illinois
November 1984*

In their reading program, students learn many different prefixes and suffixes, some with similar meanings and similar spellings, such as *in-*, *im-*, *dis-*, and *un-* (meaning "not") and *-ous*, *-ious*, and *-eous* (meaning "full of"). These affixes can be confusing elements in unfamiliar words, but they provide important clues to pronunciation and meaning.

To help children understand and later use the affixes, have them make "affixionaries." An affixionary is a personalized dictionary in which students record newly taught affixes, their meanings, and examples of words, sentences, and pictures that illustrate each one.

An Affixionary Entry

dis-
The prefix *dis-* means "not."

disappear	The magician made the rabbit disappear.
disobey	The naughty children disobeyed their uncle.
disarm	The policeman disarmed the robber by taking his gun.

Affixionaries can be used for reading, language, and writing assignments among students at virtually any level. Here are the steps for making an affixionary:

1. Make a record booklet by folding sheets of white typing paper in half and adding a heavier paper cover. The number of pages should correspond with the number of affixes to be taught.

2. The first page is reserved for a table of contents.

3. The student writes one target affix at the top of a page.

4. Under the affix (but still close to the top of the page), the student writes the affix's meaning.

5. The rest of the page is divided into two columns. In the skinny left-hand column, the student writes examples of words having the target affix and, in the wider right-hand column, sentences using the examples. (Primary grade children might illustrate the word rather than write sentences.)

The entries may be made in alphabetical order, or the student may want to list the prefixes in the front of the booklet and the suffixes in the back.

Handing out a ready-made affixionary will not do the trick. It is the act of making one—selecting the examples, placing them in the book, writing them down (which involves repetition), and adding items to the table of contents—that turns the booklet into an effective learning tool.

The affixionary helps each child internalize and transfer affix usage. It is personal. As a reference tool, it is a concrete example of the structural analysis strategy for word recognition and learning word meanings.

Using Cloze to Explore Writers' Word Choices

Christine Porter
Douglas County, Colorado
April 1987

When a student chooses a word to fill a space in a text where a word has been deleted, he or she is thinking like a writer as well as like a reader. This makes cloze a good procedure for working on students' writing vocabulary.

The students in my third grade class tended to overuse certain words when they write—for instance, *said* and *nice*. To encourage them to use a wider variety of words, I prepared a cloze passage by deleting 20 words—including nouns, verbs, and adjectives—from a 120-word passage from a children's book. (After the opening sentence, I deleted every fifth or so item.) I then numbered the blanks in the cloze passage. Down the left side of a worksheet, I listed the same numbers, and along the top of that page I wrote three column headings: "My Choice," "Group Choice," and "Class Choice." Students were to write their cloze answers on the worksheet instead of in the cloze passage itself, so as to keep the focus on alternatives.

After reading through the cloze selection, students wrote their individual responses in the "My Choice" column on their sheets. Then they met in small groups, discussed and compared their individual choices, and agreed upon one word choice for each blank in the passage. They entered these words on their worksheets in the "Group Choice" column. Then we read through the cloze passage as a class. When we came to a blank, one volunteer from each group read aloud the group's choice for that blank. As a class, students decided which of the group choices they liked best for each missing word, and they wrote those in the "Class Choice" column. After these decisions had been made, we discussed why an author might choose one word over another. I asked questions such as: "Why would you choose *whispered* over *said*? When might you want to use *soared* instead of *flew*? What difference would it make if you used *heartbroken* instead of *sad*?"

Finally the children brainstormed ways to add colorful words and phrases to their own writing. These included listing adjectives and verbs associated with a second topic, asking a friend for suggestions, and consulting a thesaurus.

Students then selected a piece of their own writing to revise to eliminate overused words. They were encouraged to use one or several of the strategies previously discussed. Part of the writing session was spent on independent revising and the other part in peer conferences during which the students gave each other feedback on the changes they had made and suggested other possible revisions.

I set up special sessions over the next several weeks to focus on language usage to reinforce the strategies brainstormed earlier.

Creating Connections

Blanche Solomon
Brooklyn, New York
May 1988

Prior to direct reading instruction, I encourage children to discuss key story vocabulary and concepts contained in the next basal selection. This strategy results in long lists of information elicited from the group as the children share their prior knowledge about narrative text. The lists are often lengthy enough to categorize, and together we make connections between words and find relationships among ideas.

For example, when discussing parades as a prereading activity with second graders, I recorded the following:

Parades have:

lots of people	horses	police	masks
music	soldiers	streamers	cars
dancing	balloons	special blowers	pompoms
horns	floats	majorettes	signs
drums	noisemakers	batons	fireworks
tooters	trombones	bands	confetti
clowns	dragons	uniforms	leaders
crowds	costumes	flags	flowers

The children suggested the following topics for categorizing the list:

People	Sounds	Transportation	Decorations
lots of people	trombones	cars	signs
crowds	drums	floats	streamers
clowns	bands	horses	masks
majorettes	tooters		balloons
soldiers	music		confetti
			flowers

When a category was of limited scope, the children suggested a broader topic. Thus, *vehicles* became *transportation* and *instruments* changed to *sounds*.

The following day the concept was extended when the class composed a list of familiar parades.

Parades celebrate:

Thanksgiving	Brooklyn-Queens	Martin Luther King
the circus	Day	Veterans' Day
Mardi Gras	Easter	Chinese New Year
St. Patrick's Day	Labor Day	World Series winners
astronauts	beauty contests	Halloween
	Columbus Day	

The children gained a wealth of vocabulary from this experience. We then used the list to form semantic maps from which the children learned to write simple sentences:

- Parades have horses.
- Parades have floats.
- Parades have costumes.
- Parades have flags.

Later the simple sentences became:

- Parades have horses and floats.
- Parades have costumes and flags.

Eventually the children were able to choose categories to write paragraphs. Finally all the lists were used as sources of information for writing complete pieces of prose. Brainstorming and writing lists with the children facilitated a flow of ideas, organized their thinking, promoted deeper understanding of key concepts, increased oral fluency, and served as springboards for creativity.

Each child copied the lists into special "We Know About" reading notebooks. The books serve as resources for ongoing independent activities as the children use the information to:

- add to the list,
- write sentences with the words,
- form semantic maps,
- write paragraphs about a category,
- categorize lists with different headings,
- find synonyms on lists,
- make up questions about a topic,
- write an original story,
- make ABC books about some of the concepts,
- read other books about an interesting topic,
- illustrate the items on a list, and
- make a group mural about one of the topics.

When children join together as a community of learners to create their own resources, they become motivated to work independently in a meaningful process. These strategies (which can be used with all grade levels) are invaluable throughout the school year as children help each other to expand their prior knowledge, make connections between ideas, and use those connections to produce original thought from the wealth of information they have shared.

Chapter 4

Comprehending Text

Students who succeed in comprehending a text are actively involved in the reading process—a process that requires the ability to make predictions, to confirm or disaffirm those predictions, and to monitor understanding throughout the process. Skilled readers have schemata for particular topics, text structures, metacognitive activities, and forms of language, and they draw on those schemata when they read. These readers use prior knowledge interactively with new information in the text. They also simultaneously apply a variety of strategies that facilitate comprehension (Pearson, 1986). Reading is clearly not the mastery of isolated skills or the verbatim reproduction of information as it appears on a page.

Students must have three types of knowledge if they are to develop into skilled readers (Winograd & Hare, 1988). First, they need declarative knowledge, which involves understanding the goals of reading and the thought processes needed to complete a particular reading task. For example, skilled readers understand that the goal of reading is to comprehend the text, while unskilled readers may believe the goal of reading is to sound out each word correctly. Students also need procedural knowledge, which involves understanding how to use different reading strategies or procedures (Jacobs & Paris, 1987). Procedural knowledge might include knowledge of how to process different text structures, how to read for different purposes, or how to relate new knowledge to prior knowledge. For example, students need to know that summaries are short versions of a longer text and use superordinate terms, omit extraneous and redundant information, and depend on sentences that capture main ideas. Finally, students need conditional or metacognitive knowledge, which involves understanding when and why a particular strategy is appropriate (Paris, Lipson, & Wixson, 1983). Students use conditional knowledge to apply the most appropriate reading strategy after considering the demands of a task. Unless students know when to use conditional knowledge, they will be unlikely to develop into skillful readers.

Teachers can facilitate the translation of declarative knowledge into procedural and conditional knowledge by using both structured and unstructured activities. Structured activities, which involve direct instruction, include "think alouds," reciprocal teaching, an explanation of question types, a discussion of reading tasks, or the presentation of strategies for various reading tasks. Unstructured activities are built around free reading time both during and outside of school. Both kinds of activities are well represented here. Chosen and used carefully, they can contribute to children's successful reading comprehension.

References

Jacobs, J.E., & Paris, S.G. (1987). Children's metacognition about reading: Issues in definition, measurement, and instruction. *Educational Psychologist, 22,* 313-332.

Paris, S.G., Lipson, M.Y., & Wixson, K.K. (1983). Becoming a strategic reader. *Contemporary Educational Psychology, 8,* 293-316.

Pearson, P.D. (1986). Twenty years of research in reading instruction. In T.E. Raphael (Ed.), *Contexts of school-based literacy.* New York: Random House.

Winograd, P., & Hare, V.C. (1988). Direct instruction of reading comprehension strategies: The nature of teacher explanation. In C. Weinstein, E. Goetz, & P. Alexander (Eds.), *Learning and study strategies: Issues in assessment, instruction, and evaluation* (pp. 121-139). San Diego, CA: Academic.

Further Reading

Anderson, R.C., & Pearson, P.D. (1984). A schema-theoretic view of basic process in reading comprehension. In P.D. Pearson (Ed.), *Handbook of reading research* (Vol. 1, pp. 255-292). White Plains, NY: Longman.

Arnold, R.D. (1989). Teaching cohesive ties to children. *The Reading Teacher, 42,* 106-111.

Babbs, P.J., & Moe, A.J. (1983). Metacognition: A key for independent learning from text. *The Reading Teacher, 36,* 422-426.

Fitzgerald, J. (1983). Helping readers gain self-control over reading comprehension. *The Reading Teacher, 37,* 249-253.

Flynn, L.L. (1989). Developing critical reading skills through cooperative problem solving. *The Reading Teacher, 42,* 664-669.

Hansen, J., & Hubbard, R. (1984). Poor readers can draw inferences. *The Reading Teacher, 37,* 586-589.

Holmes, B.C., & Roser, N.L. (1987). Five ways to assess readers' prior knowledge. *The Reading Teacher, 40,* 646-649.

Koskinen, P.S., Gambrell, L.B., Kapinus, B.A., & Heathington, B.S. (1988). Retelling: A strategy for enhancing students' reading comprehension. *The Reading Teacher, 41,* 892-897.

Pearson, P.D. (1985). Changing the face of reading comprehension instruction. *The Reading Teacher, 38,* 724-738.

Poindexter, C.A., & Prescott, S. (1986). A technique for teaching students to draw inferences from text. *The Reading Teacher, 39,* 908-911.

Raphael, T.E. (1986). Question-answering relationships for children. *The Reading Teacher, 36,* 516-522.

Singer, H. (1978). Active comprehension: From answering to asking questions. *The Reading Teacher, 31,* 901-909.

Tierney, R.J., & Cunningham, J.W. (1984). Research on teaching reading comprehension. In P.D. Pearson (Ed.), *Handbook of reading research* (Vol. 1, pp. 609-652). White Plains, NY: Longman.

Wilson, C.R. (1983). Teaching reading comprehension by connecting the known to the new. *The Reading Teacher, 36,* 382-390.

Winograd, P., & Smith, L.A. (1987). Improving the climate for reading comprehension instruction. *The Reading Teacher, 41,* 304-310.

Do students get as much as they can out of sustained silent reading (SSR)? SSR is a time when students read for pleasure; it can also be a time for them to reflect on the processes as well as the content of their reading.

Rather than having my students merely close their books at the end of SSR, I use a few minutes for them to discuss the nature, quality, and quantity of silent reading they have accomplished. This allows students to monitor and gain insight into their own reading and respond to what they read.

In *Forging ahead in Reading*, Lyman Hunt suggests using questions to generate the discussion. Decide which questions to use according to the students' needs.

1. Did you have a good reading period today? Did you read well? Did you get a lot done?

2. Did you read better today than yesterday?

3. Were you able to concentrate today on your silent reading?

4. Did the ideas in the book hold your attention?

5. Did you have the feeling of wanting to go ahead faster to find out what happened?

6. Was it hard to keep your mind on what you were reading today?

7. Were you bothered by others or outside noises?

8. Could you keep the ideas in your book straight in your mind?

9. Did you get mixed up in any place? Did you have to go back and straighten yourself out?

10. Were there words you didn't know? How did you figure them out?

11. What did you do when you got to the good parts? Did you read faster or slower?

12. Were you always counting to see how many pages you had to go? Were you wondering how long it would take you to finish?

13. Were you hoping that the book would go on and on—that it wouldn't really end?

In addition to these questions, I ask "Why?" For example, "Why were you able to concentrate better today than yesterday?" Talking about "why" enables students to reflect more on their reading.

The format for this discussion can be varied. In addition to a whole-class discussion, the students can talk in small

Marcee Hobbs
Aspen, Colorado
March 1989

groups or pairs, or even answer the questions independently in literature logs.

My third graders enjoy talking about their reading after SSR. They are eager to share their concerns or feelings about what they read, and they learn from each other. The discussion also gives them a chance to reflect on their reading and develop new insights by sharing their thoughts with the class.

Adjusting Reading Rate: Metacognitive Awareness

Rona F. Flippo
Fitchburg, Massachusetts
Robert L. Lecheler
Parkside, Wisconsin
March 1987

The term *metacognition* represents an idea that is much simpler than it seems. For readers, metacognitive awareness means knowing when they do or do not understand what they are reading. In the intermediate grades (grades four to six), teachers can emphasize metacognitive awareness by using a simple rate adjustment activity that encourages children to modify their reading rates and concentration according to the difficulty of the material. This procedure causes students to become aware of how fast they can read something and still understand it. It requires them to decide whether they need to read certain material "slowly," "moderately," or "fast" (words that youngsters can easily understand).

Begin by explaining to students the reason for varying reading rates ("Because some sentences are more difficult than others, your reading rate shouldn't always be the same.") Explain "difficulty of sentences"—how hard they are to read—and "rate"—the speed at which words in sentences are read. Use several sentences to illustrate what you mean and explain why you would read these slowly, moderately, or fast: "Bill ate peanuts" would be read "fast"; "I could not quickly say 'unique New York'" would be read "moderately"; and "There are cool reds and hot blues" would be read "slowly."

Now ask students why some sentences are read faster than others. List the students' responses on the board. Reasons may be because of unfamiliar words, concepts, language, or style; implied relationships; use of pronouns, punctuation marks, different types of clauses; or lengths of sentences.

Ask the children to suggest some sentences that they would read slowly, moderately, or fast. Write these on the board exactly as they dictate them and ask them to explain why they would read those sentences at those rates. Accept their individual reasons and responses. (What is difficult for one student to understand might not be for another.)

Next explain that comprehension means understanding what is read. Ask students to comprehend the sentences before stating what their reading rates actually were. Then have them find sentences from a variety of materials and textbooks, read them silently, and give the rates they suggest for themselves. Establish this as an ongoing assignment.

Allow many opportunities for the children to share their sentences, suggested rates, and reasons. This can be done individually or in small or large groups. This helps students develop metacognitive awareness. Here are some examples of sentences, rates, and reasons given by fifth graders:

- *Shirley always eats M&M's.* Rate, moderate; reason, "I had to look back and see what M&M's means."

- *Phil is not like Shirley; does he eat M&M's?* Rate, slow; reason, "I had to look at both parts of the sentence before I could answer the question."

- *The marshmallows disappeared.* Rate, fast; reason, "I could see what it said right away."

- *The sun warms the planet Earth, which rotates on its axis and revolves around this star.* Rate, slow; reason, "I had to look at each part, and some of the words are hard."

This activity makes students aware of their own comprehension and teaches them that decisions about difficulty of material are often personal. They learn to adjust their own speed and concentration accordingly.

Some components of reciprocal teaching, which is usually used with secondary students, can be modified for a Directed Reading Activity (DRA) to encourage more active participation and independence among primary-grade readers. This technique has met with great success in occasional use with second graders.

1. The teacher prepares questions about a story. Take both the needs of individuals and group goals into consideration when deciding which types of questions to use. Write these questions on strips of paper, one for each member of the group.

2. The group meets with the teacher. During this session, the teacher and students share background information and set purpose questions for the group to answer.

Reciprocal Teaching: Begin in Second Grade

Constance G. Stark
Cheltenham, Pennsylvania
May 1986

3. The teacher distributes the question strips to the youngsters. This is not done randomly; individuals' needs are considered. For example, a child who needs specific practice in areas such as vocabulary development or appreciation of story setting would be assigned a question dealing with these areas.

4. The group members go off to read the story, answer the purpose questions set by the group, and become experts on their individual questions. The students must each look for the answer to their question and be able to verify it.

5. Later in the day, the group reassembles to answer the questions. Youngsters take turns being the expert, asking each other the questions, exchanging responses, and offering proof. The teacher can structure the order of the questions to develop skills in areas such as cause and effect and sequencing.

6. The teacher provides three or four activities for follow-up, extension, or enrichment. Again, these may be individually assigned or chosen by members of the group. This then becomes the seatwork for the following day.

Eventually, as students gain experience with this technique and more proficiency at setting purposes, they can write their own question strips, thus integrating the reading and writing processes.

Add SQ to the DRTA and Write

Teresa Smyers
Evanston, Illinois
December 1987

How do you motivate disabled readers with low self-esteem and high frustration levels to become active participatory readers? The DRTA (Directed Reading-Thinking Activity) is one of the best approaches to foster active, purposeful reading. The DRTA is a three-step process: (1) predict—the teacher elicits predictions prior to reading; (2) read—the students read a predetermined portion of the story; and (3) prove—the students prove or disprove their predictions based on what they have just read. Add questioning and writing to this procedure and you have a well-rounded comprehension activity for every student.

Basic DRTA

The DRTA can be used in both oral and silent reading as well as to encourage independence in silent reading.

Teachers should follow these steps to prepare for the usual DRTA:

1. Select an exciting story.
2. Mark off three to four good predicting stops.
3. For each segment, write two fact-related questions and one question designed to elicit predictions for student discussion.

The steps for doing the DRTA are these:

1. Students make their initial predictions as to what the story is about. This is often done by using the title and pictures on the first page or by reading the first paragraph.
2. Students read to the next stopping point in order to prove or disprove what they have predicted.
3. At each stopping point they answer the two fact-related questions and the prediction or inference question.

Thus the predict-read-prove cycle is established. This approach is most effective when used with a small group in which the students are reading at the same level and the same rate.

Children with different reading rates pose a difficult problem. What do you do when one child in the group is much slower than the others? The dilemma is how to maintain the integrity of the DRTA without losing students' interest.

Plus SQ and Writing

Writing is the answer. Students can benefit by seeing the interrelationship between reading and writing, especially when they are directly involved through a modification of the DRTA that adds SQ—Directed Reading-Thinking Activity plus Student Questions.

Follow the same steps as for the DRTA but do *not* prepare questions. Instead, at each stopping point ask the students to write two good questions while you do the same thing; remember to have them include a prediction-eliciting question. At each stop, go around the group, allowing each student to ask a question. When a student asks a question, she or he becomes the teacher and gets to call on another student to answer.

By changing the DRTA to DRTA + SQ, the teacher does three important things: (1) involves the students even more in the text (students with the best questions almost always have the best comprehension of the text); (2) stops boredom (students who read rapidly must often go back and reread in order to come up with questions, so they don't just sit there while the slow readers finish); and (3) cuts down on preparation time, thus freeing more time for the teacher to search for well-written, exciting stories.

After sufficient practice, students become much more aware of what makes a good question. Sometimes they will criticize the questions at the end of a story because theirs are so much better; other times they will congratulate themselves on writing the same good question as is provided in the text. Either way it is a powerful self-motivated reading activity.

The DRTA + SQ also acts as a springboard to teach other reading skills. After reading the following list of suggestions, add some of your own ideas.

- Model silent reading, neat handwriting, clear questions, and critical thinking.

- Use the questions generated to teach and label types of questions. Is it a "right there" (in the text) question, a "think and search" question, or an "on my own" question?

- Teach the parts of a story. Is that question about the plot, a character, the setting...?

- Have students work on writing in complete sentences by asking them to write answers to each other's questions.

- Help students develop good communication skills. Ask: How can we vary that question? How can we answer that question more clearly?

- Use the questions as a diagnostic tool. Look for good questions. This reflects good comprehension.

- Help balance the student-teacher exchange. Class observations indicate that 80 percent of these exchanges are initiated by the teacher; can you increase the students' share?

- Motivate disabled or slow readers by making their problems less central.

- Foster independent reading and critical thinking.

Reading requires purposeful, active involvement. The Directed Reading-Thinking Activity plus Student Questions ensures student involvement and fosters independence.

The ability to summarize apparently increases with age, often developing fully by the end of high school, but even third graders can locate important events in well-developed stories, and fifth graders are able to delete unimportant and redundant information in text when direct instruction is provided. This activity, which can be used in grades three through eight, provides direct instruction in summarizing as well as practice in sequencing, another important skill. It offers students maximum involvement in a meaningful reading/writing activity that provides an alternative to typical seatwork. There are seven steps.

Step 1: Reading a selection to determine the essential plot. Choose a selection for your group—a story from a basal reader, a chapter from a book, or a sequential passage from a nonfiction text. Avoid highly descriptive or narrative passages or nonfiction that delivers information without a sequence. If you choose a complete story from a basal reader, introduce it and let students read it silently to see how the plot develops. Then guide students to develop a story frame that clearly states the essential plot.

Step 2: Provide instruction in writing one- or two-sentence summaries for small segments of text. At the time of the next lesson, direct students to reread the first page (or some other clearly delineated segment) to determine the most important ideas. Then ask the group, "What helps us know about the problem [or its solution]?" or ask students to draw a mental picture of the events of the page. Encourage students to state their ideas in their own words rather than those of the author.

When several ideas have been suggested and written on the board, guide students to delete unimportant words, combine ideas, and use more inclusive words to replace a long list (e.g., use "everyone in the family" for a list of characters' names). When one or two sentences have been decided upon for that page (or segment), write the summary on large chart paper. Continue the procedure until the entire selection has been summarized.

Step 3: Code summaries for easy checking (optional). When the next lesson begins, teach students to code the order of their summaries for self-checking. Page numbers, letters, or a code word may be used to indicate the correct sequence.

Step 4: Cut apart summary statements and mix them. Now cut apart the summaries, rearrange them, and guide students to put them back in order as a group. They may do so without looking back at the story, or they may use the selection to verify what they think—as you choose. When the group is satisfied with the arrangement, the code on the back can be used as a final check.

Summaries and Sequence for Active Comprehension

Joyce E. Eddy
Blue Island, Illinois
May 1988

Step 5: Have students make their own summary strips.
After students have learned the procedure, they are ready to
use it with other selections. Each student prepares a set of
summary sentences, putting answers or codes on the back.

A list of "rules" for writing summary sentences may be
provided for assistance, as shown in the Figure. Younger students may need to be reminded to write on only one side of
the paper so the summaries can be cut apart. Students may be
provided with slips of paper cut uniformly or they can be
directed to cut the summaries apart with straight edges so the
sentences must be read rather than reassembled by shape.

How to Write Summaries

1. Look for the most important ideas. (What helps us
   know about the problem or the solution?)
2. State important ideas in your own words.
3. Combine ideas into one or two sentences.
4. Leave out anything that repeats information, *explains*
   important ideas, or seems unimportant.

Step 6: Trade summary statements. In this step, children
work as partners, exchanging sets of summaries that have
been thoroughly mixed. Each student places the partner's summary in sequential order. This activity may be self-checking or
returned to the writer for checking.

After the summaries have been put in order and
checked for accuracy, they may be glued to construction paper
and illustrated.

Step 7: Use reconstructed summaries in group activities.
The summaries may be used in group discussion and oral
reading. For example, you might suggest changing a story
event in some way and then have students discuss how that
change would affect their summaries. Another option is to
have one student choose a summary statement to read aloud;
a second student then reads the summary statement that pre-
cedes or follows the first reader's statement.

This activity has a number of features that help students better comprehend what they read. First, students are
taught to locate significant information and to begin the important task of learning to summarize. Second, they practice
sequencing in an interesting and meaningful way. Third, since
students read for a specific purpose, they are likely to become
actively involved. Fourth, they must write and spell so that a

partner can read what has been written, thus providing another audience besides the teacher. (In fact, once students have become proficient at summarizing, the teacher is involved only in the follow-up phase.) Finally, since students are putting considerable energy into the literal interpretation of the selection, the teacher may use group discussion time to focus on the inferential and critical/evaluative aspects of the selection.

THINK-WINK-DECIDE for Comprehension

Susann K. Barbour
Hampstead, Maryland
May 1989

A variety of graphic organizers have been developed to enhance classroom instruction in many different learning areas. One called THINK-WINK-DECIDE is great for helping children with comprehension of expository selections. It also encourages them to go beyond the assigned reading selection and read other resource materials for information.

THINK-WINK-DECIDE is an acronym for THings I Now Know—What I Need to Know—DECIDE. This graphic organizer consists of three columns. In the first column, THINK, children list everything they know about the subject about which they are going to read. This gets children to draw on their background experiences prior to reading, which in turn helps them increase comprehension. The second column, WINK, establishes the purpose for reading by having the children generate questions about things they hope to learn from reading the selection. After reading, the children DECIDE whether their background knowledge was accurate and whether the selection answered all of their questions.

When I introduce this graphic organizer to my reading groups, I give all the children a copy of the THINK-WINK-DECIDE diagram and ask them to look at the title and the pictures of the expository selection. From this information they are to list in the THINK column everything they think they know about the subject. When they have had ample time to make this list, I ask them to think about things they don't know about the subject but would like to learn. They then write their questions in the WINK column. Next the children share things they have written in the two columns with the group, and I record their ideas on a chart for all to see. This sharing time helps children remember things they think they know about the topic but forgot to put down. It also generates new questions.

At this point, I ask the children to read the selection carefully and then to look again at their THINK-WINK-DECIDE organizer and decide whether the things they thought about the topic were accurate. If they had some inaccurate information, they should indicate in the DECIDE column what was inaccurate and correct it. In this column the children can also decide whether the author accomplished his or her purpose for writing the article and explain their decision.

A third use for the DECIDE column is to help the children determine which of their questions were answered by the selection and which were not. I have them write the answers next to those questions that were answered. We then discuss the questions that were not answered and how the children might find the answers. I have available in my classroom an array of nonfiction books and other resource materials on the topic so students can research and then write a report that will answer those questions.

This organizer can also be used for writing reports on topics that do not come from assigned reading selections. The children can choose their own topic and then list all the things they think they know about that topic in the THINK column and all the questions they have about their topic in the WINK column. As they do their research, they can use the DECIDE column to correct any misinformation under THINK and answer the questions under WINK. When they feel they know their topic adequately, they can decide on their audience and write their rough drafts.

THINK-WINK-DECIDE need not be confined to reading and writing. It can also be used in content areas like social studies, health, and science. It is used with the text for these subjects in the same way it is used for reading stories. One benefit this organizer provides for content subjects is that it helps the children focus on what they are learning. It can also provide a study guide to prepare for tests.

THINK-WINK-DECIDE is a versatile graphic organizer. Teachers can use their imagination to come up with other uses for it.

Space Travel in Reading

Maria Valeri-Gold
Marietta, Georgia
November 1986

To enhance the teaching of critical reading skills to a class of intermediate-grade students, introduce the class to this space travel activity. Designed to appeal to students' interest in space adventure, it combines the teaching of critical reading with the reinforcement of concepts taught in content area subjects. Evaluation of texts with respect to fact and opinion, tone, bias, purpose and intent, and propaganda is emphasized. In this activity, sentences, paragraphs, and questions are written on 4" x 6" index cards. These brief texts reinforce the concepts taught in class in the areas of science, social studies, math, and language arts. Here are some examples:

Fact and opinion. "The capital of Florida is Tallahassee." Is this a fact or an opinion statement? (Fact)

"President Kennedy was the best president of the United States." Is this a fact or an opinion statement? (Opinion)

Tone. "It was pitch dark. As I walked up the street, I could hear heavy footsteps following close behind me. I didn't turn around. I ran as fast as I could until I was home and safe in my bed." What is the author's tone? (Frightened)

Bias. "I feel that smoking should be prohibited in the workplace. A designated smoking area should be set aside for smokers." What is the author's bias? (Against smoking)

Purpose. "A tropical depression has wind gusts of up to 39 miles an hour, while a tropical storm has winds of 39 miles per hour or more. When the wind gusts reach 74 miles per hour, a hurricane is born." What is the author's purpose? (To explain the difference between a tropical depression, a tropical storm, and a hurricane)

Propaganda. "Everybody is trying the new peanut butter yogurt. Have you tried it? Everyone else has tasted it." What is the propaganda technique? (Bandwagon)

Playing the Game

Before the game, type each text and corresponding question on one side of a 4" x 6" index card. The other side is a "ticket" to a specified planet: Mercury, Venus, Mars, Jupiter, Saturn, Uranus, Neptune, or Pluto. The ticket side of the card may be colored with felt-tip pens of different colors for the different planets. Easy critical reading questions appear on tickets to nearby planets, such as Venus or Mars; harder questions appear on tickets to more distant planets. The tickets are assigned appropriate values: for instance, a traveler earns ten points and goes to Pluto by answering a hard question; he or she earns only two points for answering an easier Mars question. The tickets are placed in a large box that is wrapped in aluminum foil and labeled "Space Travel Tickets." If you want, you can mark the "planets" (different areas in the room) with placards and make different colored headbands to identify members of the two space adventure teams.

Once you're set up, divide the class into two teams and distribute the colored headbands. A space captain (scorekeeper) records the points earned by each team and sends the travelers to their destinations. The first traveler selects a ticket from the ticket box and reads aloud the critical reading question. If he or she answers the question correctly, the team receives the specified number of points and the traveler proceeds to the designated planet. If he or she cannot answer the question correctly, it is given to the next traveler from the opposing team. If neither traveler can answer the question correctly, the answer is explained and no points are awarded. Play continues until each student has had a turn. The team that has accumulated the most points (and whose players have traveled the furthest distance) is declared the winner of Space Travel in Reading.

Developing Comprehension: Evaluating What Is Read

Bette N. Greene
Skokie, Illinois
April 1986

The ability to evaluate what is read actually requires many abilities, including distinguishing between fact and opinion; telling what is real and what is fantasy; determining an author's qualifications, purposes, and attitude; and noting the currentness of information.

Fact or opinion. To distinguish between fact and opinion, students might do the following:

1. Analyze newspaper reports to determine whether they present facts or opinions.

2. Study news reports and editorials to determine the differences between the two types of writing.

3. Locate statements of opinion in a selection.

4. Indicate which of a series of statements express facts, then rewrite any others so that they do not express an opinion.

5. Rewrite statements that mix fact and opinion to take the opposing point of view (e.g., showing antipathy toward a person or event rather than sympathy).

6. Delete from paragraphs or longer selections statements that are not entirely factual.

Real or fanciful. To become more adept at judging whether written material is of a fanciful or factual nature, students might do the following:

1. Find examples in stories of means by which the author indicated that the story is fanciful.

2. Draw up a list of expressions often used in stories to show that they are fanciful (for example, "Once upon a time").

3. Decide whether a story is real or fanciful and give the reason for the decision.

4. Read a story that is fictional but based in part on fact, and then determine which statements are likely to be true and which are more likely to be fictional.

Author's qualifications. To learn to determine an author's qualifications, students might do these activities:

1. Think of two people, each of whom is qualified to speak or write on a given subject but who have different background experiences. How would the two people differ in the way they addressed the subject?

2. Look at the qualifications of two authors, then decide which one would be better qualified to write on a given topic.

3. Working with a group, decide on questions to ask when determining an author's qualifications. For example, does the author have much information about the subject? Does the author have a good reputation as a writer? Is there a reason the author might wish to promote one point of view over another?

4. Determine what the author's purpose was in writing a given selection.

5. Given a list of sentences, decide which are sympathetic toward a person or situation and which are unsympathetic.

Up-to-dateness. The following activities might help students decide on the currentness of information.

1. Note the copyright date of books.

2. Determine which books written long ago are valuable for a stated purpose and which are not.

3. Find an item of information reported in an old book that would be as valuable as one in a recent book.

The following activities can improve students' ability to predict outcomes.

1. Look at the pictures in a story and state what the outcome of the story is likely to be.

2. Arrange in order pictures illustrating a story that has not been read yet.

3. Given multiple choices, indicate what is likely to happen next in a story or article.

4. Stop in the middle of reading a story or article and tell what is likely to happen next.

Developing Comprehension: Predicting Outcomes

Bette N. Greene
Skokie, Illinois
May 1986

5. Predict what will happen next after listening to part of an account of an experience another pupil has had.

6. Discuss why things happened as they did in a story or other account.

7. Make up endings for unfinished stories.

8. Estimate answers to arithmetic problems.

9. Compare a current event to a previous one in history and decide what might happen as a result of present conditions.

10. Before beginning a science activity, discuss what is likely to happen.

11. Evaluate plans the class is making in terms of expected outcomes.

12. List on the board known points about a situation and possible outcomes, then discuss the probability of certain results.

13. Predict the weather and give reasons for the prediction. Later check it.

14. After reading a news report, predict what will happen and later check to see if the prediction was correct.

Drawing: Homework for Remedial Readers

Tina Marie Costantino
Brea, California
March 1986

I capitalize on students' drawing ability to motivate them to complete weekly homework assignments, to promote class discussions, and to use as a prewriting activity for structured writing assignments. Students' drawings often provide a reliable way to check reading comprehension without having to factor in any writing deficiencies they might have.

With this strategy, bored students who are tired of the same old homework assignments perk up and begin to ask, "What's the drawing assignment this week?" But more important, many children feel less threatened and more comfortable drawing than writing. This is especially true of some remedial students.

Here are some possible drawing strategies. The drawing task is explained in class after a story has been read and is then assigned as homework. I always tell students what the reading comprehension focus is, provide them with paper, and tell them how many details to include. I also remind them that they should be prepared to share their drawing the next day during a class discussion.

Focus: Compare and contrast. Home activity: Students draw an unlabeled before-and-after picture of a character in the story who has made a major personality change. Discussion questions (in class): Which is the before and after picture, and how do you know? What trait did everyone include in his or her drawing? What drawing don't you understand? What do you think caused this personality change?

Focus: Sequencing. Home activity: Students draw a specified number of important events from the story in comic book style. Discussion questions: Why did you choose these events? Are these events in the correct order? If you took out event 2 would event 3 have happened? Which event had the most effect on the story's outcome?

Focus: Prediction. Home activity: Draw a picture of the setting and character 20 years later. Discussion questions: What changes has the character made? Were these positive or negative changes? How is the setting different? Will the character remain in the setting?

Focus: Effect. Activity: In class, the teacher draws an event in the story. At home, the students do a series of small drawings showing the effects of that event. Students can infer some effects not mentioned in the story. Discussion questions: Which drawings illustrate an effect mentioned in the story? Which effects are inferences? Are these inferences plausible? Which characters were affected by this event?

Focus: Cause. Activity: At home, students draw their favorite scene from the story on the top half of a piece of paper. In class, this drawing is passed to three different students. Each student must write a cause for the event drawn. If there are not three causes, the students must make an inference. Discussion questions: Which cause was given in the story? What causes were inferred? Is there usually only one cause for a given event? Which cause justified the event?

Each drawing activity is related to a specific reading comprehension focus and serves as (1) a prompt during class discussions of a story (it reminds students of details of the story and helps them feel more self-assured during discussion); (2) a comprehension worksheet; and (3) a tool for understanding different interpretations of a story, drawing inferences, rethinking what is read, making predictions, or perhaps just clarifying the plot.

Drawing should certainly not replace formal writing assignments in either a remedial or a regular classroom, but it is important to realize that remedial reading students' writing skills are often even lower than their reading skills. When other means of demonstrating comprehension are easier and more appealing than writing, they should be used from time to time. Through the peer interaction that follows the drawing, students gain a varied and thorough understanding of the story and can then write more fluently and confidently about it. This frees the teacher to work with students on the mechanics and structure of composition. A formal writing assignment following the drawing and discussion can be as simple as writing two or three complete sentences or as complicated as writing a character analysis.

This drawing strategy serves three basic functions. It is a homework activity that children enjoy, a discussion prompt, and a prewriting activity. Reading, writing, speaking, and thinking are essential components of a remedial reading program. Why not add drawing? Students may find that drawing conclusions was never easier.

Children Make Reading Skills Cards

Vita Monastero
Brooklyn, New York
December 1985

We know that children learn by doing. My fifth graders proved this when I had them make their own reading skills cards. The activity described here reinforces the WH question skills (who, what, where, why, when, and how), creative writing skills, and paraphrasing and summarizing skills. It works well with middle- and upper-grade children.

Before this activity is introduced, we work as a class to write a creative story, develop six WH questions (one of each), and then answer the questions. We also summarize a short story and develop and answer six WH questions about it. In this way the students get some practice in the skills involved before they write their own cards. Then I introduce the skills card activity, with these steps:

1. Tell the children they are to choose a topic and either read something on it from the library or write their own short story about it using personal experience or imagination. Some broad topics include holidays, science, sports, and famous people.

2. Give them five 5" x 8" (13 cm x 20 cm) index cards. Tell them they will be paraphrasing what they read or wrote and putting it on the cards to make a game for others to use.

3. At this point, review the WH questions and explain that students may use as many cards as they need to provide enough information to ask WH questions about their topic.

4. On the lined sides of one or more index cards, the youngsters neatly print their summaries. At the top

right they put their topic and the source on which they have based their information; to the left they draw a small picture to act as an eye-catcher for their classmates who will read the card later.

5. Now tell the children to take a separate card and print at least six WH questions about their summaries—one of each type.

6. On another card, they write the answers to their questions in complete sentences.

7. On still another card, they develop a game to reinforce vocabulary. Some game suggestions include word find, word jumbles, and secret codes. The game is based on the summaries from the first information card(s). Game answers are printed on the back of the same card that answers the six WH questions.

8. Assign a number to each child and write that number on the top of each card in the child's set. Numbers are important, as answer cards are kept separately; the others are stapled together.

9. Finally, check all cards for spelling, writing, and correctness of answers before they are used by other class members.

This activity serves as independent work after children finish other assignments. Some days are set aside specifically for students to begin writing their cards or to read others' completed cards.

Each time we start making a new set of cards, I review the meaning of WH questions. I generally give children about two weeks to complete writing a set, although some need more time.

Finished cards are placed in number order in two piles. One pile contains the answer cards. When the finished cards are to be used, call children a few at a time to choose a card. After students read a card and try to answer the questions, they match their responses with those on the answer card. Answers to the questions and to the vocabulary game are written in their notebooks. As the children improve in writing and answering their own questions, I begin to have them write specific reading cards about sequence. (For more ideas about teaching skills this way, see Harvey Alpert and Margaret Carvo, *Selected Strategies for Teaching Decoding and Comprehension*, Casil Publications, 1984.)

Students not only improve their reading skills with this activity, they also enjoy developing their cards to share with the class.

Unscramble Me!

Maria Valeri-Gold
Marietta, Georgia
May 1985

Outlines can help students understand the main idea of a selection and distinguish between major points, important supporting details, and minor supporting details. Unscrambling a list of related words into outlines can help students learn to order their ideas.

Sample of a Science-Related Word List and Outline Form

Word List

Tyrannosaurus Rex, Herbivores, Triceratops, Types of Dinosaurs, Stegosaurus, Allosaurus, Brontosaurus, Carnivores, Pleisosaurus.

Completed Outline Form

Main Idea: _Types of Dinosaurs_

  I. _Herbivores_
    A. _Triceratops_
    B. _Stegosaurus_
    C. _Brontosaurus_

  II. _Carnivores_
    A. _Tyrannosaurus Rex_
    B. _Allosaurus_
    C. _Pleisosaurus_

I developed unscrambling word exercises for students in intermediate grades who were learning how to outline. I used high-interest words from their science and social studies textbooks to integrate reading, the content areas, and vocabulary development. Here are the teaching steps involved.

1. Define outlining as a visual way of displaying key ideas and details.

2. Tell students that numbers, letters, and indentations show the importance of ideas in an outline (see Figure). Roman numerals state the major ideas, uppercase letters identify important supporting details, Arabic numbers represent minor supporting details, and indentations tell the significance of ideas and details. The further from the left margin a word is placed, the lower its priority.

3. Write lists of related words on transparencies. Give students the same lists of words, representing scrambled major ideas and supporting details, on duplicated worksheets.

4. Ask students to read the word lists and answer three questions: Which words fit into groups? Which describe larger categories? What word describes the whole topic?

5. Students unscramble the related word lists by identifying the main ideas, major points, and supporting details and rewriting them on the outline forms provided.

6. As an individual activity, students create their own word lists using their science or social studies textbooks.

7. Finally, students exchange their word lists with classmates who unscramble and rewrite them on outline forms.

Teaching Theme to Elementary Students

Edna K. Smit
Grand Rapids, Michigan
May 1990

Because the theme of a story is abstract, it can be a difficult concept to teach. I have devised several methods for teaching theme that have been quite successful.

The first method requires selecting two stories with the same theme but very different settings, problems, attempts to solve the problems, events, outcomes, and endings. (For example, I used this method with *Why the Chimes Rang* by Raymond MacDonald Alden and a Japanese folktale entitled *The Grateful Statues*. Both of these stories have the theme of giving.) The method uses the following steps: Read the first story and then ask, "In one word, what was this story about?" Have the students form small groups to answer this question and discuss their answers for a few minutes. Follow this by receiving a report from each group and writing the responses on the board.

After each group has reported and the students have reached a consensus on the theme, read the second story. When you have finished, ask again, "In one word, what was this story about?" The students should immediately recognize that the two stories have the same theme.

As a follow-up writing activity, have students write the elements of story grammar on the left-hand side of a piece of paper and then fill in the elements for each story. At the top, they should write the theme. The completed papers should look something like the example in Figure 1.

Figure 1
Theme: Giving

Story:	*Why the Chimes Rang*	*The Grateful Statues*
Characters:	Pedro and Little Brother	An old Japanese couple
Setting—		
Where:	In a far-away country	Japan
When:	Christmas Eve	New Year's Eve
Problem—		
Event:	On the way to the Christmas Eve service, Pedro and Little Brother came upon a woman in the snow.	The old man took hats to sell at the market but did not sell them.
Event:	Little Brother took Pedro's only coin and laid it on the altar when no one was watching as a gift to the Holy Child.	On the way home in a snowstorm, he came upon six stone statues of Jizo, the patron saint of lost children. He gave up his own hat, as well as the hats he was to sell, placing them on the statues.
Resolution and ending:	After Little Brother placed the gift on the altar, the chimes rang.	The stone Jizo rewarded him with the biggest rice cake they had ever seen.

The other method I have used involves the following steps: Before giving children the books, say, "I want you to read this book. When you have finished, I want you to think of one word that tells what it is about."

When the students have finished reading, have them discuss the book with a partner. Ask for volunteers to tell the words they thought of, writing all their responses on the board. Discuss these responses and point out that some are either too inclusive or too exclusive. See if the students can reach a consensus about the author's purpose and thus the theme. Then complete a story chart on the board (this might look like the example in Figure 2).

Figure 2
Theme: Jealousy

Story:	*One Frog Too Many* by Mercer and Marianna Meyer
Characters:	Big Frog, Little Frog, Boy, Turtle, Dog
Problem:	The boy gets a new Little Frog and Big Frog is jealous.
Attempts to solve the problem:	Big Frog bites Little Frog on the leg. Big Frog kicks Little Frog off Turtle's back. Big Frog kicks Little Frog off the raft and everyone thinks he's dead and is sad.
Resolution:	Little Frog comes back and Big Frog puts his arm around him, showing that he wants to be friends.

Next, ask the students to close their eyes and think of something personal relating to the theme. After a few minutes, have them talk about their experience in groups of three or four. For grades three to five, have the students write a story with the theme. To aid them, refer them to the story grammar on the board. They can select their own characters, setting, and attempts to solve the problem. When they have done this, they realize that they have developed many different stories with the same theme. For grades one and two, the class can write a book collaboratively. First and second grade children who are comfortable with invented spelling can write their own stories.

Aside from giving and jealousy, common themes in children's literature include determination, friendship, survival, courage, responsibility, good and evil, inner versus outer beauty, the value of home, the consequences of trying to be something you aren't, and faithfulness.

Teaching Comprehension with Editorials

Mary A. Furleigh
Fallbrook, California
March 1991

Reading and writing editorials are good ways to develop skills in reading for the main idea, inferential comprehension, and critical thinking. I use this activity with eighth graders, but the level can be adjusted by changing the reading level and subject matter of the editorials.

This procedure comprises three steps: selection, directions, and evaluation. Editorials are selected from a variety of sources, such as local newspapers, news magazines, or school newspapers. The subject of the editorials should be relevant to the students. Initially students can select from teacher-provided editorials but can gradually begin to bring their own editorials.

The students are then given the following directions:

1. Read the editorial and discuss it with an adult or another student.
2. Answer the questions on the Editorial Response Form (see Figure).
3. Based on your answers, write one sentence to answer each of the following questions: What is the subject of the editorial? What is the writer's opinion? What is your opinion on the subject?
4. Turn in the sentences, editorial, and completed response form.

Editorial Response Form

Statement of Main Idea

1. Who or what is the editorial about? _____

2. Is the title intended to inform or to interest the reader? _____

3. What is the most important point the writer makes about the subject?_____

Statement of Inference

1. What is the author writing about?_____

2. Is the author for or against this subject?_____

3. List one or two reasons the author gives for his or her position._____
   _____

4. What is the author's opinion on the subject of the editorial? _____

Student Response

1. Why do you believe the writer is for or against this subject? _____

2. Do you agree or disagree? _____

3. Why do you feel as you do on the subject? _____

This activity can be evaluated by the teacher or by peers. Peer evaluation is actually a review activity since the peer must read, ask and answer questions, and judge the writing of the editorial. (If this method of evaluation is used, students can write on their papers a code known only to the teacher, rather than their names.) For variety, the peer evaluation can also be conducted as a small-group activity in which three or four students evaluate one another's work.

Extra Readings: Reading outside the Classroom

Sandra Bennett
*Jonesboro, Louisiana
(now College Station, Texas)
March 1991*

Students need to be aware of the various types of reading materials that they will encounter outside the classroom. In order to prepare my junior high students for these materials, I created "Extra Readings." Each week I assign students a particular type of reading material that they must bring to class from home. I make the assignment on Monday, and the students have until Friday to bring the material to class. At the beginning of class on Friday, we discuss the material collected, and then I give the students questions or a specific activity to complete using their reading material.

Several types of material can be assigned, and several activities can be used for each to reinforce reading comprehension. Listed below are a few examples.

1. *Recipe*: Have students rewrite the directions in their own words.

2. *Menu*: Formulate questions that require students to locate particular information on the menu (for example, "How much does a particular item cost?" or "Where is the restaurant located?").

3. *Comic strip*: Have students rewrite the comic strip using synonyms.

4. *Can label or cereal box*: Ask the students certain questions concerning the information given (for example, "How many calories does it have?" or "How much iron is in it?").

5. *Weather map from newspaper*: Have students identify symbols and weather vocabulary.

6. *Contents page of a magazine*: Pose questions and have the students identify the page or section in which the answer is found.

7. *Sale advertisements*: Have students determine how much they can save by buying sale items, how to go

about buying a particular item, and how to use ads in making selections (see Figure 1).

8. *Newspaper articles.* Use various newspaper articles for several activities, such as (1) find all the words with prefixes, suffixes, or both; (2) determine the topic sentence; (3) find all pronoun referents and list the noun to which they refer; (4) write the main idea; or (5) outline the article.

Figure 1
Specific Questions for Specific Ads

Automobile Ads

1. What makes are the automobiles being advertised (Ford, Pontiac, Chevrolet, etc.)?
2. What types of automobiles are they advertising (convertible, van, etc.)?
3. List the cost of each of the automobiles.
4. Do they require a down payment? If so, how much is it for each car?
5. Do they offer a rebate? If so, how much is it for each car?
6. Where could you purchase these automobiles?
7. Do they offer a finance plan? If so, explain the type of plan they offer.

Classified Ads

1. What category (or categories) of ads do you have?
2. What basic information is given in each of the ads?
3. List any abbreviations used and explain what they stand for.
4. Read over the ads carefully. Explain how they are written as opposed to an ordinary paragraph or passage.
5. Select one of the ads that interests you and explain how you would respond to it.

Real Estate Ads

1. What type of real estate is being advertised?
2. Where is this real estate located?
3. How much does it cost?
4. How would you find out more information about the real estate?
5. List some other important information that is given (if any).
6. In your own words, define "real estate."

Commercial Ads

1. What company or store is being promoted in your ad?
2. Where are they located?
3. What is their phone number?
4. What are they advertising?
5. What is their slogan or title?
6. Do you think the product is a bargain? Why or why not?
7. Do you think someone would really notice this ad? Why or why not?
8. What do you think is the purpose of ads?

To begin the day each Friday, we have an Extra Reading session. I display questions or specific instructions for the students to follow that are appropriate for the type of readings they have collected. Students then attempt to carry these out on their own, using the material they have brought to class. After they have completed the independent portion of the session, we hold a class discussion about the information they have collected. I begin by going over the steps, questions, or directions given. Next, I allow the students to express their opinions, ask questions of their own, elaborate on why particular information is important, and point out why being able to read this information is essential (see Figure 2).

I relate each week's Extra Reading to a subject being discussed in class or use it to reinforce a specific skill for that week. When materials are more difficult to locate or are not available to students, I have extra materials on hand.

My students look forward to these Extra Readings each week and enjoy trying to bring them from home. They consider it "fun homework" and are highly motivated and involved with the activity.

As the year progresses, watch for students' improvement in newspaper reading skills, locating information, relating information and numbers, study skills, word structure skills, and vocabulary. The Extra Readings serve as an indirect way to teach skills needed for better reading while increasing students' knowledge about the application of reading outside the classroom.

Figure 2
Sample Discussion

Extra Reading: Cereal box

Discussion: After specifically stating the answers to any questions and pointing out where information can be found, allow students to elaborate on this information by stating opinions, asking additional questions, and generating discussions. The following is an example of this type of discussion.

Teacher: Does anyone have any points to make or questions to ask about the information on this cereal box?

Student 1: Is it really important for the company to list *two* columns of nutritional information—one for the cereal *with* milk and one without?

Student 2: I don't think so because most people eat cereal with milk.

Teacher: Does anyone have a different answer?

Student 3: I think it might be because some people use dry cereal in recipes and would need to know the nutritional information.

(continued next page)

Figure 2 (continued)
Sample Discussion

Student 4: Some people may use skim milk or low-fat milk which would be different than the milk on the box.

Student 1: Why is it important to know the number of calories?

Student 2: Some people are trying to lose weight and count the calories they eat.

Student 3: Other people may be on special diets and have to count calories.

Teacher: The information says that calcium is found in milk. Do you know what calcium is?

Student 1: In science class we found out that calcium is an element found in a lot of substances.

Student 2: It builds stronger bones and teeth.

Student 1: After looking at the guarantee, my question is do you think any people actually write in or call for their money back?

Student 2: Well, I think some probably do. Some people really demand satisfaction and will do anything to get what they are entitled to.

Student 3: I think that most people really don't take the time to call or write if they don't like the cereal.

Teacher: Do you think it's important for companies to include all of this information on their products?

Student 1: Yes, because there are many people who are really conscious of nutrition and health.

Student 2: I think it's good because the company is not trying to hide anything about the products.

Student 3: Well, I think that most people are going to buy the product they like the best no matter what nutritional information or guarantee is provided.

Story frames are a form of probed text recall. The story frame is a skeletal outline of the text—in a way, a story-level cloze. The skeleton contains just enough information to probe the child's recall of the story. In the Figure shown here, the sentence beginnings (set in type) are the teacher's frame; the handwritten endings to the sentences show how a six-year-old filled in the frame after reading the story.

Story Frames— Story Cloze

Trevor H. Cairney
Wagga Wagga (now Kingswood), NSW, Australia
November 1987

A Story Frame for Maurice Sendak's
Where the Wild Things Are

Max gets himself into trouble when he _is cheky to His mother and he said he will Eat His Mother up._

His mother _Sent Him to bed without any supper._

That night in Max's room _a forist grew._

So Max sailed away to _to the wold of wild things._

and met _the wild things_

Max tamed them and they made him _King of all ths wild things._

But Max became lonely and wanted _someone who Loved Him._

So he left the Land of Wild Things and when he reached home _his dinner was wating for Him._

The frame that you construct after reading the story in preparation for class should not be too detailed or the activity will become far too restrictive. (Avoid restrictiveness at all times.) Children can complete the frame individually or in small groups; I feel that group collaboration is preferable for this lesson.

Presenting the original text to the class can be done in a variety of ways. You might use books beyond the children's current reading level and read the texts to them. On the other hand, you might use a text that the children can read and have them read it silently.

After the story is read, each child attempts to fill in the story frame by recalling the text. If they are working in groups, a leader asks the members to suggest the content to be placed in each slot. Once the frame is complete, it is read right through and the content is discussed. Children are encouraged to consider individually how accurately they feel the completed frame reflects the meaning they created for themselves as they read the original story. A useful extension to this technique is to ask children to create story frames for other children to use.

This story frame or story cloze technique is not designed to test memory of text. Rather, its aim is to help readers construct a coherent understanding of text. One of the difficulties some readers face is not being able to organize the information they take in from reading; they may remember only isolated segments. This framing technique helps them to construct a coherent representation of the text.

Transformations

Evelyn T. Cudd
Gainesville, Florida
December 1988

First graders can enjoy instant success as writers and at the same time reinforce sight vocabulary by transforming sentences from their basal readers or read-aloud stories. When a sentence is transformed, the structure or syntax remains the same, but the words change—for instance, "On every branch there was a monkey" becomes "On every clothesline there was a bird."

Most basal reading series have good complex sentences to transform as early as the third preprimer or primer. If you do not want to use basal sentences, draw from read-aloud literature. Use the following procedure for selecting and assigning sentence transformations:

1. Choose a sentence that does not follow the normal noun-verb-object sentence construction. This will provide practice in understanding and using complex and varied sentence patterns.

2. Write the sentence on the chalkboard and underline with colored chalk the words or phrases to be transformed (for instance, "At the <u>flower shop</u> there was a <u>little red pony</u>.").

3. Explain that you will be transforming or changing the underlined words to make a new sentence. (Children easily understand the word *transform*. Do not hesitate to use it.)

4. Brainstorm possible substitutions for the underlined words. As a child gives his or her response, write it on the board, and then have the child read the new sentence. This reinforces the sentence structure and vocabulary.

5. After five to ten minutes of brainstorming (this time will decrease once children understand the procedure), tell students that they are to transform the sentence twice. To demonstrate, have one child give two sentences. Write them both on the board or on an overhead transparency. Before children begin, erase the words to be transformed.

6. Tell children that if another child has given an idea out loud during the brainstorming period, that sentence belongs to him or her and cannot be used by anyone else in the class. Each child must write unique sentences. This encourages productive thinking and ownership of ideas.

7. Tell the children that after they have written their two sentences, they are to illustrate each one. Emphasize adding enough appropriate details to convey the specific meaning of each sentence. (You may need to demonstrate by drawing an illustration on the board and adding specific details.) Remember that illustrating is not busywork. It facilitates visual imagery and therefore enhances comprehension. Formulating a mental picture further aids the retention of vocabulary as well as the understanding of a particular sentence structure. Story paper 12" x 18" (30 cm x 45 cm) is excellent for this activity because it provides a space for illustration.

In place of worksheets, my colleagues and I use sentence transformations two to three times a week as seatwork. We have found this activity to be an extremely productive way to reinforce vocabulary and practice complex sentence patterns, both of which are essential for effective reading and writing.

Sentence Elaboration

Cynthia Tyler
Rockford, Illinois
February 1987

Do your students have difficulty writing elaborated sentences? Here is a concrete way to teach children to expand their sentences and have fun while doing so.

To begin you need a piece of paper for each student, folded into three equal sections labeled 1, 2, and 3. Next write a simple sentence on the chalkboard and have students copy it in the first section of their papers. (Perhaps elicit this sentence from a child.) Then have the student illustrate the meaning of the sentence in the space under it. Next ask children to tell more about the first sentence they illustrated—to expand on the sentence. For the example in the Figure, some common answers would involve the flower's size, color, or shape. Then either you or a student can write the expanded sentence in section 2 and the student can illustrate it. Do the same for an elaborated sentence in the third section.

This technique can be used with individual children in early elementary grades and is a good class or small-group activity with more sophisticated children. In groups, several students can suggest elaborations before each child writes down her or his own variant.

Elaborating sentences has a spin-off for bilingual students, too: it's a good way to learn sentence structures.

Sentence Elaboration Example

1 The flower grew.	2 The _____ flower grew.	3 The _____ flower grew _____.

Chapter 5

Reading and Writing in the Content Areas

Content area reading refers to reading and learning from subject area textbooks or other subject-oriented material, usually expository text that explains or analyzes information about that subject. Content reading instruction includes guiding students' readings and understanding of science, social studies, health, and math texts, usually through structured activities (Schallert & Roser, 1989).

It is important to help children learn to read expository texts skillfully, for several reasons. First, children need to develop proficiency with simple expository texts in order to keep pace with the increasingly complex subject area textbooks they will encounter as they progress through school. Second, although children certainly build knowledge about the world through daily experiences, they cannot get all their information from experience. For example, children may learn about the physical sciences in and out of school through discovery, experimentation, and observation, but much science information is impractical, or even dangerous, to learn in these ways; science textbooks are necessary to supplement children's knowledge of science.

Learning new or additional information through expository text may be difficult for some children, however (Alvermann & Boothby, 1982; Olson, 1985). Expository texts have special characteristics that make them harder for children to comprehend than stories. For instance, readers may have limited background knowledge to link to new information presented in text. Content area textbooks are written to inform rather than entertain, which may lower children's motivation to read them. Children meet unfamiliar organizational structures that are difficult for them to follow in expository writing, which often lacks logical connectives and transition words and thus requires increased cognitive effort. Specialized vocabulary further hinders comprehension, particularly for younger readers.

Content area reading instruction clearly deserves time and attention. Children need much guidance and many experiences reading expository text in order to deal successfully with content books. The purpose of teaching students to read expository text is obviously to help them learn from those texts. Reading to learn is closely allied to instruction in metacognition, text structure, and general comprehension; therefore, many strategies and ideas useful for promoting comprehension of stories can be adapted for content area material. Any reading instruction should certainly touch on traditional organizing skills such as summarizing, outlining, note taking, and underlining, as well as such abilities as monitoring reading rate, locating information, following directions, and interpreting graphic aids. This instruction, along with instruction in text patterns and opportunities for discussion, appears to boost students' comprehension of content texts.

Having students write about a topic has several benefits. Students are more likely to remember content they write about (Emig, 1977; Moffett, 1981). In addition, students who manipulate what they know about a topic in order to compose will eventually understand it better (Applebee, 1984; Fulwiler & Young, 1982). When students think about what they know about a subject, they shift and rearrange their knowledge and are apt to come to a deeper understanding of that subject. The "writing across the curriculum" movement urges teachers to use writing as a way to increase students' mastery of content as well as to help students become better writers. However, unless students actively engage in planning and reviewing their writing, they probably will not reap the full benefits of this activity. It is thinking about a topic and manipulating information about it that seem to hold the most promise for writing as a way to learn. Teachers should therefore do more than simply hand out writing assignments in content classes.

The strategies in this chapter are suggestions for teachers to use as they help children learn how to learn from content texts. Teachers can select from both reading and writing activities to suit the needs of particular children.

References

Applebee, A. (1984). *Contexts for learning to write: Studies of secondary school instruction*. Norwood, NJ: Ablex.

Alvermann, D.E., & Boothby, P.R. (1982). Text differences: Children's perceptions at the transition stage in reading. *The Reading Teacher, 36*, 298-302.

Emig, J. (1977). Writing as a mode of learning. *College Composition and Communication, 28*, 122-128.

Fulwiler, T., & Young, A. (Eds.). (1982). *Language connections: Writing and reading across the curriculum*. Urbana, IL: National Council of Teachers of English.

Moffett, J. (1981). *Active voice: A writing program across the curriculum*. Portsmouth, NH: Boynton/Cook.

Olson, M.W. (1985). Text type and reader ability: The effects on paraphrase and text-based inference questions. *Journal of Reading Behavior, 17*, 199-215.

Schallert, D.L., & Roser, N.L. (1989). The role of reading in content area instruction. In D. Lapp, J. Flood, & N. Farnan (Eds.), *Content area reading and learning: Instructional strategies* (pp. 25-33). Englewood Cliffs, NJ: Prentice Hall.

Further Reading

Cudd, E.T., & Roberts, L. (1989). Using writing to enhance content area learning in the primary grades. *The Reading Teacher, 42*, 392-405.

Cunningham, P.M., & Cunningham, J.W. (1987). Content area reading and writing lessons. *The Reading Teacher, 40*, 506-513.

Ferguson, A.M., & Fairburn, J. (1985). Language experience for problem solving in mathematics. *The Reading Teacher, 38*, 504-507.

Flood, J., & Lapp, D. (1988). Conceptual mapping for understanding information texts. *The Reading Teacher, 41*, 780-783.

Just, M.A., & Carpenter, P.A. (1987). *The psychology of reading and language comprehension.* Needham Heights, MA: Allyn & Bacon.

Maring, G.H., Furman, G.C., & Blum-Anderson, J. (1985). Five cooperative learning strategies for mainstreamed youngsters in content area classrooms. *The Reading Teacher, 39*, 310-313.

Ogle, D.M. (1986). K-W-L: A teaching model that develops active reading of expository text. *The Reading Teacher, 39*, 564-571.

Raphael, T.E., & Englert, C.S. (1990). Writing and reading: Partners in constructing meaning. *The Reading Teacher, 43*, 388-400.

Wood, K.D. (1988). Guiding students through informational text. *The Reading Teacher, 41*, 912-920.

Zarnowski, M. (1988). Learning about fictionalized biographies: A reading and writing approach. *The Reading Teacher, 42*, 136-143.

Teach Map Reading through Self-Assessment

Rona F. Flippo
Fitchburg, Massachusetts
Clayton R. Frounfelker, III
Milwaukee, Wisconsin
December 1988

Map reading abilities are necessary for reading textbooks in the social sciences. Here's an activity that teaches basic map reading concepts, vocabulary, and symbol interpretation to intermediate-level students and encourages them to assess their own understanding and knowledge.

Begin by briefly introducing the subject of map study and displaying a variety of maps. Distribute the self-assessment sheets (see Figure). Ask one student to volunteer to read a question aloud from the sheet. After allowing time for students to answer the question for themselves, ask another volunteer to answer and, if possible, tell how she or he arrived at the answer. If the student gives a full and accurate answer, say, "You knew the answer" and tell others that if they responded similarly, they should check the "I knew the answer" space following the question on the self-assessment sheet. If an answer

Self-Assessment of Sample Map Reading Skills

Questions	I knew the answer	I knew part of the answer	I did not know the answer	Unknown words
1. What is a map?	___	___	___	___
2. What is a compass rose?	___	___	___	___
3. What are the four cardinal directions?	___	___	___	___
4. What is a map scale?	___	___	___	___
5. What is a map key or legend?	___	___	___	___
6. What are symbols used in a map key?	___	___	___	___
7. What is a map grid?	___	___	___	___
8. What does parallel mean?	___	___	___	___
9. What does perpendicular mean?	___	___	___	___
10. What are coordinates?	___	___	___	___
11. What is a political map?	___	___	___	___
12. What is a boundary?	___	___	___	___
13. What is a capital?	___	___	___	___
14. Name one common kind of map that is a political map.	___	___	___	___
15. What is a physical map?	___	___	___	___
16. How are things or features shown on a physical map?	___	___	___	___
17. What is an elevation map?	___	___	___	___
18. What are contour lines?	___	___	___	___
19. What is a demographic map?	___	___	___	___
20. Name two things you can learn from a demographic map.	___	___	___	___

is partially accurate, say, "You know part of the answer. Keep thinking, maybe you will get the rest of it." Other students with similar responses should check the "I knew part of the answer" space. Solicit a more complete answer from volunteers. If the answer is inaccurate, say, "You don't know the answer, but it was a good try." Students with similar responses would check the "I did not know the answer" space. Again, let volunteers try to come up with the correct answer.

As the questions are read in turn, have students write any words they do not know in the space at the right of the sheet. These words later can serve as individual vocabulary lists.

Once all the questions have been reviewed and checked, use the information provided by the self-assessment to make instructional decisions. Provide instruction for different types of maps, as appropriate. At the end of the unit, allow students to reassess their understanding using the same procedure.

Sharing and clarifying information, along with the self-assessment activity, enhance learning and motivate intermediate-level students.

Science and Language: An "Egg"sperience

**Susanne Christensen
Stana Lennox
Mary Jane Savage**
Wayne, Pennsylvania
December 1987

In April, third and fourth graders can experience spring in a special way. Our students nurtured and held new life, and we all became embryology "egg"sperts. Each of our classrooms received six fertile chicken eggs, an incubator, and a brooding box. The program was sponsored by the 4-H club, which in turn was sponsored by the Agricultural Department of Pennsylvania State University.

When the chicks arrived at school, the 4-H club representative showed the children a film called *How to Hatch Chicks*. Each child received a 4-H club pin and agreed to memorize the 4-H pledge. The children were now official 4-H club members. In addition, each class was considered a club of its own and consequently had to find a name to represent itself.

All the students became intensely involved in this program. As adoptive mother hens, the children assumed the responsibilities that come with parenting a chick. A turning chart was set up for each group of six eggs. The eggs had to be turned four times a day, for four days. Twice a day the temperature was checked. Once a week, the children controlled the humidity of the incubator by adding water.

The program was a language experience as well as a scientific experience. Each day children read the "Chick Event Calendar" to see what was occurring inside the eggs. They completed worksheets on development and terminology. In addition, they cracked open infertile eggs to see how their components matched those of our developing fertile eggs. Their learning continued outside of class as the children brought in literature concerning the chicks, opened infertile eggs at home, and wrote about their "eggs"periences in other classes.

To reinforce the reading and writing aspects of the project, we read folk, fiction, and factual books to the students (*Henny Penny, The Little Red Hen*, and *Horton Hatches the Egg*, for example), as well as poems and scientific books. The writing experiences varied. We wrote factual reports on hatching chickens and creative stories that made the children assume the role of a hatching chick. Scientific terminology as well as "chick expressions" were included in these writing experiences. Expressions like "Don't put all your eggs in one basket" and "It sounds like a hen house" were analyzed and illustrated.

Chick crafts were also an important aspect of the "egg"sperience. Students used painted eggshells and yellow cotton balls to make hatching chicks; they also filled eggshell halves with soil and grass seeds, painted a face on the eggshells, and waited for the grass to sprout.

As hatching time approached, the children's "egg"citement was like that of any new parents. The children created birth announcements and sent them throughout the school. At that point, other classrooms, as well as faculty members, became involved. They visited and wrote about this experience in their own classrooms. Community members and parents came in to film "The Hatch."

To say farewell, we gave the chicks a bon voyage party. We made a chick cake, chick chocolates, and chocolate eggs. We dedicated a "Farewell to the Chicks" poster, adorned with student poetry, to the chicks. When we were done, the children received a 4-H certificate that certified each of them as an embryology "egg"spert.

A fall unit on leaves can include a variety of reading instructional activities. For a class of first graders, I designed a series of activities that included work on some of the basic reading skills required by the school district, reinforced spelling and handwriting skills, and involved some vocabulary and comprehension strategies. This unit is particularly appropriate in a child-centered, activity-oriented classroom.

Day 1. The unit began with a class walk in the woods. The children gathered leaves and brought them back to class for discussion. We looked at books on leaves, and the teacher read some books aloud. We tried to identify some of the leaves collected by looking at the books' pictures.

Day 2. The children were shown how to do leaf rubbings, and each child did several on a large sheet of paper. Then we discussed the size of the leaves, their colors, and the different leaf shapes and vein patterns. The children were encouraged to write on their rubbings something they liked about leaves or something they had learned during the past couple of days. Some children were able to write interesting short statements, while others wrote letters or made letter-like shapes. When youngsters asked how to spell different words, they were encouraged to write the words as best they could. All of the children were excited about writing something. When the rubbings and their accompanying writings were finished, the children shared them with the class. Every child wanted to share; even those who had written only letters "read" something to the class.

After the rubbings were collected for display, the words *leaf* and *leaves* were written on the board and discussed. The students read each word and examined them to see if they could tell how they were the same and different; then they used each word in sentences.

Day 3. Another activity that improved the first graders' reading ability involved reading graphs. Each child selected a leaf from the science table. The teacher attached a large, reusable, two-column graph to the chalkboard. Columns were marked with a drawing of the characteristic patterns of pinnate leaves at the top of one and a picture of the palmate pattern at the top of the other.

Each pupil brought his or her leaf to the front to show the class. Together the class decided on the column under which the leaf should be placed. Each child then taped the leaf into the appropriate square on the graph. The children asked if there were names for the different patterns. The teacher wrote "pinnate" and "palmate" on the board. When the graphing activity resumed, some children used the names as they classified their leaves.

First Grade Content Teaching

William E. Smith
University, Mississippi
December 1987

Once all students who wanted to do so had placed their leaves in position, the class began to "read" the graph. The following questions were asked and discussed: What does our graph compare? What kind of leaf do we have more of? How many more of one do we have than the other? If you were to go for a walk in the woods, which kind of leaf do you think you would find more of? Why do you think so?

Finally, the children were asked what they thought the graph should be called or labeled. They decided on "Pinnate and Palmate Leaves." The title was written on a sentence strip and attached to the top of the graph.

Day 4. The youngsters were given a page with the words *leaf* and *leaves* written on it. They traced the words and tried writing the words themselves.

Day 5. Children were given pieces of paper with a large outline of a leaf on it. They wrote stories about leaves inside the outline. The stories were admired and shared.

Interestingly, during the days after the unit was finished, the children continued to find reasons to use the vocabulary learned during the leaf unit. This was good evidence that teachers should provide reading instruction in a setting that permits the use of effective strategies and at the same time promotes a meaningful use of reading, allows the children to participate in reading activities with high levels of success, emphasizes whole-text, real-world reading activities, stresses process and not product, and promotes transferability of tasks being learned. During the leaf unit, it was possible to do all of this while developing vocabulary, word recognition, comprehension, spelling, composition, and handwriting.

Highlight Your Reading/Writing Program with Challenging Content Materials

Roberta Salomon
Deer Park, New York
April 1985

Tired of the same old reading instruction materials? Add some new ones by incorporating content area topics into reading/writing programs. I used materials from the science curriculum, but social studies materials would also work well.

In one successful project my third graders studied animals in science and focused particularly on pandas. They brainstormed ideas about pandas, which I wrote on the chalkboard. Then, with the help of a web, I categorized these concepts (see Figure).

Web of Student-Generated Responses

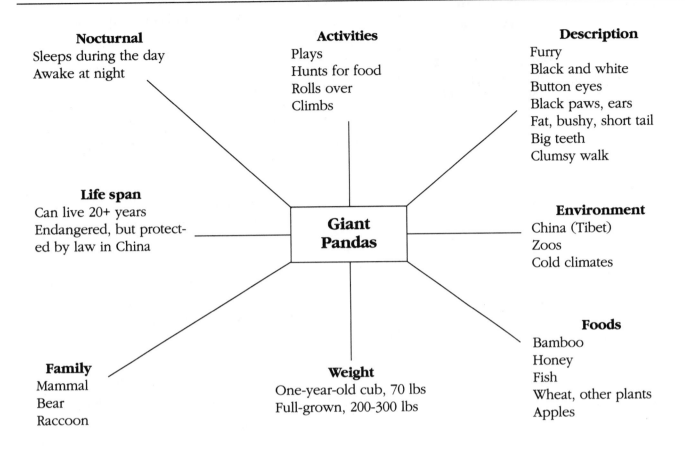

Nocturnal
Sleeps during the day
Awake at night

Activities
Plays
Hunts for food
Rolls over
Climbs

Description
Furry
Black and white
Button eyes
Black paws, ears
Fat, bushy, short tail
Big teeth
Clumsy walk

Life span
Can live 20+ years
Endangered, but protect-
ed by law in China

Giant Pandas

Environment
China (Tibet)
Zoos
Cold climates

Foods
Bamboo
Honey
Fish
Wheat, other plants
Apples

Family
Mammal
Bear
Raccoon

Weight
One-year-old cub, 70 lbs
Full-grown, 200-300 lbs

To add to their knowledge about pandas, the students listened as I read facts from science texts and library materials. I had them list the information they believed was pertinent and gave them assistance and encouragement. With this knowledge and background, students worked in pairs to write stories about pandas, which they illustrated with pictures of pandas in zoos and rolling hoops. This led to creating booklets about pandas.

As a follow-up, I taped information from the materials read aloud. Students listened to these tapes to recall facts and details and then draw conclusions. Finally, they answered written comprehension questions on the topic.

This kind of project is successful because it keeps students interested and actively involves them in the learning process.

Reading, Writing, and Art

Myrna S. Levin
Philadelphia, Pennsylvania
November 1988

Sometimes my students need extra help in reading, so I provide supplementary lessons in addition to the regular reading program. Because of my own interest in art, I decided to try adding art as a stimulus. The lesson described below was inspired by Marc Chagall's *I and My Village*. This lesson can be used with fourth, fifth, and sixth graders.

First of all, show the children a reproduction of the painting, and present a brief information sheet on the artist:

> Marc Chagall painted *I and My Village* in 1911. He was in his twenties and living in Paris. It was one of the happiest times in his life. He was surrounded by friends who were poets and artists. Picasso was also painting at the time, and the influence of Picasso's cubism is readily seen in this Chagall painting.
>
> Marc Chagall was born in a small Russian village called Vitebsk. His memories of Russian and Jewish folklore influenced his painting.

With fourth graders, study the painting with only the eyes—for color, interpretation, feeling, and story. Have them think about and write answers to these questions before discussing them as a class:

- What do we see?
- What does the painting make us feel?
- What kind of childhood do you think Chagall had?
- What kind of things did he see as a boy?

With fifth graders, teach some background through questions and discussion about the painting. Then have the students write.

- What kind of village did Chagall live in?
- What kind of things did he see?
- Why do you think some people and houses are painted upside down?
- Who could the man carrying the scythe be?
- What could the bushes at the bottom of the painting be?

With sixth graders, discuss art vocabulary and write vocabulary and questions on chart paper to use as a reference for writing.

- fantasy—an imaginative poem, story, or play
- cubism—objects or forms are cut into sections or flattened
- surrealism—like a dream; coming from the unconscious mind

- What was Chagall's childhood like?
- What kind of place did he live in?
- What things did he see?
- How can you tell he had a good imagination?
- Are there any clues in this painting that tell he thought of himself as a poet?
- Are there any details that tell he was a happy child?
- What colors did he like?
- What makes some of the painting seem like a dream?
- How can you tell he was influenced by people around him?

The students have fun, learn to look at paintings with real interest, and enjoy reading, sharing, and writing about artworks. The results will be different in each group because of the different methods used at each grade level, but all students will likely write freely and comfortably. They all have an opportunity to illustrate their writing in a style inspired by Chagall.

Teachers interested in art may want to try a similar lesson with this painting or with one of their own favorites.

When health spas and fitness centers integrated music into their exercise routines, the aerobics craze was born. Reading programs can also take advantage of the high degree of motivation, participation, and variation associated with music by using songs to help teach reading concepts. The two ideas for music/reading activities presented here can be adapted and expanded according to students' abilities and needs, even by teachers who are not experienced musicians. Songs can be effectively taught using a record player, unaccompanied singing, or simple strumming on an autoharp, ukelele, or guitar.

The first idea uses simple children's songs in which a line is repeated, such as "Skip to M'Lou," "She'll Be Coming 'Round the Mountain," and "The Farmer in the Dell." After singing through such a song, list two or three headings (such as animals, places, action) across the top of the chalkboard. The students then compose new verses by suggesting words for each heading. For example, the line "Flies in the buttermilk, shoo fly shoo" from "Skip to M'Lou" can become "Horses in the barnyard eating their hay" or "Tigers in the backyard

Enhancing Reading Instruction with Music

John A. Smith
*Chapel Hill, North Carolina
(now Logan, Utah)
February 1984*

chasing the dog." The song "She'll Be Coming 'Round the Mountain" could be modified as "She'll be swimming down the river when she comes" or "She'll be eating in the kitchen when she comes."

The second idea involves writing language experience songs. This means using students' brainstormed words and phrases to fashion a poem which is mapped onto the linguistic rhythm of a familiar tune. These are the steps:

1. The students or teacher selects a familiar topic.

2. The students brainstorm ideas and phrases about the topic, which the teacher writes on the chalkboard.

3. Using a simple rhythm pattern, rhyme scheme, and continued student input, the teacher arranges the students' words and phrases into poem form.

4. By adding and deleting words when necessary, the poem is molded to fit the tune of a familiar nursery rhyme or children's song.

The following language experience song was written by a group of learning disabled second and third grade students. They even came up with the idea of using the tune from "Jingle Bells."

Service Stations

When you go to the service station
You get some candy bars
Sometimes the soda splashes on you
While they help you with your cars.
They often fix your motor
And fill your tires with air
Wash your windows, check your oil
And try to sell you a spare. Oh...
Service stations, service stations
You go there every day
The price of gas goes up and down
But you always have to pay.

Songs to inspire these activities will not be hard to find. Most public and school libraries have children's records as well as anthologies of folk and children's songs like Alan Lomax's *The Folk Songs of North America* (Doubleday, 1960) or Ruth Seeger's *American Folk Songs for Children in Home, School, and Nursery School* (Doubleday, 1948). Music stores, other teachers, friends, and the students themselves are also good sources of songs.

Theme Cubes

Maura K. (Carrico) Sedgeman
Dearborn, Michigan
October 1988

Making a theme cube is a cooperative learning activity designed to access prior knowledge and higher order thinking. Using the six sides of a cube you can capsulize concepts from a reading selection (from basals or content area texts). The materials you will need are as follows:

- cardboard squares, 10" x 12" (25 cm x 30 cm), 6 per cube
- markers, crayons, pencils, pens, paints
- magazines, newspapers, colored paper, etc.
- tape (masking or transparent)

A model cube is shown in the Figure on the next page to give you ideas about what to include on the cube sides. A simple cube could have who, what, when, where, why, and how questions, one type per side, or each of six groups could choose a topic for each square of a class theme cube. Pairs or small heterogeneous groups could also try making their own complete theme cubes.

Making the theme cube can be a prereading activity to access prior knowledge or a postreading synthesis activity. Either way, the classroom procedure is as follows:

1. Divide the class into groups (if desired).
2. Encourage discussion of the content of the cube or individual squares.
3. Give time for students to create illustrations, cut and paste pictures, and write.
4. Each group presents its contribution.
5. Tape the squares together into a cube.
6. Share cubes with other classes, groups, or schools.

I have used theme cubes with teachers and aides, with limited English proficient students at elementary, junior high, and high school levels, with gifted students, and on one occasion with 75 grade two students—always with great success. Let cooperative groups do the work and thinking. You just provide the materials and the creative learning environment.

Important vocabulary
(5 to 6 words—defined, described, illustrated, explained, and used in context)

Personal response
(feelings, thought-provoking statements, tie-ins to other stories, texts, situations, or real-life experiences)

Title, plus something that captures the essence of the theme or concept (pictures, drawings, graphs, decorations)

Story or concept
(overview or review, including pictures, words, main ideas, interesting points to ponder, description or map of content)

Questions
(5 to 7 who, what, when, where, why, how, and higher order thinking—"What if..."—questions)

Statements of learning
(5 to 6 sentences about what has been learned or what may be learned)

Students' sometimes negative reactions to social studies may be the result of the teaching methods that are (or are not) used in conjunction with the textbook. Alternative textbook-related methods may lead students to react much more positively. The following methods can turn things around in social studies classrooms.

Selective use of the text. Social studies texts are usually jam-packed with information—much more than students can possibly learn in a year. Not all is of equal importance. Weed out less important information and develop instructional activities around what is left. This allows treatment of less information in more depth.

Structured overviews. Introduce each chapter with a structured overview—something like a flow chart. It shows, by means of categories and subcategories, how the material in the chapter is organized. This helps students in two ways: it gives them a sense of direction, and it helps them place the information they read into categories, which in turn helps them remember what they read. An example of a structured overview is shown in Figure 1.

Textbook-Related Methods in Social Studies

Marian Houseman
Polk City, Iowa
Frederick A. Duffelmeyer
Ames, Iowa
April 1987

Figure 1
Structured Overview of a Social Studies Unit

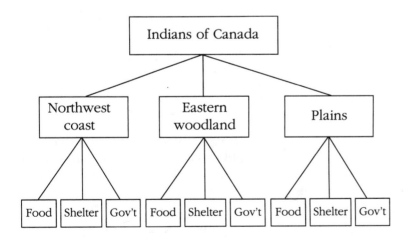

Study guides. To encourage purposeful reading, provide students with a selective guide that directs them to the paragraphs with the most basic information and provides a framework for written responses. An example of a selective study guide is shown in Figure 2.

Figure 2
Selective Study Guide for a Social Studies Unit

Page 104, paragraphs 2 and 4: These paragraphs tell how the woodland Indians got their food.

What foods did they grow?_____

What food came from rivers? _____

What food did they hunt? _____

Page 105, paragraphs 2 and 3: These paragraphs describe the Indians' homes.

What kind of homes did the eastern tribes live in?_____

_____

What kind of homes did the northern tribes live in?_____

_____

Page 106, paragraph 2: This paragraph explains the government of the woodland Indians.

How was a tribal chief selected? _____

_____

What was the purpose of the council? _____

_____

Collaborative learning. As an alternative to teacher-directed learning, give children opportunities to work together. Students can work in pairs to complete a study guide, for example, or complete one independently and then share written responses in groups of two to four. Completed study guides come in handy when students are reviewing for a test. Let students work in pairs for that purpose.

Another opportunity for collaboration offers itself in conjunction with comprehension questions after reading. As an alternative to asking questions of a large group, put questions in writing and have students react to them in small groups prior to a large group discussion.

With these strategies in place, students won't hate social studies anymore, nor will they find it boring. They may actually say things like "You made social studies easy to understand" and "Social studies is fun now." The textbook-related methods described here will have a lot to do with such a change in attitude, because they make the textbook material more comprehensible and provide multiple opportunities for student participation.

"Little Books" for Content Area Vocabulary

Pamela Beth Heukerott
Scarsdale, New York
January 1987

Fifth grade math and science curricula make very challenging vocabulary demands. To assimilate technical terms, students need to know definitions and have opportunities to use these terms meaningfully. To motivate my students and to emphasize the importance of key concepts and vocabulary, I implemented "little books," which a colleague had used successfully in social studies classes.

Before beginning a unit, I identify important vocabulary and construct a "little book" packet for every student. The packet consists of sheets of white paper divided into quarters. On the top left quarter of the first sheet are instructions on how to make the book. The top right quarter is the title page, which instructs students to fill in the name of the unit and to print their name after the words "Concepts by." On each of the remaining quarters, a vocabulary word appears, followed by a dash. The students are given these instructions:

- Define each concept in your own words.
- Draw a picture or diagram illustrating the concept and explain what you have drawn. Remember to color it, too.
- Draw an attractive title page.
- Cut out the pages.
- Staple your book together.

The class has a week to complete the "little books." Students may work on them during allotted class time, study halls, and at home. It is each student's choice to work alone, in small groups, or with a partner. Information on the concepts may be drawn from textbooks, magazines, booklets, experiments, and their own experience. Use of dictionaries alone is discouraged.

Fifth graders approach this project enthusiastically. It permits students to pace themselves, to select appropriate source materials, and to work in a social setting that best promotes learning. Students have lively discussions, stimulate one another's thinking, and willingly share materials and ideas.

The "little books" assignment is a pleasant alternative to the routine of writing definitions and using terms in meaningful sentences on notebook paper. While the latter task is done in a matter-of-fact, efficient manner, the former elicits self-direction, care, thought, creativity, and flexibility. The resulting definitions tend to be more complete, since the students must synthesize information from the different sources they select and state the meanings in their own words. The illustrations serve as a springboard for the students to articulate their understanding of the concepts since they require the students to apply the terms in a meaningful context and explain them.

Students can keep their "little books" inside a pocket folder in their notebooks and use them as a handy glossary or for review. "Little books" provide a unique and enjoyable opportunity for fifth graders to formalize their understanding of key concepts and vocabulary, and they give the teacher a means of thoroughly assessing the students' grasp of those concepts and vocabulary.

Writing for Students to Read in Hands-on Science

John David Butler
Eagle River, Alaska
January 1985

Some elementary school science programs have improved on the textbook-lecture approach to science education by adopting a hands-on process approach in which children learn by doing. Students may collect, open, and force buds, or find the hardness of minerals by doing scratch tests.

To make better use of hands-on activities, as well as to help students develop a deeper understanding of science and improve their reading comprehension, I write material for my fourth graders to read. This article describes how I write to help students get more from their experiences and readings in science.

Planning and writing. The average time for planning and writing material for one lesson is about an hour. Planning is essential to make the writing go smoothly. First research the topic by reading school texts, trade books, and manuals from hands-on science kits. Find out why certain results occur. What causes leaves to burst from buds? What use do people have for minerals that are hard or soft? Sometimes a quick review of a page or two is enough. If I can't visualize the experience, I try the children's science activity to appreciate exactly what they will be doing. For example, I might try opening buds to find folded leaves and peeling back the scales to see the beautiful symmetry of the folds.

Through each preparatory step to writing, hold the objectives of the lesson in mind. This helps your writing stick to the point, ensuring that the students' learning will be focused. In the writing, list and include vocabulary derived from the children's activity, from related ideas, and from individual students.

At this point in the planning, questions may come to mind. Which characteristics of the students will be important in their learning process? What out-of-school experiences have they already had? What happened in class last year? By answering such questions, you can match the writing to the students.

The final planning step is to find a twist to engage students in the lesson. The twist often includes probing questions, like "Can leafless trees be alive? If not, how do trees 'come back to life' in the spring? What enables them to bear leaves, make food, and shade us?" Plan how to use the special twist to hook students early in the writing. What they read about themselves and their experiences pulls them in as they read on.

Now comes the actual writing. Include ideas from your research. For example, to understand where leaf buds fit in the scheme of a tree's life cycle, children need to know the role of leaves and why leaves fall off in autumn. When a bud is opened, a waxy substance is left, so include that phrase in the writing. Since the prime objective in a lesson about buds is for students to understand what buds are, buds should frequently be related to leaves in the writing. An engaging twist might challenge children to think about life and death in trees.

Certain mechanical elements help students read your writing. The written material should fit on one sheet of paper and be broken into clear paragraphs. Simple diagrams and drawings add interest and increase understanding.

Working in class. There are three parts to the actual lesson: discussion, experience, and reading. Begin classroom discussions by engaging students with an interesting twist: "Look out the window at those birch trees. They have no leaves. Are they alive?" The children tell what they know. In the discussion, students often use specialized vocabulary related to the lesson. Guide the discussion to fill vocabulary gaps and prompt the children to recall what words mean.

Next, make sure the activity part of the lesson will move smoothly by checking that all children know what to do, why, and what they may learn. Two things are essential here:

each student must be involved with the materials and each should be encouraged to talk freely. Circulate among them, questioning, extending, checking for problems, and repeating important student statements so all can hear. With comments like "Kristi says her bud covering feels waxy" or "Aaron says the leaves in this bud are wet," every student's chance of success during the science experience and in the reading that follows is increased.

Finally, the children settle back to read about what they have done. Each student should have a copy of the material you've written. Have them review the material and see how the new knowledge fits in with broader scientific concepts and processes. The students can put their copies of the writing in their science folders.

To extend the lesson, let children write in their notebooks about what they have learned. The teacher's writing becomes ready reference material. The children can illustrate their writing and tape in samples like twigs or mineral chips.

A combination of discussion, hands-on experiences, and follow-up reading is a potent force for teaching science. The approach described here takes increased teacher preparation time, but the gains in reading comprehension, student understanding, and application of science concepts are worth the extra effort.

Planning for a Content Area Reading Assignment

Paul Borthwick
Cleveland, Mississippi
February 1984

The processes involved in reading and interpreting content area textbooks are much more complex than reading from a basal reader. Look at the contrast in these two types of writing:

- Style: basals—narrative; content texts—expository.
- Vocabulary: basals—controlled; content texts—uncontrolled, uncommon, technical.
- Content: basals—generally familiar, usually narrative and involving characters; content texts—generally unfamiliar, presented by facts, sequence, cause/effect, problem/solution, maps, graphs, tables, printed directions, examples, questions.
- Skills needed: basals—basic reading skills; content texts—basic reading skills plus skills unique to each subject.

Interpreting and remembering information from content area textbooks is a real problem for many youngsters, regardless of their reading level. They may know how to apply the basic word identification, comprehension, and study skills, but transferring those skills to other subjects is not automatic. In addition, some subject areas require specific reading skills. Each area uses special vocabulary—familiar words used in an unfamiliar way or words totally new in both form and meaning. If these items are crucial to understanding the passage, the teacher needs to alert the children to them. Also, young readers need to be urged to give attention to special textbook aids—like marginal notes, pictures, or diagrams—and to be told when to skim and when to slow down and analyze. Textbooks often contain prequestions, interspersed questions, and end-of-the-unit questions and students need instruction in using these aids.

Each subject has unique features with which readers must contend. Science material, for example, involves interrelationships among symbols, words, formulas, diagrams, graphs, and charts; math uses all these plus many abbreviations, equations, and tables; social studies materials often demand interpretation of maps, charts, pictures, globes, and captions. Content area teachers can prepare well for reading assignments in these complex subject areas with a quick preplan and a differentiated lesson plan—one that provides help tailored for readers of different ability and with different needs.

Preplan. For the preplan, look for things you need to know about both the text and the students:

1. Read the selection carefully.

2. Estimate its readability level. (Easy formulas are the Fry or the Fog index, either of which your local reading teacher can show you in a few minutes or can be found in most textbooks on teaching reading.)

3. Note the function of each paragraph in the selection—is it introductory, definitional, narrative, summary, transitional, explanatory, or descriptive?

4. Identify connective or signal words, such as *but* (shows contrast), *also* (addition), *thus* (summary), *absolutely* (reflect on this idea!), *finally* (time), *since* (cause and effect), and *many* (degree).

5. Identify major concepts, technical terms, and question strategies used.

Differentiated lesson plan. For the differentiated lesson plan, follow these steps:

1. Note the wide range of reading levels in the class; differentiate instruction by grouping students or varying the assignments.

2. Use a variety of activities to familiarize the students with the vocabulary before they start reading the selection.

3. Give the poorer readers some topic-related material written at their level.

4. Give average and good readers a study guide to accompany their reading assignment.

5. In planning activities that will either precede or follow the reading, include (a) some concrete "doing" type experiences like creative writing, constructing models, and doing experiments; (b) some listening/observing experiences like field trips, exhibits, and films; and (c) some abstract, symbol-unlocking tasks using maps, charts, other reading, or lectures.

6. Try to include some instruction that matches each child's preferred way of learning (different media, surroundings, teaching methods).

Since reading activities are interwoven with work on the content to be learned, the children get double benefit from your plans. It's worth the effort and, with a bit of practice, this sort of planning becomes natural and easy.

Mr. Three Feet

Sharon E. Wilson
Mt. Pleasant, South Carolina
March 1989

Mr. Three Feet became a very common name in my third grade classroom. He solved a big problem for me and became a longtime friend of the students.

For months students had worked on measurement conversions: 12 inches=1 foot; 3 feet=1 yard; 36 inches=1 yard. While trying to find a way to make these conversions stick by relating them in some way to the students, I created a silly story that helped—the story of Mr. Three Feet:

There's an old, old man who lives down the road near the creek. I'm not sure what his real name is, but I've always heard of him as "Mr. Three Feet."

Mr. Three Feet is the strangest looking fellow I've ever seen. He's not like you and me. Instead of having two feet, he has three feet!

Mr. Three Feet lives in a neat little house with a fenced-in backyard. He can be seen standing in his backyard late some afternoons, all by himself.

Last spring I was out walking and saw Mr. Three Feet standing in his backyard. He really looked odd. All of a sudden, 12 mosquitoes flew up to him and bit him on his right foot. Boy, did he start scratching! Then 12 more mosquitoes buzzed up and bit his left foot. After that, 12 mosquitoes bit his middle foot.

The poor fellow itched and scratched, itched and scratched. Just think, 12 itches on one foot, 12 itches on another foot, and 12 itches on the third foot.

The following classroom discussion illustrates how to follow up the story of Mr. Three Feet.

Teacher: Where is Mr. Three Feet standing?

A student: In his yard.

Teacher: How many feet does he have in that yard?

Another student: He has three feet.

Teacher: How many itches does he have on each foot?

Another student: He has 12 itches on each foot.

Teacher: Can you figure out how many itches were in the yard all together?

Another student: There were 36.

Teacher: What does "itches" sound a lot like—something we've been talking about in math?

Another student: It sounds like "inches."

Teacher: When you think about the number of inches that are in a foot, I want you to remember the number of itches that poor old Mr. Three Feet had on one of his feet. He had 12 itches on each foot, and there are 12 inches in a foot. When you think about the number of feet in a yard, I want you to remember the number of feet that Mr. Three Feet had when he was standing in his backyard. He had three feet in his backyard, and there are three feet in a yard. If you need to remember the number of inches in a yard, think about the total number of itches in the yard—the three feet that Mr. Three Feet had times the 12 itches on each foot. There are 36 itches in the yard, and 36 inches in a yard.

After telling the story to my students, I simplified it for them to use in making Mr. Three Feet books. The purpose of the student-made books was not only to reinforce the math skill, but also to incorporate sight words being covered and reading skills recently taught.

I displayed a chart with a sample of each page to go in the book. Samples contained only the text for each page and the page number, not pictures. Students were to draw their own creations for each page.

Students took their books home to read with their families. They then brought them back to share with their classmates and finally put them in the library for other students to read.

Reinforcing Language in Arithmetic Problem Solving

Joanna Sullivan
*Boca Raton, Florida
(now Carbondale, Illinois)
October 1985*

A major challenge teachers face is helping the learning disabled child achieve independence in arithmetic problem-solving tasks. Although LD students may perform adequately on computation skills, many are unable to develop correct procedures for solving math problems. While teachers often use many reinforcement devices (such as objects and pictures) to help the LD child understand the task, they may be overlooking an important aspect of the child's problem—difficulty in using "inner language" effectively when thinking through the problem. This is an important process in organizing problem information.

For this reason, language cards—large blank cards used to record each word separately as the child verbalizes a problem—are very useful as a supplement to other reinforcement devices. These cards help children organize and monitor their thinking and allow them to examine their own verbal interpretation of a problem. They also serve as a vehicle for expanding vocabulary.

To apply language cards to basic addition and subtraction with younger learners, begin by placing like objects, such as eight disks, in a pile. Write the problem on cards (one word or number per card) and tell your students to separate the discs as shown here—circles represent disks and rectangles represent the cards.

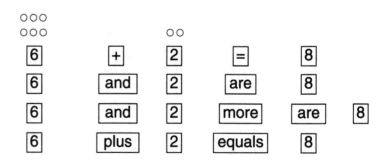

Since problems can be stated in different ways, prompt the child to verbalize the problem in as many ways as possible. In the example given here, the child stated the problem in four ways, and the teacher made cards for each.

Checking comprehension is a critical step in the process. To do so, remove each set of cards (one at a time), shuffle them, and ask the learner to place them in the correct order.

Among older LD pupils, key-word reading is essential to interpreting word problems, and language cards can be used as key-word identifiers. Three steps are necessary in applying language cards to word problems.

Step 1. Instruct the pupils to read the problem and underline the most important words, as seen here:

> <u>Two jars</u> are the <u>same size</u>. <u>One half</u> of the <u>first jar</u> is dry <u>dog food</u> and <u>one half</u> of the <u>other jar</u> holds <u>bird seed</u>. Weigh each jar to find <u>which is heavier</u>. <u>How much</u> heavier <u>is</u> the <u>heaviest jar</u>?

Step 2. Place key words on individual language cards and organize each key word under either a quantitative or descriptive category.

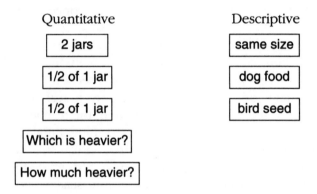

Quantitative	Descriptive
2 jars	same size
1/2 of 1 jar	dog food
1/2 of 1 jar	bird seed
Which is heavier?	
How much heavier?	

Step 3. After discussing the problem, have students manipulate the cards in different ways in order to simplify the problem.

Jar 1	Jar 2
1/2 dog food	1/2 bird seed
8 oz.	10 oz.

There may be a good deal of trial and error until this approach has been applied to a number of problems. Soon, however, children recognize a pattern and the task is simplified.

The purpose of using language cards with LD children throughout the grades is to improve their ability to verbalize a mathematical problem, help them understand terminology, and, on the cognitive level, assist them in organizing information and reviewing the process of reaching a solution.

Understanding Content Material

Lane Roy Gauthier
Houston, Texas
December 1989

Intermediate-grade students often have trouble understanding concepts in content material. Textbooks in which concepts are presented in rapid-fire fashion certainly make the task no easier. Following is a strategy designed to improve students' comprehension of content material by having them read, discuss, and give written responses to items pertaining to short content texts.

In this activity, the teacher chooses a short selection from a content text (e.g., science or social studies). The length of the excerpt may vary from one paragraph to one page depending on concept load and the purpose of the lesson. The teacher then prepares a list of the major concepts for students to learn. Next, the teacher selects a small group to participate in the lesson. For this activity, a cooperative group comprising children of different abilities works well. Initially, the teacher previews the content of the short selection. These brief comments may address vocabulary terms (technical and/or specialized) or major concepts. In addition, the teacher should ask if anyone in the group already knows a few things about the subject, so that students with information can share their knowledge with the rest of the group. One fifth grade teacher doing a science lesson about the Earth's four seasons got responses such as "I know that the winter is a lot colder when you go north" and "When the Earth goes around the sun it helps the seasons to change."

Before the students read the selection, the teacher should ask them to look at the following questions and to be aware that they will be asked them in written form after the reading is complete. These prequestions will help students set purposes for reading.

1. What have you learned from reading this selection?

2. How does the information in this selection connect to the other things you know about this subject?

3. List any words in the selection you did not fully understand.

After the students have read the selection and have written responses to the three questions, the teacher leads a discussion. For example, the fifth grade teacher elicited responses such as "That the world going around the sun is only some of why we get the seasons" (for item 1); "I knew the Earth went around the sun, but not that it was tilted a little" (for item 2); and "Revolve, axis, solstice, rotate, equinox, Tropic of Cancer" (for item 3).

When the students have had sufficient time to conduct their own discussion of their written answers, the teacher should join in the exchange to help solidify the students' understanding of the topic by asking key questions and providing explanations of unfamiliar concepts and vocabulary.

Key questions should be based on the major concepts the teacher listed before the lesson began.

By limiting the amount of text to be read at one time, connecting the material to prior knowledge, attending to content vocabulary, and involving the students in cooperative learning, this technique can lessen the usual difficulties associated with understanding content material.

Classroom Big Books: Links between Reading and Writing Nonfiction

Diane Snowball
Melbourne, Australia
December 1989

Children are often asked to write about nonfiction topics. This activity presents a process for researching and presenting information in the form of nonfiction Big Books that allow children to read for information and write to inform.

Step 1. Select a topic that interests the class and ask children to suggest words related to that topic.

Step 2. Ask children to describe the relationship between the topic word and each of the words they have suggested. Assist them in classifying the words into categories that describe different aspects of the topic. This organization will help the students retain information when reading about the topic. It will also help students organize notes from other sources.

Step 3. Choose one of the categories to write about as a class. It's important to model the processes involved in gathering further information about the topic:

- List what is known about the category.
- List questions students would like to explore.
- Discuss where the necessary information might be found.

119

If necessary, the teacher should demonstrate how children might write letters to obtain information, how to interview people, or how to use various resources such as telephone books, a variety of informational texts, brochures, magazines, audiovisual materials, and computer databases.

Step 4. Relate newly acquired information about the category to original known data. Explain that all of this information will be written as one of the chapters of a book about the topic. Then discuss ways the information can be organized, perhaps using other suitable nonfiction books as models. Make use of headings, subheadings, and layout, and remember that often information is best presented in tables, diagrams, flow charts, or graphs.

Working with the teacher, the class should now decide on the best way to organize the information—reorganizing, revising, and perhaps even deciding to delete some information or to find out more. This chapter is then written on large sheets of paper as part of a class Big Book.

Step 5. Allow groups of children to select one of the other topic categories to research. This activity should follow the model of the class example given above.

Step 6. Collate all of the groups' chapters into a total class Big Book and decide on an appropriate title. Have the class create a cover, a table of contents, an index, and other book elements such as a glossary, suggestions for further reading, a title page, acknowledgments, and a back cover blurb. Use other books as models.

Step 7. Encourage the children to work in groups, pairs, or as individuals to write other nonfiction books in a variety of curriculum areas.

This process involves a variety of reading, writing, and oral language tasks, as well as cooperative learning strategies. Learning of this type broadens the range of options for children and allows them to choose their own resources for reading literary forms and styles of writing. In addition, it gives teachers a scaffolding method that can work with all age groups.

By the end of November, my first graders had acquired sufficient skills through basal reader instruction to enjoy independent recreational reading. Most of the books they selected from the classroom library tended to be fiction, very often the storybooks I had read aloud to them. When we began a science unit on the solar system, their high interest level inspired me to introduce them to the concept of reading for research.

At the beginning of the unit, we brainstormed a list of questions about the solar system. These ranged from the answerable ("How hot is the sun?") to the imponderable ("How do you make a planet?"). We recorded all the questions and discussed the fact that some might be easier to answer than others. Then the children had time to share information they already had. In some cases this was considerable.

Over the course of the next week, I read to the students about the earth, the sun, the moon, and the planets. Based on the reading, we formed human models to demonstrate the relationship between the earth, moon, and sun. We used a flashlight and a mirror in our darkened room to demonstrate the concept of reflected light.

At the end of the week, we talked about all we'd learned from the books that I'd read to them. I introduced the term "research" and told the children that they were going to do some research on their own. I showed them the books they were going to use: a variety of simply written texts on the solar system, including some copies of controlled-vocabulary first grade science texts.

The children's research task was simple and open-ended enough to ensure success: they were to read in any of the available books in order to learn something new about the solar system. Each child would then write a sentence telling what she or he had learned. We talked about the difference between reporting what was learned and copying out of the book. To give the children the opportunity to practice, I read a paragraph aloud to them and had them report the material back in their own words.

I chose to have the children work with partners for the research project. I thought working in pairs would give them confidence in approaching the material. I decided not to pair stronger with weaker readers—a plot that children always recognize—but instead let them choose their own partners.

The children selected their own reading material, too. Some teams initially chose books that were too difficult for them, but then traded them for more manageable material. Even those with the least developed skills were comfortable with the first grade science texts. The children wrote their one-sentence reports in pencil on strips of chart paper. After check-

Anita Page
Warwick, New York
May 1988

ing their work, I had the youngsters trace over the sentences with fine-tipped markers for display purposes. We pasted the sentences on blue chart paper decorated with clouds and entitled "Facts about the Sky." The children enjoyed reading their facts to each other. I kept the research books available for weeks after the project was completed. Some children consistently chose them for their free-time reading material.

The research period took an hour of class time. The students had the satisfaction of seeing their work immediately displayed. Their concept of reading was broadened and the sense of the power that reading gives—the autonomy that comes with literacy—was enhanced.

Chapter 6

Understanding Text Structures

When writers compose text, they generally organize that text around an internal structure or pattern. The texts that children encounter in school are usually either narratives or expositions. Narrative texts, or stories, chronicle events involving characters in a particular setting, while expository texts seek to explain a phenomenon. Teaching children about text structure is one way to help them increase their comprehension of narratives and expositions. For example, if children expect a story to have a setting, characters, events, and a conclusion, they will be able to fill those expectations with information unique to the particular story they are reading; the text's structure provides a framework to help them organize and remember the things they read about.

Just as traditional grammar organizes our language structure, story grammar describes the structures that are usually found in well-formed narratives. According to Stein and Glenn (1977), a story basically consists of two parts: the setting plus one or more episodes. These two parts are what the story grammar depicts.

As illustrated in the Figure on the next page, the setting introduces the main characters and outlines the time, place, and context in which the episodes occur. In this example, five categories are subsumed under episode: the *initiating event* allows the story to begin; the *internal response* describes the protagonist's reaction to the initiating event and results in some feeling or goal that motivates subsequent action; the *attempt* is the action or series of actions that the protagonist undertakes to attain the goal; the *consequences* are what happens as a result of the attempt (success or failure in attaining the goal); and the *reaction* is the protagonist's internal response to the outcome of the actions and may include broad or long-term consequences of the actions.

Story grammar research consistently concludes that knowledge of story structure is critical to understanding stories. This knowledge seems to begin forming during the preschool years and is refined throughout elementary school (Baker & Stein, 1981). Teachers can help this knowledge develop by providing many opportunities for children to experience stories—by reading to them and having plenty of books

Story Grammar of a Simple Text

Setting	Once there was a herd of wild horses led by an appaloosa stallion. The herd usually grazed in a pasture at the edge of some foothills.
Episode	
Initiating event:	One afternoon as they were eating, the stallion saw several rattlesnakes sunning themselves in the pasture.
Internal response:	The stallion knew how dangerous rattlesnakes were, particularly for colts and fillies, and wanted to warn his herd.
Attempt:	He neighed loudly to warn the other horses and loped into the foothills.
Consequences:	Fortunately, all the mares and their young followed him immediately, so the rattlesnakes did no harm.
Reaction:	The stallion was pleased with the herd's response and knew the horses were all safe.

for them to read. Answering comprehension questions based on story grammar categories or completing stories with missing categories gives children additional experiences with stories and their structures (Whaley, 1981).

Expository texts (e.g., science or social studies textbooks) may have one of several organizational patterns or rhetorical structures. Meyer (1975) identified five possibilities: (1) causation; (2) response (question and answer, problem and solution); (3) comparison; (4) collection or sequence; and (5) description. The relationships among the ideas or facts about a topic determine the structure a writer selects when conveying particular information. For instance, a writer who wished to chronicle the events leading up to the American Revolutionary War would probably use a sequential pattern to convey the information.

Writers use semantic and syntactic techniques to signal the various structures. A writer composing a passage that explained the reasons for branding calves, for example, might use signal words like *because, consequently, as a result, caused,* or *thus* in the composition. Words such as *first, next,* and *finally* signal a different text structure. When children are aware of how and why writers use signal words, they can use them to organize and remember the information they are reading about.

Research on text structure provides some guidance for teachers. First, older readers and better readers seem to have greater understanding of expository text structures, and they use their knowledge to comprehend material as they read (Taylor, 1980). Second, awareness of the rhetorical structures of exposition develops later than knowledge of narrative text structure (Englert & Hiebert, 1984), perhaps because children have fewer experiences with expository texts in the preschool and early elementary years. This finding suggests that younger children and poorer readers can benefit from experiences with expository texts and instruction in their structure. Finally, some structures have a clearer organizational pattern than others: texts that are organized around causes and effects or comparisons seem easier to comprehend than content presented as a collection or description (Meyer & Freedle, 1984).

Conscious or unconscious recognition of the organizational structure of a narrative or an expository text is a characteristic of good readers, who seem to expect information to be arranged in a pattern that they can use to construct meaning. In other words, they seem to have a schema for text structures. Helping children understand how each text type is organized is a wise instructional goal for teachers. Certainly less skilled readers can become more proficient at understanding text structures with direct instruction. The following strategies were designed to help children learn about text structures and use that knowledge to increase their comprehension of what they read.

References

Baker, L., & Stein, N.L. (1981). The development of prose comprehension skills. In C.M. Santa & B.L. Hayes (Eds.), *Children's prose comprehension* (pp. 7-43). Newark, DE: International Reading Association.

Englert, C., & Hiebert, E. (1984). Children's developing awareness of text structures in expository materials. *Journal of Educational Psychology, 75*, 65-74.

Meyer, B. (1975). *The organization of prose and its effects on memory.* Amsterdam: New Holland.

Meyer, B., & Freedle, R.O. (1984). Effects of discourse type on recall. *American Educational Research Journal, 21*, 121-144.

Stein, N.L., & Glenn, C.G. (1977). *A developmental study of children's construction of stories.* Paper presented at the Society for Research in Child Development, New Orleans, LA.

Taylor, B.M. (1980). Children's memory for expository text after reading. *Reading Research Quarterly, 15*, 399-411.

Whaley, J.F. (1981). Story grammars and reading instruction. *The Reading Teacher, 34*, 762-771.

Further Reading

Armbruster, B.B., Anderson, T.H., & Ostertag, J. (1989). Teaching text structure to improve reading and writing. *The Reading Teacher, 43*, 130-137.

Brennan, A.D., Bridge, C.A., & Winograd, P.E. (1986). The effects of structural variations on children's recall of basal reader stories. *Reading Research Quarterly, 21*, 99-104.

Flood, J., Lapp, D., & Farnan, N. (1986). A reading-writing procedure that teaches expository paragraph structure. *The Reading Teacher, 39*, 556-563.

Golden, J.M. (1984). Children's concept of story in reading and writing. *The Reading Teacher, 37*, 578-584.

Marshall, N. (1983). Using story grammar to assess reading comprehension. *The Reading Teacher, 36*, 616-620.

McGee, L.M., & Richgels, D.J. (1985). Teaching expository text structure to elementary students. *The Reading Teacher, 38*, 739-749.

Meyer, R.J.F., & Rice, G.E. (1984). The structure of text. In P.D. Pearson (Ed.), *Handbook of reading research* (Vol. 1, pp. 319-352). White Plains, NY: Longman.

Piccolo, J.A. (1987). Expository text structure: Teaching and learning strategies. *The Reading Teacher, 40*, 838-847.

Reutzel, D.R. (1986). Clozing in on comprehension: The cloze story map. *The Reading Teacher, 39*, 524-529.

Spiegel, D.L., & Fitzgerald, J. (1986). Improving reading comprehension through instruction about story parts. *The Reading Teacher, 39*, 676-683.

The Story Circle is a technique to help students' comprehension, discussion, and summarizing skills. The Story Circle pattern works with groups or individuals. It is an excellent aid for students, who benefit from a combination of oral discussion, meaningful print, and illustrations to synthesize what they have read.

The first step is for the teacher to draw a circle on the board, an overhead transparency, or a handout. The circle is then divided into six to eight pie-shaped parts. It is helpful to number the parts so each student will follow the sequence in the proper direction. The student then reads the selected story either orally with the teacher or silently, using the ordinary text.

An after-reading discussion should help the student focus on significant events in the story. As the child relates the story events, she or he should be encouraged to recall them in sequence and to limit their number to the number of pie-

Story Circles Teach Sequence

Jane A. Vogel
Bloomingdale, Illinois
November 1987

Completed Story Circle
(Based on Ann McGovern's *Too Much Noise*)

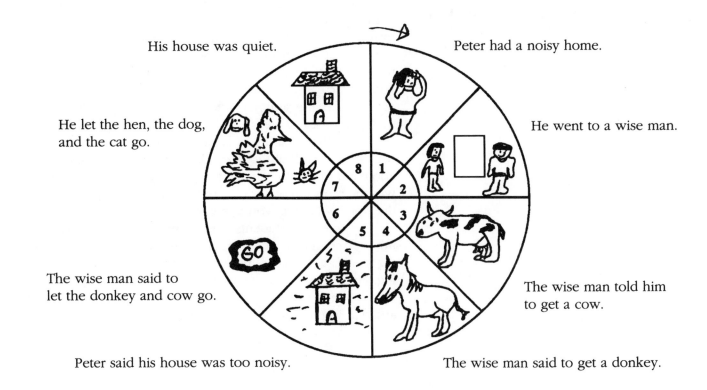

His house was quiet.

Peter had a noisy home.

He let the hen, the dog, and the cat go.

He went to a wise man.

The wise man told him to get a cow.

The wise man said to let the donkey and cow go.

The wise man said to get a donkey.

Peter said his house was too noisy.

shaped segments in the Story Circle. The student then records the main story events on the outside of the circle frame, as in the Figure. Lower ability children can dictate events as the teacher records them.

By limiting story events to a set number, the teacher allows the student to develop accurate and concise summarizing skills in response to a reading selection. Main ideas may be isolated and restated during the discussion and may be reinforced during the recording of events.

After the recording is complete, the student can illustrate the events that were selected (as in the Figure). In this manner, children are encouraged to use three cueing systems (oral, word clues, and picture clues) to demonstrate understanding of a literature selection.

Thinking about Stories

Nancy J. Farnan
San Marcos, California
April 1986

This reading/writing activity for intermediate-grade students is designed to promote thoughtful reading and written responses based on pupils' own experiences. The teacher prepares students by directing them to read or listen to a story with the following purposes in mind: (1) to think about the events of the story and their feelings about the events; (2) to think about the characters in the story and the reasons they act the way they do; and (3) to draw mental pictures of the setting and characters of the story.

After the story has been read or heard, students write their responses to the story, guided by the purposes that were set before their reading or listening. These questions may be used to aid recall of the story: What was most memorable about the story—the characters, the plot, the ending? What was the most important picture you saw as you read or heard the story? What will you remember best about the story?

When the students have completed their writing, editing is done in teams of two, beginning with peer reading of the story. Revisions are based on both peer and teacher editing. Finished stories may be bound or posted on the bulletin board, along with a copy of the story that was read or heard and that inspired the pupils' writing.

Book Maps

Clifford J. Kramer
Cross Plains, Wisconsin
December 1987

Making a book map is a motivating reading project that has resulted in better reading and thinking by the students in my reading classes. Book maps work well with remedial reading students in second through sixth grades; children in grades one to six who read an entire book in regular or advanced reading classes also enjoy making book maps.

Each day my students spend the majority of the reading period reading and discussing a chapter from a book. The discussions focus on the characters, setting, episodes, and conflict in each chapter. After the discussion is complete, the students eagerly begin to work on their book map.

A book map is an oversize version of a story map. To make it, the students use a really large piece of paper, 5' x 3' (150 cm x 90 cm). The paper is divided into three sections, as shown in the Figure.

A Book Map Outline

Characters	*Setting and Events*
(Students list characters and write a few words to describe each one.)	(Students draw the setting and some of the action.)
Chapter Summaries	
(In two or three sentences, students describe the chapter's main episodes. A final sentence tells of new conflict.)	

In one section of the map, the students compile a list of the book's characters and write a short description of each one. As they continue to read the book, they add more characters and descriptive words to the list. (More mature readers might also add character development—how and why the characters change.) On the bottom third of the map, the students—with help from the teacher, if necessary—write chapter summaries that give the main episodes of each chapter in two or three sentences. The last sentence of each summary tells of the new conflict that has arisen. In the third and largest section of the book map, the students illustrate their concept of the chapter settings and the main action.

Working on a book map results in better concentration when the students read each chapter. As they read, they search for additional characters, a new setting, the main episodes, and a different conflict. They appear to have a better understanding of the book and to enjoy reading more.

Story Mapping for Primary Students

Sheila E. Felber
*San Diego (now Chula Vista),
California
October 1989*

Understanding the components of story structure is critical to good reading. Story mapping is an effective graphic strategy to teach first and second graders the basic story elements of main characters, setting, and story sequence. The terminology of various story parts has become a common factor in middle-grade language arts curricula. However, primary grade students can also learn more about story structure through the simple technique of story mapping.

By introducing this graphic technique, teachers can familiarize students with the common elements found in many stories. Building on this foundation, children begin to anticipate the characters, action, main idea, and setting in new stories they read. This increases motivation, the ability to predict story events, comprehension, and reading enjoyment.

During initial instruction, the students follow the teacher's model to complete the story map. Each student is provided with a story map frame that includes the story title and the words *main characters, setting,* and *sequence.* On the chalkboard or an overhead transparency, the teacher draws an enlarged version of the map and begins by discussing the title's importance in terms of its relevance as the central and connecting idea, theme, or person of the story. Next, the teacher generates active class discussion and completes either the character or setting portion. Primary students find sequence the most difficult story element to complete, so it is best left for last.

By comparing and contrasting the students' suggestions, the teacher models the metacognitive skills needed to discriminate important story elements. In this way, the teacher leads the class to understand the importance of main characters and selected setting elements. As the class agrees on the importance of certain characters, the teacher draws a picture of them on the correct portion of the map. The students do the same thing on their papers. Focusing on one story portion at a time, the teacher continues in this manner until the entire story

map in complete. The Figure shows a possible map for the story "Cinderella."

A critical component of this teaching strategy is the repetition of each section of the story map as it is completed. Proceeding from one portion to the next, enumerate both the story element and the structural component. When students become more adept at this procedure, the pictures can be replaced with written phrases. Through the repetition of this teaching strategy, young readers develop a sense that they understand story parts and learn to look for these elements in the stories they hear and read.

Story and Poetry Maps

Jennie Livingston Munson
Houston, Texas
May 1989

How about an "off the wall" approach to reading instruction? First and second graders at my school often create mural-like story maps and colorful renditions of favorite poems which, when hung on classroom and corridor walls, not only are read and enjoyed, but also serve an instructional purpose.

You will need a supply of butcher paper, some markers, and various colors of construction paper for both of these wall ideas.

A story map requires about 6 feet of butcher paper. Draw and label the shapes as in the Figure. Then choose a story amenable to mapping, one that has a definite sequence of events and strong characters, such as "The Three Little Pigs." Place the story map on the floor in front of the students. (This works best if they form a semicircle around the paper.) Explain that as they listen to the story they should identify the parts listed on the map: characters, setting, problem, beginning, middle, and end. After you have discussed the various parts of the map, choose one or two students to walk slowly over each shape, beginning with the "characters" square and moving along until they reach the "end" rectangle. This walking especially helps kinesthetic learners.

Once the story has been read, go through its parts with the students, asking them to apply what they heard to the story map. Ask "Who were the characters in this story?" and

Story Map for a Wall Display

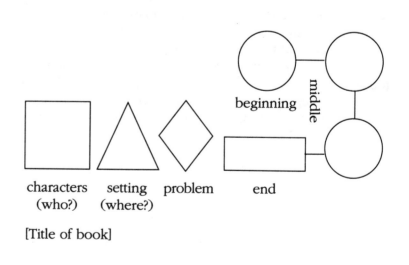

characters (who?)   setting (where?)   problem   end   beginning   middle

[Title of book]

132

"Where did most of the story take place?" and so on. Check for participation by all students.

When students demonstrate understanding, explain that the class will recreate the story within the shapes on the map. Divide the class into small, manageable groups of two or three and give each group the responsibility of illustrating one part of the story map. (To avoid crowding around the map, provide construction paper so the students can draw the illustrations separately and then glue them on the map.) Depending upon the reading and independence level of the students, you may want to establish definite assignments for students in the groups. Ask, for example, "Who would like to draw the three pigs for the 'characters' square?" If allowed to design a particular part of the story map, though, most groups will follow the process in creative and interesting ways without much teacher guidance.

Once the students have glued on all their illustrations, attach each end of the map to an available wall in the classroom or hallway. Allow members of each group enough time to explain what they included in their shape of the story map, and write specific details on the map for each group.

Students can learn to enjoy poetry in a similar way. Instead of having the groups work on different parts of the map, give each group one or two lines of poetry to illustrate on construction paper. They then glue their pictures under or near the matching lines of poetry on the butcher paper.

These "off the wall" creations help comprehension and enrich the print environment so vital to helping reading and writing become meaningful and purposeful to students.

Story Map Raps

Mark Howard
Denver, Colorado
October 1988

Story mapping helps students identify and better understand the relationships among story elements. However, students often become passive and uninterested if mapping is used over and over in the same way. Story map raps motivate students while maintaining the technique's effectiveness.

I used the following cooperative lesson with my sixth grade reading class. My students had had extensive experience with story mapping; however, since this time they were to transform a written story map outline into a rap song (a popu-

A Story Map and Rap

Story Map

Title: *The Three Little Pigs*

Setting: A forest; pigs' houses

Characters: Mother Pig, three little pigs, wolf

Problem: Pigs were sent out to live on their own but needed to find secure homes to keep safe from the wolf.

Events: 1. First pig bought hay for house; wolf blew down the house and ate the pig.
2. Second pig bought sticks for house; wolf blew down the house and ate the pig.
3. Third pig bought bricks and built house; wolf was unable to blow down house.

Solution: Third pig built a strong, secure house and was able to outfox the wolf and eat him for dinner.

Story Map Rap

In a forest far away at mama piggy's house, lived three little pigs with very hungry mouths.

Money was a problem and mama couldn't pay, so she sent the little piggies out and on their way.

So sad, so sad, Mama felt real bad.

Real bad, real bad, Mama wasn't so rad.

The piggies were afraid and sought a place to stay, 'cause the big, bad wolf was hard to keep away.

The first little piggy rounded up a bunch of hay and he built his flimsy house in less than half a day.

Good job, good job, he thought he was real cool.

Real cool, real cool, but he really was a fool.

The wolf came huffin' and puffin' to blow the house down, he had that pig for lunch and that was no ground round.

The second pig found sticks to build his house anew, this would provide support, for sticks were strong he knew.

So smart, so smart, this pig thought he was smart.

So smart, so smart, soon to be part of the meat mart.

The wolf took in a breath and huffed and puffed a little, soon the pig was dead because his house it was too brittle.

So the third little piggy had his work cut out for him, but he found some bricks to use and his future was not so dim.

Hurray, hurray, this pig he used his brain.

Hurray, hurray, but the wolf was such a pain.

Again came the wolf his breath which smelled of pork a huffin' and a puffin' but this pig he was no dork.

The wolf tried many tricks to have this pig to eat, but the pig he tricked the wolf and wolf became dead meat.

Dead meat, dead meat, oh the wolf was such a pain.

But the third little piggy used his brain for his own gain.

lar style of "spoken" musical verse), I modeled how to apply story mapping, using a familiar fairy tale. I hoped that by giving the students visual examples of how to separate the elements of the story map (setting, characters, problem, events, solution) and translating each element into musical verse, I would help their understanding. (The story map and story map rap I used are shown in the Figure on the opposite page.) Although most students find the task simple after it is modeled, a lesson on rhyming words and developing word families might be helpful.

The students moved into small groups to create their own rap song. They cooperatively developed a story map of a novel recently studied in class. Their excitement led them to begin writing the rap song without the story map outline. To keep them from eliminating this important step, I suggested that they present the story map and rap song separately and had the small groups turn in a written story map along with their song. Using the elements of the story map, the groups wrote their raps, incorporating familiar rap language, music, and tempo.

The groups practiced their rap songs, including musical accompaniment, sound effects, props, costumes, and dance movements. We videotaped each group's performance for the class to evaluate and enjoy.

In a large group discussion of the story map process, we reflected on what was accomplished, how it was done, and what was gained. This helped students think about the strategies and cognitive processes they used.

While assessing these students' written story maps and rap songs, I noticed that they easily identified story elements and were able to differentiate between important and unimportant events within the story. I also observed improved comprehension of story elements (as determined by a comprehension test), active processing and participation in decision making, use of higher-level thinking skills, deeper-level processing using analysis and synthesis of information, increased awareness of metacognitive processes, and increased group interaction and improved social skills.

Map a Story's Framework

Evelyn F. Searls
Tampa, Florida
October 1987

Most children's stories have certain key elements in common: (1) major characters, (2) a setting (including both place and time, if time is important to the story), (3) a problem (most stories represent characters' attempts to solve problems), (4) the main characters' goal (usually to alleviate the problem), (5) attempts to achieve the goal (usually the story's major events), and (6) a resolution (usually achieving the goal and solving the problem).

After much experience in listening to and reading stories, children develop an internal "sense of story," or a general framework into which they can fit what happens in a particular story. Many children develop and use this framework subconsciously; others require direct instruction.

Identifying a story's key elements and using them as a guide to asking comprehension questions accomplishes four good things: first, such a story map helps children develop a general framework for stories that they will consciously use to predict as they read; second, it gives them practice in identifying the main idea of a story, since the problem and its solution are usually the main idea; third, using a story map helps children focus on and remember a story's sequence of events; and fourth, it helps children see cause-effect relationships—that is, that the events do not happen in random order but one leads to or causes the next.

Not every basal story lends itself to story mapping, but many do. The questions in the teacher's manual often include those that will be generated by following the story map, but they are mixed in with many other kinds of questions. If you follow the questioning sequence given in the manual, there is no focus on the framework of stories in general.

To construct a story map, make up a form like the one shown in the Figure to list the key elements. Using the story map as a guide, ask the children a sequence of questions to elicit the story's elements.

In some stories it may not be necessary to include both a problem and a goal question because one may encompass the other. Also, in longer stories there may be more than one problem or goal or the problem may develop later in the story, as illustrated in the Figure.

Although some primary school children already have an unconscious grasp of story structure, this teaching technique works best with children in grade four and up. Students do see the logic in it and benefit in the ways mentioned.

136

Partially Completed Story Form
with Teacher Questions

Teacher's Questions

Who were the major characters?

Where did the story take place?

What did Mary wish for at the beginning?

Did the something special happen at school?

When Father's truck slid off the road on the way home from school, what did Mary find in the snow?

What did Mary want to do with the puppy?

Why couldn't Mary keep the puppy?

Where did Mary take the puppy first to try to get rid of him?

•
•
•

How did Mary reach her first goal?

How was the problem solved?

Story: *Mary of Mile 18*

Story Map

Characters: Mary and her father

Setting: Northern British Columbia, where winters are very cold and long.

Goal 1: Mary wanted something special to happen.

Event 1: No, it was an ordinary school day.

Event 2: Mary found a puppy that was part wolf.

Goal 2: Mary wanted to keep the puppy as a pet.

Problem: The family didn't have enough money to keep a pet--their animals had to work or give food.

Event 3: Mary took the puppy into the woods and left him.

Events 4-8:
•
•
•

Resolution: Finding the puppy was something special that Mary had wanted. The puppy proved he could be valuable to the family.

137

Charting Effect and Cause in Informational Texts

Lori L. Conrad
Littleton, Colorado
February 1989

Many children know a great deal about the structures and structural cues authors use in stories. Their notion of "storyness" helps them comprehend new stories, retell old favorites, and create pieces of their own. This recognition and use of a text's structure is not as developed or as readily used with expository texts. Children need additional experience with informational writing to further their intuitive knowledge of its structures.

Since cause and effect is one of the most widely used and more easily detected structures in elementary informational texts, I decided that this would be a good starting place to increase my students' knowledge of text structure. I began by charting the two elements side by side but I placed "Effect" to the left of "Cause" (see the Figure). Some children have more difficulty expressing cause and effect relationships when they try to explain the cause first. They often want to tell what happened followed by a "because" phrase—the reverse of many workbook exercises. When I asked for the effect first and *then* the cause, the relationships seemed to fit better with students' natural explanations. It also made it easier for me to decide whether they understood the concept or if the procedures for answering were confusing them.

The first time I used this procedure, I chose four well-written informational texts that utilized cause and effect relationships to explain their information. The books related to a class thematic unit on winter. Before reading any of the informational texts, I presented a blank chart to the class (see example 1 in the Figure). We discussed the words *effect* and *cause,* their meanings, and possible applications to the upcoming shared reading experience. The children predicted relationships the author might try to explain about winter.

After sharing the first text, we returned to the blank chart. I demonstrated how the chart could be filled, "thinking aloud" the process used to explore and note the effect and cause relationships remembered from the text. Then I turned the chart over to the children and asked them to help fill in the missing information (see example 2 in the Figure).

Sharing of the second informational book was followed by the display of an "effect and cause" chart with the "effect" side already completed (see example 3). The children then filled in what they believed to have been the reasons the effects happened. We discussed the finished charts as a whole group, and ideas were compared, confirmed, and expanded using other students and the original text as information sources.

138

Example 1

Effect	Cause
1.	1.
2.	2.
3.	3.

Example 2

Effect	Cause
1. Some birds fly south when winter comes	1. because they can find more food there.
2. Bats stay in their caves during the winter	2. because it is warmer in the cave—there is no wind or snow inside.

Example 3

Effect	Cause
1. Most trees lose their leaves in the winter	1.
2. Trees have hard buds on their stems where the leaves once were	2.

Example 4

Effect	Cause
1.	1. because they [the flies] spend the winter in places that offer protection from the cold.
2.	2. because the mother grasshopper lays them [eggs] in deep holes in the soft earth.

Then the third informational book was shared, followed by an "effect and cause" chart that had the "cause" side completed (see example 4). After the children finished the matching effects, they discussed their findings in small groups.

Finally, the children were asked to fill in an entire "effect and cause" chart on their own. Since none of the relationships was established beforehand, this chart led to the greatest amount of discussion.

These steps can be repeated and elaborated upon if the children do not understand the intended process. Reversing the "effect" and "cause" terms helps children note the information's relationships more easily.

The Shape of Content: Four Semantic Map Structures for Expository Paragraphs

Marion B. Schmidt
Trumbull, Connecticut
October 1986

Semantic mapping is a strategy by which students represent the relationships in a prose passage with geometric shapes. This produces a diagram that represents the message of the passage. It is an excellent aid to reading comprehension and to learning content.

I have found it useful to show my fourth, fifth, and sixth grade students ways to identify and map the four most common paragraph patterns using four agreed-upon shapes. In this way the shape alone communicates some essential relationships.

The simplest and most common map is the "spider" diagram used to map paragraphs of enumeration, or main idea with supporting details. The spider image is particularly useful because it encourages students to draw the "legs" horizontally so they can read the words without rotating the paper. For the literal-minded student, I point out that these spiders may have any number of legs. Figure 1 gives an example of this kind of paragraph and its spider map. (A variation is the "one-legged spider" as in Figure 2. It is used with paragraphs that state a generalization and give an example).

The time-order or sequence paragraph involves either narration or a step-by-step description of a process. Both can

Figure 1
The Spider Map: Main Ideas and Details

The Jackson family has a favorite vacation place. There is a lake nearby for water skiing and boating. They can also go hiking and horseback riding. Tennis courts and a swimming pool are close to their cabin.

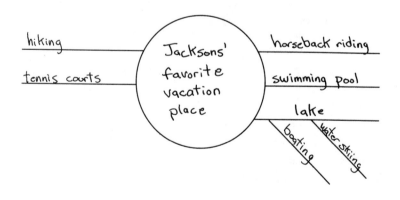

Figure 2
The One-Legged Spider Map: Generalization Plus Examples

Many places have a traditional food. In Boston, baked beans are flavored with molasses and baked slowly in a special pot. Steaming brown bread is usually served with the beans. This traditional Boston dish is often served on Saturday night, but it may also be enjoyed at other times.

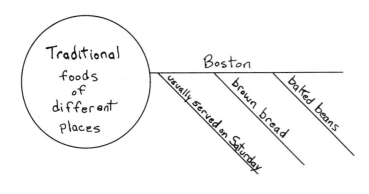

be mapped as a descending ladder (Figure 3 on the next page).

Another common paragraph pattern is comparison-contrast. This is clearly illustrated by the map in Figure 4, which reveals the areas of overlap between concepts.

The fourth common pattern is cause-effect. Figure 5 presents an example of such a paragraph and its map. Some paragraphs of this type give multiple causes, multiple effects, or chain reactions. Students may map such paragraphs in one of the ways shown in Figure 6.

Mapping can be used with a wide variety of text material. Students may develop combinations and variations of these basic mapping patterns depending on the length and complexity of the text to be mapped. There is no one correct way to construct a map, but relationships within the text should be evident in the map. Figure 7 presents a passage with two different student maps. No doubt the reader could suggest other ways to map the passage because the technique is flexible.

Some paragraphs defy mapping. Extraneous sentences and confusing comments abound in some texts and practice materials. My solution to this problem is to avoid such passages when possible or to use them as examples of poor writing and to work with students to rewrite them.

A useful modification of the mapping technique involves incomplete maps. These can be used as advance

Figure 3
The Time Ladder Map

It was already dark by the time Beth and Mary left the library. They immediately started walking as quickly as possible to the bus stop. Unfortunately, the bus had already left when they got there. They had to telephone Mary's mother for a ride hame.

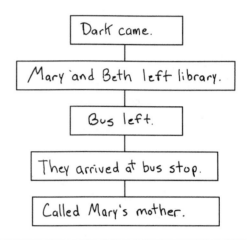

Figure 4
The Compare-Contrast Overlay Map

The computer and the human mind are very much alike. Both can store and recall information. However, the computer must be told what to do with the information. The human mind can invent new and different ways to use information.

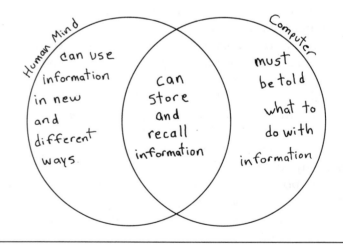

142

organizers for students' reading and writing, as a questioning technique, or as an aid to review and recall.

Semantic mapping can be a powerful tool. It can increase student involvement, comprehension, and recall. It really works for me.

Figure 5
The Cause-Effect Map

Hundreds of years ago a fierce group of people called the Huns attacked China. The Huns wanted to conquer China. The Chinese built a huge wall 1,500 miles long to keep the Huns out of China. The Great Wall is still standing today.

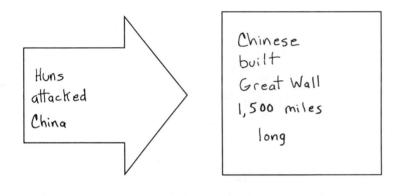

Figure 6
The Multiple Cause, Multiple Effect, or Chain Reaction Map

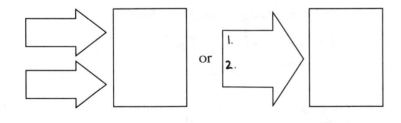

Figure 7
Combined Maps

The Pilgrims left England in September of 1620. They started out with two ships. One, the *Speedwell*, developed a leak and could not make the journey. The Pilgrims decided to make the trip in just one ship, the *Mayflower*. Many of the *Speedwell's* passengers crowded aboard the *Mayflower*. The Pilgrims were very crowded and uncomfortable. They had to eat, sleep, dress, and pass the time between decks. Each person had less than 6 square feet of space.

It took the *Mayflower* 65 days to cross the Atlantic. The voyage was very rough, windy, and cold. There was not enough medicine or supplies. There was no doctor on the ship. The Pilgrims were sick, weak, and tired when they arrived at Plymouth Rock in November.

Time Ladder with Embedded Spider

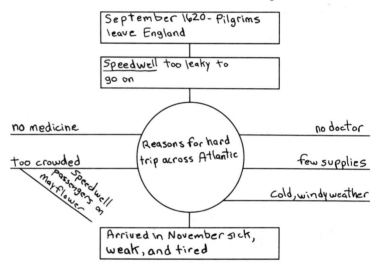

Time Ladder Plus Chain Reactions

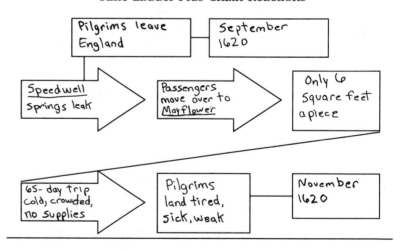

144

Reading teachers routinely evaluate students' reading comprehension, traditionally by asking questions at different comprehension levels. An alternative has been provided by story grammar for narrative selections: teachers can build questions around the story elements and make question frames to use with any story. Wouldn't it be helpful to have such useful frames for content area materials?

To build content area question frames, I first identified three elements typical of content material: main idea, supporting information, and causal relationships. I used these three elements along with a category called "reactions"—whose purpose is to elicit critical thinking and personalize the material—to make the following question frames. When using them, the teacher must fill in the information called for by the brackets.

Main idea. The author states that [supporting information] and [supporting information]. What does that information point out?

A sample main idea question: The author states that *the tombs of blacksmiths, weavers, gardeners, and dressmakers are among those found in the Roman catacombs.* What does this point out? (Answer: Humble people, as well as renowned people, are buried in the catacombs.)

Supporting information. The author states that [main idea]. What information does the author provide to support that statement?

A sample question for supporting information: The author states that *there are some misconceptions about the catacombs.* What information does the author provide to support that statement? (Answer: The catacombs were built openly as burial places, not as secret places of worship or hideaways for persecuted Christians).

Causal relationships. The author states that [cause]. What effect did that have? The author states that [effect]. What was the cause of that?

A sample question for causal relations: The author states that *during the tenth century there were earth tremors near the catacombs.* What effect did that have? (Answer: The catacombs collapsed and were not visited for centuries.)

Reactions. What are some things you learned about [topic]? What was the most interesting thing you learned about [topic]? Why did that interest you the most? How do you feel about [event/practice/idea]? What is your opinion concerning what the author says about [event/practice/idea]?

A sample reaction question: How do you feel about *allowing visitors to tour the catacombs?*

Question frames suit virtually any content area selection. With them, the teacher is not merely an actor following a

Question Frames for Content Area Reading Material

Frederick A. Duffelmeyer
Ames, Iowa
May 1984

145

script. Even with the basic framework for posing questions, the teacher still must decide what information is significant, from the standpoint of both retention of information and critical thinking. The question frame can help the teacher focus on significant information and so conduct a worthwhile evaluation of students' reading comprehension.

FAN Out Your Facts on the Board

Barbara Swaby
Colorado Springs, Colorado
May 1984

Visual aids are good for extending elementary school children's comprehension and stimulating divergent thinking. A strategy called semantic webbing (described by Freedman and Reynolds in the March 1980 issue of *The Reading Teacher*) has been widely accepted and used successfully. Cleland (March '81 *RT*) showed how semantic webbing could be used to extend elementary students' appreciation of children's literature. I want to show how it can be used with science texts or other expository materials in such a way that it extends students' comprehension of new facts and helps them think about how the selection relates to their own experiences. The strategy is called the Fact Analyzer, or FAN.

The FAN starts out with a crescent in which the title of the selection is written. Emerging from it are the selection's major facts. Filling in these blanks stimulates students to recall facts and decide what information is most important. Once this is done, two semantic webs are applied. Two types of core questions are hung below the crescent. The first extends the text. It is a question (provided by the teacher) that helps the children think divergently about the material read and thus extend the text's information. The question may require children to draw some answers from the text, but they must also go beyond the text and draw from experience.

The second core question asks the children about their own experiences. Here they are helped to understand how certain aspects of the text may be relevant in their own environments and experiences. This type of question is vital, yet it is seldom asked in the content areas. (Teachers are more apt to have children draw personal implications from literature than from science or social studies texts.) The experience web helps children realize that they indeed "live" social studies or science.

For example, a selection about Australia's Great Barrier Reef was presented to a group of average fourth graders. After they read the piece, we applied the FAN. Student responses are recorded verbatim in the Figure to show how the strategy works.

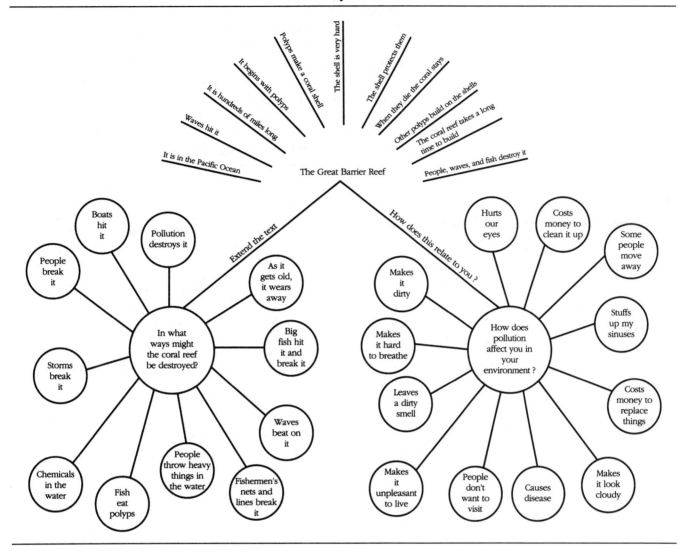

After the selection was read, I said, "Close your books. Okay, now what was the title of the selection? Tell me all the important facts that you remember from the passage." As the children gave their comments, we discussed them all briefly. The result is shown in the fan at the top of the Figure. This structure helps children recall the facts and also provides a way to review material.

Once we recalled the facts, I wrote on the chalkboard the core question for extending the text, and this elicited the responses shown. The children's responses represented both the material in the text and predictions based on the text. Once the ideas were exhausted, I added the core question for expanding students' experiences. Obviously, the core questions are up to the individual teacher, who chooses any aspect he or she wants to relate to the children's experience. I chose pollution because the children had just finished a unit on ecology and I wanted to link this to the science passage.

The FAN has been used successfully in clinical and classroom situations, and has been modified for grades one through six. It is a helpful strategy for developing both recall and divergent thinking abilities and for helping children relate content material to their own experiences. If it is used regularly, the children learn that whenever they read they should think about how the text extends to the outer world and how it ties into their own lives.

Chapter 7

Composing Text

During the 1970s and '80s the study of writing focused on the cognitive processes writers use when they compose and their mental representation of texts, as well as the social and communicative context of writing (Graves, 1981). Flower and Hayes's (1980, 1981) cognitive model of the writing process provides the most complete account of the processes involved in composing and is in the problem-solving tradition. The most powerful aspect of their model is the idea that the primary sub-processes used in writing identified by Flower et al. (1986) as planning, translating, and reviewing occur simultaneously and include other subprocesses. This notion, called "recursion," explains that writers move among different subprocesses as they compose rather than proceeding in a linear fashion from planning to editing. For example, writers may evaluate their texts as they alter their structure, or set new goals as they translate the original plans to paper. In other words, writing is not a series of steps that can be followed in a prescribed fashion.

"Planning" means generating ideas about content and organizing those ideas into a plan that guides the creation of the text. This concept presupposes that the writer has prior knowledge of the topic, "discourse knowledge" of rhetorical structures such as narrative, persuasion, argument, or exposition, and the ability to access both. Skilled writers exhibit conscious control of discourse knowledge and have a sense of audience, purpose, and voice; novice writers seem to make little or no use of discourse knowledge. Overall, the amount of time devoted to planning, and the skill with which plans are made, separate skilled writers from novice writers. Classroom instruction that focuses on prewriting activities is an attempt to help students become more efficient planners. For example, teachers may list topic-related words students might use, have them recall all they know about a topic, or guide a decision to create a narrative, exposition, or argument.

"Translating" refers to taking the plans for a composition and using them to create written text. It is the step of actually putting pen to paper. As writers draft their compositions, they may revise their plans, include new information, or delete superfluous details—such is the recursive nature of composing. Translating also involves using the conventions of written language, including the rules governing punctuation, capitalization, and language usage. Skilled writers seem to use little cognitive energy to meet these surface needs of a text; in contrast, novice writers often have difficulty with these conventions and devote much attention to them. In an effort to help children attend more closely to content and organization, teachers often urge beginning writers to ignore the conventions of language in their first drafts. The idea is that children can "clean up" their writing later.

"Reviewing" includes evaluating the text, revising it on the basis of that evaluation, and completing the final editing. To succeed at this stage, writers must know about discourse characteristics and surface structures, recognize problems in these areas, and know how to address those problems. A connection between reading and writing occurs here because writers must review their own texts to determine which revisions are necessary. Skilled writers tend to review their work frequently, making revisions that change a composition by modifying, adding, or deleting content; novice writers often see revision as an editing process and make only a few surface revisions. Holding teacher-student conferences is one way teachers can help children focus on their work and gain a sense of how an audience sees their writing. Specific (rather than evaluative) written feedback is another tool that can help children improve. Certainly providing adequate time for children to think about and revise their compositions is critical.

The social and communicative context of writing centers on the meanings that composing has for children. Children write more easily on familiar topics or about things they want to share with someone else (e.g., a letter to grandmother about a new puppy). In fact, letting young children write about things that interest them significantly increases the amount they write (Graves, 1975). Teachers create a social and communicative climate that encourages writing by allowing students to select their own topics, make unique interpretations of assigned topics, and share their creations with audiences.

Writers usually know the audience for whom they are writing, and this knowledge affects the form and content of their text. For example, students writing in a personal journal or log will use a different form and include different content than students writing a formal class assignment. A student writing a letter to his or her grandmother about a new puppy would use a different style (or voice) if the letter were to the local veterinarian. When teachers create a social climate that is supportive of writing, such as exists in writing workshops, children begin to grasp the idea that writing is a communicative as well as a cognitive activity.

In any discussion of writing it is important to note that skill in reading is vital to developing skill in writing. Reading, rather than writing, offers a foundation for children's knowledge of composing—both procedural knowledge and discourse knowledge. For example, through reading, children gain a sense of grapheme-phoneme correspondence and begin to understand spelling; they become familiar with what makes a story and thus know what elements to include when they write stories themselves; and they come to realize that writing conventions help readers understand what is written.

The strategies included in this section are suggestions for teachers to consider in terms of their own classrooms, the writing climate they have created, and the children they teach. Teachers should remember, though, that one of the best ways to teach writing is to teach reading.

References

Flower, L., & Hayes, J.R. (1980). The cognition of discovery: Defining a rhetorical problem. *College Composition and Communication, 31,* 21-32.

Flower, L., & Hayes, J.R. (1981). The pregnant pause: An inquiry into the nature of planning. *Research in the Teaching of English, 15,* 229-244.

Flower, L., Hayes, J.R., Carey, L., Schriver, K., & Stratman, J. (1986). Detection, diagnosis, and the strategies of revision. *College Composition and Communication, 37,* 16-55.

Graves, D.H. (1975). An examination of the writing processes of seven-year-old children. *Research in the Teaching of English, 9,* 227-241.

Graves, D.H. (1981). Writing research for the eighties: What is needed. *Language Arts, 58,* 197-206.

Further Reading

Calkins, L.M. (1980). When children want to punctuate: Basic skills belong in context. *Language Arts, 57,* 567-573.

Calkins, L.M. (1986). *The art of teaching writing.* Portsmouth, NH: Heinemann.

Clark, A. (1989). Helping primary children write about reality. *The Reading Teacher, 42,* 414-416.

Fitzgerald, J. (1988). Helping young writers to revise: A brief review for teachers. *The Reading Teacher, 42,* 124-129.

Freeman, R.H. (1983). Poetry writing in the upper elementary grades. *The Reading Teacher, 37,* 238-242.

Gunderson, L., & Shapiro, J. (1988). Whole language instruction: Writing in 1st grade. *The Reading Teacher, 41,* 430-439.

Heald-Taylor, B.G. (1984). Scribble in first grade writing. *The Reading Teacher, 38,* 4-9.

Jones, M.B., & Nessel, D.D. (1985). Enhancing the curriculum with experience stories. *The Reading Teacher, 39,* 18-23.

Olson, M.W. (1984). A dash of story grammar and...presto! A book report. *The Reading Teacher, 37,* 458-461.

Reutzel, D.R. (1986). The reading basal: A sentence combining composing book. *The Reading Teacher, 40,* 194-199.

Spivey, N.N., & King, J.R. (1989). Readers as writers composing from sources. *Reading Research Quarterly, 24,* 7-26.

Tierney, R.J., Soter, A., O'Flahavan, J.F., & McGinley, W. (1989). The effects of reading and writing upon thinking critically. *Reading Research Quarterly, 24,* 134-173.

Use Writing Folders to Show the Process

Betsy L. Lanzen
Rocky River, Ohio
January 1987

If writing is to be a part of the elementary classroom, every student should keep a writing folder: a place to experiment, plan, and collect thoughts. The folder includes all the ideas, webs, and pieces of writing a student has worked on throughout the year. It provides a record for evaluation of papers and of progress from beginning to end. The writing folder becomes a handy source for documenting strengths and weaknesses as well as for setting goals for writing and documenting achievements.

Introduce students to the idea of writing folders over the course of several days. Begin by asking them to decorate their writing folders. This helps instill a sense of ownership: the folders students will be working on belong to them just as much as the writing they put into the folders. Then you can model brainstorming ideas for writing topics. Afterwards, students brainstorm, and list possible topics in their writing folders. Next, model narrowing down the topic and provide opportunities for students to practice this activity. When ready, students can narrow their own topics. The next step is to model webbing a subject. Provide practice by selecting common topics for students to web as a class and individually. Finally, model writing a rough draft and then provide guidance as students begin to write their drafts. Writing is not an event. Feedback should come during the process and not just when the writing is completed. Find something positive to say to every student. Positive reinforcement makes us feel confident about what we are doing even though we may need to revise and correct.

For clarity and guidance, give each student a checklist to include in the writing folder. The checklist expands the writing process into seven steps that guide the student from beginning to end. Students can refer to the checklist as they proceed, and each step can be checked off by the teacher or student to keep track of progress. Here are the seven steps, with complete explanations; briefer descriptions can be used on the students' checklists.

1. *Prewriting.* First brainstorm to find a topic. Make a list of all the ideas you can think of to write about. Think of things you have done, something you have seen, a place you have been, something special to you, or a feeling. Talk to a friend or talk to your teacher—they can be helpful in suggesting ideas. Look at your list. Decide what you want to write about.

   Narrow the topic—a broad subject can be narrowed to something more specific.

Web the topic—write the topic inside a circle, and then write words or phrases about the topic around the circle.

2. *Rough draft.* A rough draft is a practice story. Include ideas from your web. Do you need to tell who, what, where, when, why, or how? Read your story to yourself. How does it sound? Does anything need to be added? Should anything be left out? Read it to a friend. What is his or her opinion of your story? Write several rough drafts.

   Content conference—choose the rough draft you like best and meet with your teacher for a conference.

3. *Revision.* Following the conference, make any changes needed in the content of your story.

   Organization conference—meet with your teacher again to discuss your story's organization. Make any needed changes in the organization.

   Editing conference—meet with your teacher again to discuss the changes you have made. Is there anything else you need to fix?

4. *Proofread.* Find any spelling errors. Check with word lists or a dictionary for spelling correctness. Are capital letters needed anywhere? Are punctuation marks used correctly?

5. *Final copy.* Write your story neatly with all the necessary corrections in your creative writing folder.

6. *Publish.* Is this a special story? Should it be published? Decide how your story will be published. Will it be typed and bound? Is the story to be illustrated?

7. *Share your book.* Share your published piece of writing with your class, the principal, a parent, a friend, another class, the school newspaper, or your parent-teacher association.

They key to improved student writing lies in developing the whole process, not just assigning topics and correcting papers. Our goal should be to encourage each student's creativity. Prewriting activities trigger ideas. Modeling demonstrates how more experienced writers approach the task of writing. Revision helps students develop independence and ownership. Teacher conferences guide students through the process. Writing is not a lonely experience; it's done in cooperation with others.

Guided Writing for Beginners

Judith A. Munk
Honolulu, Hawaii
February 1987

Try turning Manzo's Guided Reading Procedure into the Guided Writing Procedure (GWP) for kindergarten and grade one. At this grade level, use a structured overview instead of an outline. A chart displaying a clustering of the children's ideas will help the students write a comprehensive, organized language experience story. The GWP strategy has three basic parts:

Gathering information. When possible, begin with a Directed Seeing-Thinking Activity (DSTA) that yields a line drawing of the topic. Draw this in the center of a large chart. For example, if the theme is spiders, use a spider in the DSTA drawing and then write the word *spider* inside it. Then begin eliciting information from the children. Write this information in clusters or categories on the chart as the students are giving it to you (see Figure).

After a few items in one category are written on the chart, the students should be able to come up with the main idea for that category. Write the category name above the

DSTA Chart

What They Do (Behavior)	Feelings
1. make spiderwebs	1. scares me
2. crawl	2. sad
3. carry food around	3. frightened
4. live on a spiderweb	4. happy
5. make orb, messy webs	5. upset
6. make spider silk	6. I like them
7. wait for enemies (some spiders are poisonous)	

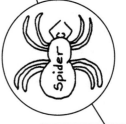

Appearance
1. looks like a peanut
2. 8 legs
3. 2 body parts (thorax, abdomen; legs come out of thorax)
4. some have dots
5. 2 palpi
6. 2 fangs

information and circle or box it. Later, add information from other sources (field trips, books, films, etc.) to the chart.

In this approach, students' prior knowledge and new knowledge are visually organized and represented on the structured overview. The group has been doing a combination of prediction, story mapping, and semantic webbing, all starting from the children's own knowledge about the topic.

Guided writing. Begin the writing activity by selecting one category on the chart. Encourage students to give sentences derived from the ideas in that category, and write the sentences on another large chart or the chalkboard. The children may use all of the information from the category, some of it, or new information to formulate their sentences. However, they should stick to the category. After the information is used, cross it off the chart.

Tell the children the sentences written for each category are a paragraph with one idea. Show how each paragraph begins with an indentation that marks where the idea begins.

During the guided writing, model and elicit complete sentences from the students, being careful to use the students' language but also allowing them to revise sentences they've offered that do not sound right after they are written. Correct language thus filters into the story and correct sentence patterns are formed and practiced by the children. Later, when they write their own stories, they will have a better grasp of a correctly formed sentence.

The Guided Writing Procedure creates a very meaty, enjoyable story with the language experience approach. It gives lower primary students a sense of what a sentence is and an awareness of how ideas are connected and developed into a story.

Working the story. The completed story is used according to the needs of the children. For example, the story may lend itself to teaching certain structural analysis skills (such as compound words) or phonetic skills (such as short or long vowels). Examine the story to determine what skills to teach.

The GWP provides a writing framework for students. The children see and experience writing because the teacher models the writing process by visually representing the ideas, clustering them, and guiding the organization of the writing. Using the GWP, the teacher has the opportunity to develop the students' oral language ability, enrich their vocabulary, and develop sentence and paragraph sense, all while teaching the concept of clustering ideas into larger units. The result is a comprehensive, cohesive story. Furthermore, with a richer text developed through the students' own ideas, there is the possibility that they will need to use fewer inferencing skills to read and comprehend the story. Thus, the teacher has effectively guided the students to better thinking in language, writing, and reading.

Successful Peer Conferencing

Jean M. Daly
Setauket, New York
November 1990

Peer conferencing is an important part of the writing process. However, it is difficult to monitor the conferences and children often stray from the task, so the results are less than expected. The temptation for teachers to collect the papers, get out the red pencil, and revise the pieces is great. However, with a little structure, modeling, and practice, peer conferencing can become a rewarding experience for both students and the teacher.

I organized my class for peer conferencing using cooperative learning guidelines for team set-ups. Specifically, I placed an equal number of students on each team, being careful to distribute students according to ability so that each team was heterogeneous. To help the students remain on task, I developed a set of peer conference cards that were printed on 8" x 12" (20 cm x 30 cm) colored construction paper and laminated. I made one set of cards for each group of students.

Card A was the *Reader Card*. It directed the chosen reader to perform these tasks for the group:

1. Tell the group which part you want them to listen to with special care. It may be a new beginning you tried. It may be a new ending. You may need suggestions for a title, or you may only want an audience to hear your piece.
2. Read your piece twice to your listeners. Do it clearly and slowly.

Card B was the *Summarizer Card*. This task requires the student to summarize what he or she heard from the reader. The card suggested formats for the summarizer to use. For example:

- I heard you say....
- Your main point was....
- This is what I heard....

Card C was the *Questioner Card*. It directed the conference member to ask questions such as:

- Could you tell me more about...?
- Will you explain more about...?
- Could you please clarify...for me?

Card D was the *Suggester Card*. It directed a child to make suggestions to the author based on group conversation. The card offered these suggestions:

- These possible titles came to me as you read for us....

- Have you thought about trying...?

- Have you talked with...? He/she had the same problem before.

Card E was the *Praiser Card*. It gave hints about how to praise the author and the piece. Some suggested compliments were:

- I liked the part where you....

- I especially enjoyed....

- You made me (laugh/cry/smile) when you....

- You really made some good changes in this draft.

Card F is the *Observer Card*. I prepared this one in case groups needed rearranging at the last minute due to absences or additions to the class. The holder kept a checklist and marked it off as each group member completed his or her task.

The cards were rotated clockwise around the group until each member had been the reader. When each member had had a turn to use each card, the floor opened for any member of the group to add closing comments.

The author often made notes as peers spoke and then decided what to do with the information the peer group offered. The author maintained ownership of the piece, since the decision to act or not act upon the information obtained in the peer conference resided solely with the author.

When I first introduced these cards to the class, we modeled the procedure using a group of volunteers. I stood nearby to coach members if they got confused. Within a week, the class no longer needed modeling. Within two to three weeks, I noticed less dependence on the cards and more confidence in my students' peer conferencing skills. Now I no longer need to pass out the cards, although occasionally a group may take the cards and use them for the session. Peer conferencing has become an efficient use of classroom time, and student writing does benefit from the process.

Cite and Write on the Class Calendar

Anne E. Murdock
Wayne, Pennsylvania
January 1987

My third graders focus on a student-made calendar for language arts writing activities. Each week a child is assigned to enter the day's date every morning. Ample space is provided for each day of the month where the students write bits of significant information from their own lives. Included are birthdates, pending trips, holidays, sports events, or happenings they think are of high interest. I encourage children to write in complete sentences, applying their best writing skills. If they wish to elaborate on their calendar contribution, they express themselves further in a daily journal entry.

A calendar kaleidoscope of events unfolds and becomes self-prescribed required reading. Children with statements that might be of high interest to others are invited to share them. They either read from their journals or give an oral presentation. Questions and discussion naturally ensue.

Wide margins are left around the calendar's borders. Student drawings with descriptive captions representative of that month occupy this area. For example, drawings depicting the month of April are accompanied by the following comments: "Magnificent spring is here at last!" "Yellow is everywhere." "Easter. I like to walk in the rain." "Daffodils are my favorite flowers!"

This calendar activity touches on many aspects of language arts. It provides the students with opportunities for expressive writing, reading, oral expression, developing a descriptive word vocabulary, and keener perception of time and space.

When the last bit of writing space has been used, a new month is conveniently tacked directly over the old one. With continued enthusiasm, children begin citing and writing in the many blank spaces that await their important news.

There's Magic in Giving Directions

Barbara Snyder
Glastonbury, Connecticut
October 1986

Because magic intrigues people of all ages, I chose that topic to motivate second graders who needed remedial reading help. I provided each student with a copy of instructions for executing the same simple magic trick. Each child read the directions and was able to perform the trick well enough to go home and try it on the family.

I asked each child to come back with a trick that needed only a few props we could find around the school. Everyone knows some magic! The next day each child tried her/his magic trick on the group.

The next step was for the children to write directions explaining how to do their individual tricks. The directions had to be numbered and written very clearly so other students could perform the trick. It took a lot of careful writing (and some help from me) to make the directions inclusive and clear enough for another person to follow. The children attached their written directions to a piece of construction paper and drew a picture that would interest another second grader in doing the trick.

When everyone was finished, I gave one of these "trick posters" to each child in another class. I made sure the recipient's ability level was similar to that of the originator. Each child performed the trick for her/his class. Afterwards each student wrote a letter to tell the originator of the trick how it went.

The children gained self-confidence performing in front of a group of peers, read for understanding, wrote very clearly for someone else to understand, and had fun.

With notewriting, students have a purpose for reading and writing. Follow these suggestions to encourage notewriting in a controlled way.

- Write a note to someone in the class the very first day of school. Always ask a question so that the student will need to respond. Respond to your students' notes—you will see an abundance of notewriting when students receive an immediate reply from the teacher. "Sticky" notes are great for this—just stick a note on the student's desk.

- Announce the first week of school that notewriting will be permitted when students have time. Make a list of things students can do with reading and writing when they finish their work. Notewriting will become a high priority. Let children tape notes they've written to their friends around the doorway, to be distributed after lunch by the classroom helper. Watch for students who never receive a note, and write one to them. Make sure to respond to any notes you receive.

- Display the notes you receive on the bulletin board, or glue them in a spiral notebook and make it available for students to read. They will be able to see their own progress if notes are placed in the notebook throughout the year.

Stimulating Noatewriting

Karen L. Milliron
Sterling, Illinois
December 1988

- When you collect writing journals, write frequent comments and questions. Students may answer in writing. Talk less and respond in writing.

- Stick notes on students' desks when you see positive behavior, especially in students who need constant reinforcement. Written words are often heeded more than spoken ones.

- When a student is absent, send notes from the class along with the homework (a friend may volunteer to drop these things off).

- Send notes to students who don't understand their work, explaining what they didn't understand.

- Look for reasons to write—it promotes reading, too. Have your students respond with a class note to any other class that does something for them.

- Save verbal comments. Tell students about the work that you like with a note.

- Don't photocopy information for parents—let the students write notes to explain any activities their parents need to know about.

- If another teacher has been absent for a period of time, welcome that teacher back by taping children's notes around the doorway or putting them on banners.

- Have your students interview adults and write notes to each other about what they learned.

- Write compliments to one another. Each day choose a student and have the others write letters telling that person all the things they like about her or him. Choose a day for everyone to open the compliments and read them. These will become prized possessions.

- Instead of telling classroom news, students can write it down in notes.

Penn's Principal Person

Sara Lee Schoenmaker
Iowa City, Iowa
May 1987

"You want to interview me for Women's History Month?" Our principal was slightly shaken, but after recovering from the thought of being a historical artifact, she was delighted with the benefits of this whole language activity.

I had told the students that they would be reporters for an interview with a "special person." I used role playing with them to show how to take notes. "I can't write down every-thing you say!" students protested, so we talked about how reporters cope. After deciding that a tape recorder would be useful, I explained about key words; then I let students make up statements about things they were interested in and we practiced finding the key word in their sentences.

Finally, I revealed that the subject of the interview was to be the principal of the school. Now the task was to brain-storm appropriate questions to ask her. These ranged from the mundane ("Where were you born?") to the more imaginative ("How does it feel to be boss of the school?"). Nitty gritty questions like "Who pays for the reading books?" as well as the personal ("Did you have a lot of boyfriends?") would pro-vide opportunities for the principal to build concepts as well as present herself as a humane, caring person.

We went through the list of questions, eliminated some, categorized the rest, and then decided on a logical sequence—all important skills for students. One student was selected to be the moderator to welcome the principal and begin the interview. Each student was responsible for asking designated questions and recording the answers.

After the interview, I explained how reporters write an interesting story from their notes. The students then went through their own notes to determine which bits of informa-tion would interest readers. Everyone had a chance to write an article, and then we shared these by reading them aloud. (This helped authors see some changes they wanted to make.) After rewriting, the class participated in a peer-editing process.

Finally, I typed up the final drafts and compiled them into a booklet entitled "Penn's [the name of our school] Principal Person," which was illustrated with computer graph-ics. Students avidly read their own and others' articles.

Celebrations of Women's History Month can be enjoy-able and enlightening and can encourage pupils to develop a cluster of language abilities. Mothers, grandmothers, teachers—the list of female history-makers is endless. There will likely be some fascinating subjects near at hand.

A School Newspaper: *The Crown Press*

Judy Kissell
Coronado, California
November 1990

During Newspaper in Education month, a group of third grade students and I decided to put together a newspaper for our school, Crown Elementary. The outcome was so well received that we decided to publish four editions over the course of the year, using different students as editors for each edition. Here are the procedures we used to publish issues of *The Crown Press*.

Session 1. We began by looking at several different newspapers in the area to obtain an understanding of the types of things found in newspapers and the way papers are laid out. Students discovered items such as want ads, comics, interviews, and news articles. We then brainstormed ideas about newsworthy events and people at school. This was difficult for the children and there was much discussion among the group, but finally they came up with the news that they wanted to print.

Now the children agreed on article writing assignments. Some students conducted interviews with specific staff members; some wrote articles about past or upcoming events; some wrote riddles or drew cartoons. Students were to complete the interviews and write a rough draft of the articles for the second meeting, to take place the following week.

Session 2. When the children brought their drafts to the meeting, we discussed the editing process. We made a list of things to look for in the articles. Spelling was the most obvious concern, but in time the list included these questions:

1. Will other people be interested in the material?
2. Is the material easy to read and understand?
3. Is the spelling correct?
4. Are complete sentences used?
5. Is correct punctuation used?

The children then read their own articles and were encouraged to revise and edit them as needed. They exchanged articles and proofread each other's work. After they reached agreement on a final form, the articles were ready to go into the computer.

Session 3. The children entered their articles on the computer, saved them, and printed them. (The articles were printed in 40-character columns so they would fit on the paper newspaper-style.)

Session 4. The next meeting was spent cutting and pasting articles and deciding on a name for the paper. The students had a wonderful time arranging and organizing the paper and began to talk about what would go in the next edition. I made sure all the children had an opportunity to be newspaper reporters and to have their work published. Students began thinking about other kinds of material to include such as movie and book reviews, advice columns, and editorials.

After the children put the paper together, I made enough copies for everyone in the school. The principal and teachers loved it. Most important, however, was that the students loved their newspaper.

Each week, usually on Wednesday, individual students in my fourth grade class write personal newsletters home, telling about current classroom activities as well as future events. After parents read and sign them (some even write messages back), the newsletters are stored in individual student folders. At the end of the year, they are bound and given to students as a diary of their year in the classroom. What started out as a communication tool became an authentic way for children to practice and master language arts skills in a meaningful context. The procedures are as follows.

First, students contribute the events and activities they think are important and that they might want to include in their newsletter. I "web" the ideas on an overhead transparency as they talk, and we discuss informally where the details need to go, what seems to fit together, and why. (An example appears in the Figure on the next page.) I share any information that the parents might especially need (for example, plans for a field trip). Each circle of the web and its details are written in a different color on the transparency to help the students locate the different categories that will become paragraphs in their newsletters.

For the first few weeks of school, the students and I write the newsletters together using the overhead. I model for them how to translate the web categories into paragraph form. Gradually they begin to write their own newsletters by selecting those parts of the web they want to share with their parents.

In using this strategy, it is important that students not write about too many topics and become overwhelmed or discouraged; therefore, one of our early minilessons focuses on limiting the events or activities to be included. Another minilesson might include using several of the children's newsletters (with permission, of course) to show how each child has a special way of communicating with his or her parents.

As students develop confidence in their writing, some may experiment with using different formats (e.g., the newspa-

Personal Newsletters for Parents

Janet Speer Johnston
Apopka, Florida
May 1989

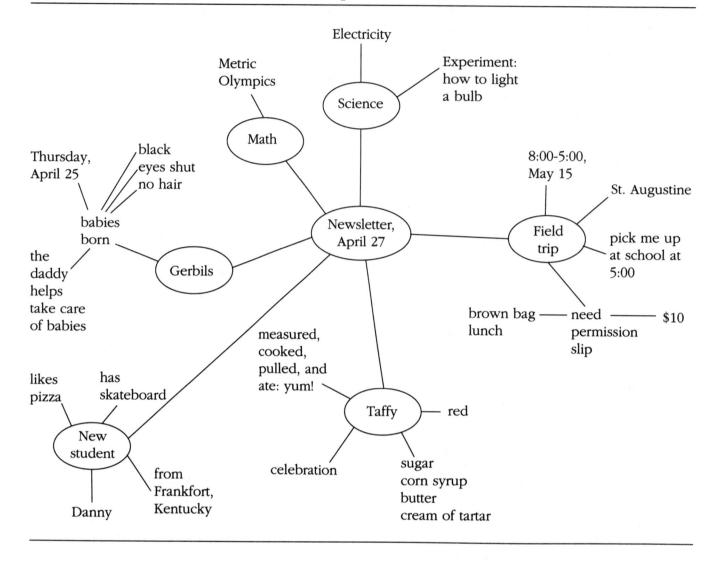

per or a news bulletin). We also have other regular minilessons on different ways to communicate meaning.

- Using punctuation: Baby gerbils!!
- Varying the print: BABY GERBILS.
- Developing an interesting lead: Guess what we found when we came into the classroom today?
- Quoting someone: We ran into the classroom when we heard Angela yelling, "We have new baby gerbils!"
- Adding feelings: I felt a tiny little butterfly in my stomach when I saw the little black dot in the cage. I loved that tiny black-dot gerbil!

- Using one or more of the five senses: I heard the softest sound of rustling in the hay. I couldn't decide if I wanted to feed the carrot to the gerbil or eat it myself. I took a bite of the crunchy carrot and gave the rest to the gerbil. Then I saw a tiny ball. What was it?

These newsletters are treated like dialogue journals. Students are encouraged to read them to a classmate, do some peer editing, and proof their work (based on skills taught through minilessons), but I do no final editing. Parents are aware (from previous communications) that I will not check or correct the newsletters, but that I will read them carefully and use them as a diagnostic tool to determine the writing skills to be addressed in future minilessons.

These bound newsletters become a chronicle of each student's creative and skill growth in writing and will bring pleasure in future years when their authors reminisce about those wonderful events, people, and learning from a fourth grade class many years in the past.

Writing Classmates' Biographies

Eunice G. Coakley
Greenville, South Carolina
November 1988

After reading several short biographies and a few fictionalized biographies, my sixth grade reading students embarked on a special activity—writing biographies of each other.

Each student selected a number, and those with the same numbers became partners. Partners conducted interviews with each other. They were given pointers on how to conduct an interview, how to take notes, and how to use direct quotations effectively. They also learned techniques writers use to make their accounts more vivid and interesting to the reader.

Though partners alternated interviewing each other, they basically followed a skeletal outline of areas they wished the interview subject to discuss.

- **Birth:** date/place of birth; family history or roots; fond childhood memories/anecdotes; major historical events during your lifetime.
- **Education:** preschool/kindergarten; elementary school; middle school.
- **Activities:** hobbies/special interests; vacations/travel.
- **Interpersonal relationships:** friends; pets.
- **Career goals**

Once the interviews were completed, each student was asked to bring to class several photos related to the interviewer's questions. (The original photos were photocopied and all originals were returned.) Each student developed his/her notes into paragraphs, organized the layout of the photos, and designed a cover for the booklet. (Booklets were handwritten or typed.) To strengthen oral reading skills, each student read aloud the biography she or he had written. One child's parent volunteered to stitch each booklet together. Finally, each student was given the biography that was written about him or her.

For extra credit, the youngsters were asked to read their biographies to their families either before or after dinner. When a signed parental note was returned, the student received extra points. Parents sent positive notes, revealing how much they enjoyed this shared activity.

As a result of this activity, students were able to define the biography as an account of a person's life and also classify it as a work of nonfiction.

Wish You Were Here

Nancy G. (Zeager) MacKenzie
Berwyn, Pennsylvania
January 1987

"What a beautiful drive we had on the Redwood Highway. We arrived in San Francisco late last night and spent today touring the Monterey Peninsula. We met lots of interesting people in Carmel, a famous art colony." So begins an imaginary trip that serves as an activity for fourth and fifth graders to develop researching and notetaking skills using the encyclopedia.

After introducing the encyclopedia and previewing an article on a particular place, ask students to jot down ten facts about that place. These facts should include information about sights to see, the people who live in the area, and the physical features, history, and climate of the region. After they gather these facts, ask students to rewrite them in an interesting way—as if they were actually visiting the place and sending a friend a postcard. This encourages students to paraphrase.

Students may find the next step to be the most fun. Pieces of white paper cut to the size of postcards are passed out, and students write their messages and the addresses. On the other side they draw a picture of something that represents the place they've written about.

This approach to researching and notetaking is always popular with children.

Children Write to a Varied Audience

Anne E. Murdock
Wayne, Pennsylvania
May 1987

By October, after six weeks or so of writing practice, my third graders had become quite comfortable with their daily, ready-made, unchanging audience of teachers and peers. They wrote, conferred, and published on carefully selected topics directed solely to one class and one teacher. They needed a wider audience.

The children decided to expand their audience beyond the classroom by selecting other listeners who might be interested in receiving their writings through the mail. Within days, the children had compiled a list that included friends and teachers from previous schools, grandparents, new neighbors, shut-ins, and an entire nursery school class.

With this new audience, there was an obvious adjustment as the third graders discovered they had to speak to the interests of a different set of listeners. They required longer and more concentrated periods of writing. Many questions arose, leading to a minilesson in which we outlined basic topics that were acceptable and others that should be avoided: Is it all right to tell a sad person that I have red hair? Will a three-year-old understand skateboarding? Can I tell Scott's grandparents that he teased me and I don't like it?

The ability to elaborate on diverse topics added dimension to the children's writings, which took on many forms. Poetry, stories, letters, and personal narratives poured forth. Many children began with a 5" x 8" (12 cm x 20 cm) pastel index card; they completed a drawing on one side, measured off the reverse side to resemble a large postcard, and completed it with a message and address.

By May the happy outcome was a response rate of 95 percent and a bulletin board overflowing with letters and greeting cards expressing enthusiasm for the activity. The third graders gained confidence as their voices were heard by a broadened audience whose ages ranged from 3 to 93 years.

New focus brought clarity to their writing. The natural spin-off of developing communication skills in general was the improvement of letter-writing skills in particular; however, the maturity children gained from acquiring a deeper social consciousness was the greatest reward.

Writing across Generations

Barbara J. Bryant
Royal Oak, Michigan
February 1989

Writing across generations was a pen-pal experience between my third/fourth grade class and local senior citizens. Eight-year-olds corresponded with 70- and 80-year olds. They loved it, and we discovered many unexpected rewards.

The project began in autumn when I had a conversation with a former teacher, Joy Wise, who had begun work as the activities director at a local senior citizen center. We both realized that we were searching for challenging, innovative activities for the groups of people we worked with and decided to collaborate on a project that would involve the children and the seniors together. An idea hit us—we would set up a pen-pal program.

I started by asking my class to respond in writing to the question "What do my grandparents mean to me?" in celebration of Grandparents' Day. Students responded enthusiastically with touching and amusing comments. They illustrated their stories with equally tender and humorous drawings. Brian told about fishing with Grandpa but having steak for dinner when they came home empty-handed. Stacey mentioned a snoring Grandpa whom she loved anyway. The stories were posted at the senior center; the older folks easily related to the stories and pictures. Joy met with the seniors and asked for some willing volunteers to write to students. I discussed the project with the third and fourth graders. Joy sent over a list of senior volunteers and the students selected pen pals at random. They were very eager to write to older people: the idea interested them much more than writing to someone of their own age.

I now had fertile ground for teaching letter-writing skills and sneaking in things like correct spelling, punctuation, and sentence structure. This was an opportunity to do these things with a real purpose. The class understood that their handwriting had to be clear and easy for the seniors to read. We didn't focus on mechanics, but good mechanics followed naturally. Since this writing comes from the heart, I didn't infringe on any student's ownership of his or her creation.

The class could not wait to finish and mail the first letters. Their enthusiasm was greater than it had been for any other writing project. Everything was not perfect, however. We needed six more seniors to match student writers, but that came later. For now the children without a pen pal wrote to their own grandparents.

Now came the most difficult time: waiting for the mail carrier. It was worth the wait. Letters came almost every day—faster than anticipated. The seniors wrote wonderful letters telling about themselves and their families and what life was like when they were young. The students were amazed at the activities in which the seniors had been involved. They enjoyed stories about life "long ago." The seniors told of walking safely on the streets at night, roller skating, and waiting for the iceman to come. The children shared each letter with the entire class, and later posted them in a hallway showcase. Other students and many teachers stopped to read the letters and passed on encouraging comments.

Again, all was not perfect. Not every letter was answered. Illness, vacations, and possibly forgetfulness all played a part in the disappointment of not receiving a letter. Joy made some new match-ups, and after a while all the students had pen pals.

After this initial correspondence, the writing continued. A regular cycle of mailing a letter and receiving a reply began. Birthday cards appeared. Postcards came from vacation spots around the country.

The pen pals decided they wanted a personal contact as well. Joy invited the class to the senior citizen complex for a party. We used Valentine's Day as the occasion, and each child made a paper rose and a Valentine for his or her pen pal. Parents willingly drove the students to the complex. It was difficult to say who was more excited—the kids, the parents, or the seniors.

The meeting was a wonderful confusion of hugs and hellos. Shy smiles turned quickly to happy grins. Hand holding pairs toured the building and visited some of the apartments. The children entertained with songs and, in turn, were entertained by the seniors' own singing group. Refreshments were served and the whole experience was videotaped to be enjoyed many times later. The local newspaper took pictures and featured the event.

After the children had met their pen pals, their correspondence took on more meaning. The class now planned to invite the seniors to school. In May, the seniors visited and watched a dress rehearsal of a spring music program. The local paper covered this event, too. Home addresses were exchanged.

We know that this was a successful educational project, but it was also much more. The two groups became friends. The seniors genuinely opened their arms and hearts to the youngsters, and the children had an opportunity to share thoughts and experiences with an "honorary grandparent." And perhaps some sad, older hearts were lifted by some young hands.

Three Motivators for Low-Reading Sixth Graders

Naomi S. Herron
Edison, New Jersey
November 1983

Teachers have always been challenged (and often defeated) by students who have given up from lack of success. Here are three approaches that have brought excitement to my reading program, especially to low-reading sixth graders, and have spurred an interest in reading which, in turn, has improved reading ability.

Bulletin boards and balloons. If you can discover a child's interests, she or he will read. However, some low achievers show little real enthusiasm for or knowledge about any field. I have found that new, genuine interests can be developed through the newspaper. I read several papers a day and clip out all articles (ideally with pictures) that present unusual, exciting, or different information and post them on a bulletin board. The students soon develop the habit of checking the board as they come into the room. Many articles generate only passing interest, but all contribute to discussion and enhance the students' store of background information.

One group had an unusually successful newspaper-related experience. They became very excited about one man's plans to balloon across the Atlantic and wanted to write to the balloonist directly. Much time and effort were spent composing a letter that included everyone's question and concerns. One student was selected by his peers to write the final draft. We sent the letter off and were delighted to receive back the information—plus pictures. This led to an interest in documenting previous attempts to balloon across the Atlantic. When this person's attempt failed, the group took the loss as a personal disaster. It spurred them to write almost lyrical articles about ballooning and to make commemorative plaques to send to the balloonist. The group was delighted and surprised when he not only acknowledged the gifts but placed them in a museum of ballooning.

Game fair. Another ploy I use regularly is to have students construct games for kindergartners and first graders to reinforce reading skills.

Kindergarten games consist of a board game for identifying upper- and lowercase letters, color word games, and picture sequence cards. Each kindergarten child receives a score card. They progress from one game station to another and are given a score at each station. After all have participated, the older children total the scores, write certificates for each participant, and award a prize to the highest scorer.

A similar game fair was developed for first grade using rhyming words, sight vocabulary, alphabetical order, and context to determine the meaning of nonsense words. This game may be done on tape: the first graders listen through headsets to a short story and then choose a definition from a choice supplied on a worksheet.

170

The creation of the games and the scoring ensure that skills are mastered by the sixth graders as well as the younger children. The admiration of the younger children boosts sagging egos and even makes the other sixth graders a little envious of my group.

The Bermuda Triangle. The third activity involves an extension of language experience techniques with a topic of common interest. For example, the Bermuda Triangle is a topic of great speculation among sixth graders. Discussion and reading provides necessary background information.

Each student writes his or her own solution to the mystery. These stories are typed and illustrated. Then the books are bound and covered with appropriate fabric. These books will be all-time reading favorites and remain so the following year. This project was so popular in one class that the students produced a series of books. Ghost, horror, and pirate stories were made into books and displayed in the school library.

It is always a challenge to motivate someone to try something that has previously been unsuccessful. Children succeed when they enjoy and are excited by what they do.

First and Fifth Graders Coauthor Books

Deborah J. Davis
Seattle, Washington
April 1989

As part of Young Author's Month at our school, my first grade class and a fifth grade class teamed together to write books. On the first day of the project, my colleague and I brought the classes together and paired each fifth grader with a first grade student. We reviewed the elements of story grammar, and the first graders shared the blank "Story Planning Chart" they use before writing a story. These charts are made by folding a piece of 15" x 18" (38 cm x 45 cm) lined newsprint to make four columns (see the Figure on the next page). We use the story grammar elements of main character, setting, other characters, story problem, and solution (on the back of the chart) as the headings for each column. With young children, symbols may be used for each heading, if desired.

Following the story grammar review, the student pairs planned a story using the chart. They then wrote chapter one of their story together. Ideas were shared by both partners, and the fifth graders wrote the stories down. The older children encouraged the younger ones to contribute ideas. On the next day of the project, the first graders composed chapter two on their own. After editing, their chapters were recopied and sent to their fifth grade partners, who read them and then wrote chapter three on their own. On the final day, the pairs rejoined to read chapter three and to coauthor the final chap-

Front

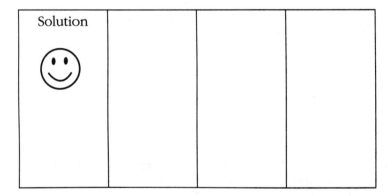

Main character	Setting	Other characters	Problem

Back

Solution			

ter of their book. The older students again served as scribes for this chapter, which they later recopied.

As final touches, the first graders made covers and title pages, and both partners drew illustrations that were interspersed throughout the chapters. The first graders also interviewed their partners and wrote an "About the Authors" page that was placed at the end of their book along with a photograph of the two children together.

Once the books were completed, the classes assembled to share their stories aloud. The entire project took about two weeks.

In addition to the enthusiasm the children displayed toward this writing experience, my colleague and I also noticed a special bonding that occurred between the classes. The intimidating "big kids" and the "nuisance" first graders became comfortable friends, and the good feelings lasted long after the project had ended.

The week of St. Patrick's Day can be a special time for your students, providing a springboard for conducting an art lesson, teaching reading, reinforcing classroom housekeeping standards, and, most important, reviewing letter-writing procedures. The story that follows should give you some ideas for an ideal activity for kindergarten or early primary grades. The sequences of activities in the story can be put into action over a four-day period, or the story can simply be told to the class as the motivation for a lesson in letter writing.

"My goodness!" said the teacher when she walked into the schoolroom. A few of the chairs were upside down, the counting man [an arithmetic device] was standing on his head, and the painting easels were in the middle of the floor. On the windowsills she found two little green footprints. [Footprints are made by dipping the outer edge of your fist in green paint and pressing down on a surface, and then using your fingertips to make toes.] "I wonder if the leprechauns were here last night."

When the children came to school they helped her put everything back in place again. "Hmmm," they said, "maybe the leprechauns *were* here last night."

The next morning when the teacher came to school she said, "My goodness!" The tables were pushed into the middle of the room, the erasers were piled on her desk, and the paint jars were in the sink. On the windowsill she found four little green footprints. "Hmmm," she said, "I'm *sure* the leprechauns were here last night."

The children helped the teacher write a note on the chalkboard that afternoon:

> Dear Little Leprechauns,
>   We are glad you like school. School is a place to have fun. Perhaps you do not know school is also a place to work and learn. We can learn more about you if you will paint a picture of your home and write about it.
>   Love,
>   Room 23

On the third morning, the teacher was very pleased, even though the books were all over the floor and the sink was messy with paint. She was pleased because there was a picture on the easel of a tree with a tiny door in the trunk. On the floor by the easel was a piece of paper with writing on it:

> We live in a tree.
> Our beds are made of green leaves.
> We eat berries.
> We drink morning dew.

When the children came to school they were very pleased. They helped the teacher put the books back in place and clean up the sink.

Leprechaun Letters

Millie Lindell
Plains, Montana
March 1985

173

That afternoon each child made a picture of what she or he thought a leprechaun looked like. All the pictures were put up on a bulletin board. Big letters were pinned across the top of the board to form a question: "Do leprechauns look like this?"

While the children were working, the teacher wrote a note on the board:

Dear Little Leprechauns,
    We like your picture and story very much. Thank you.
    We are glad you painted and wrote and read our books. Perhaps you do not know school is also a place to put things away. We are proud of our room. We work hard to keep it neat and clean.
    Love,
    Room 23

"My goodness!" said the teacher when she walked into the room the next day. It was neater, cleaner, and shinier than she had ever seen it. A bowl of flowers was on her desk, and a box wrapped in pretty green paper was on the floor by her chair.

"My goodness!" said the children when they walked in and saw the neat shiny room, the flowers, and the box. Then one child said, "Look! The bulletin board has been changed!"

"How?" asked another child.

"Two letters and a question mark are missing from the board," answered another. "Now the board says, 'Leprechauns look like this.' "

"But all our pictures are different," several children said. "What could it mean?"

"I guess everyone was right," answered the teacher. "Leprechauns must be different sizes and shapes and colors— just like people. Let's find out what they left us."

The children sat on the rug and watched the teacher open the box. It was filled with big green shamrocks [cookies or green gum drops]. On each shamrock a child's name was written in what could only be a leprechaun's own handwriting. At the bottom of the box was a note:

Dear Children,
    Thank you for teaching us to be good workers and good citizens. At midnight we will go back to our own land. We will always remember you.
    Love,
    The Little Leprechauns

Some of the thank-you letters written by the children after they received their shamrocks were put in a large envelope and mailed to the leprechauns; others were displayed on the board with the reassurance that the leprechauns would come back to read them before they returned home.

When the children asked if the leprechauns were real, the teacher just smiled and said, "It's one of the ways we have fun in our room." She felt that today's children knew the difference between fact and fancy, but still needed to have the fun of make-believe.

Ideas to Spark Creative Writing

D. Cherry Trese
Cocoa Beach, Florida
December 1986

Does your class moan each time you mention a writing assignment? Is this the only time they seem to use colorful adjectives? Take heart—this has happened to all teachers. But it need not be so!

I once agonized over the results of the common September assignment, "Tell what you did during your summer vacation." Only one response held my attention, and that was because it was disturbing and obscene. (A fifth grade boy described hurling stones at a hog during the County Fair and told precisely where they had been targeted.) But how could I fault him? My assignment was dull. Checking with the class the next day, I learned that they had had the same assignment for five consecutive Septembers. So if you strive for creative results, your assignments must be creative, too. Children must also clearly understand the reason for an assignment. Even young children recognize busywork and time fillers. If they don't know why they are writing, very little enthusiasm or spark will follow.

The techniques and ideas that follow have been refined over 19 years of teaching and have proved productive for underachievers, leisurely learners, quiet flowers, and witty clowns alike. Use these methods and anticipate good results.

- Create a file of unusual magazine pictures—pictures that beg for a caption or an explanation. (Each picture is worth a thousand words, so how can you miss?) Ask the students to choose a picture, but do not allow them to discuss the pictures before they write. The students should imagine that they are part of that scene and explain to you on paper exactly what is happening.

- Nothing motivates a class more than fresh, live mail. After studying the five main parts of a letter, have the students write and send a real letter to a prominent person. Children's authors, government officials, athletes, and rock stars all make interesting subjects, and many of them will respond. If you have a friend who teaches in another area, initiate a

Pen Pal Club. When studying states, provinces, or countries, assign each child a specific locale and have him or her write to the Bureau of Tourism or the Chamber of Commerce for information.

- Creating original greeting cards incorporates both art and writing. There are so many times when this idea fits into a school year. Some examples might be cards to wish a speedy recovery to a student recuperating from a tonsillectomy, cards to thank the park ranger who guided your class through a mosquito-infested swamp, or cards to send birthday wishes to the ungrumbling custodian who silently climbs up to the school roof to retrieve rubber balls.

- Design a hidden word puzzle for a special holiday. After the students have discovered the vocabulary words (e.g., cranberries, Pilgrims, and Mayflower for American Thanksgiving), ask them to incorporate the words into a story. This saves nerve endings by eliminating the need to spell "P-l-y-m-o-u-t-h" 15 times in 10 minutes.

- Nothing beats exposure to quality literature. Surround your class with award-winning books. Read to the children each day. Let them hear how language can flow and sense how a plot is developed. Read stories such as "The Lady or the Tiger" and let them create an ending. Pattern books are especially effective with young children. Many are so good they could stimulate creative thoughts in geraniums.

- The ultimate in creative writing is to have children produce and illustrate their own books. Unfortunately, this cannot be a first-day assignment. It takes many successful experiences to develop competent young authors. The finished books may be stapled, bound, laminated, painted, or pasted. Many different processes can be used; the best one for your students can be decided through classroom discussion. Just be certain that the final results are shared, displayed, and praised.

- A journal or log is an excellent method to reach the quiet or troubled child. I promise the children confidentiality and ask that they let their thoughts travel freely through their arms and out their pencils. This process not only encourages writing but also gives you insight and an understanding of your students that is very special. Be sure to respond individually to each child with a written comment and a pertinent question.

- Last, get rid of the red pencil. Feed it to a hungry termite or file it under "hateful." Red means stop, and a red pencil does just that. It can choke the very syllables from a young, inspired writer. Let writing class be imaginative, spontaneous, and fun. If you enjoy it, your students will, too.

The "Row"tating Story

Linda Whitaker
Worth, Illinois
December 1985

The "row"tating story has proved to be an excellent warm-up writing activity for my middle school students. I arrange the class in rows of equal numbers of students and then write a predetermined title on the chalkboard. I give students three minutes to begin their story (five minutes might be better for younger students). I remind the students to write legibly since others will be reading their writing, and then each student writes a story opener on his or her own sheet of paper.

After three minutes, the story sheets are passed—or "row"tated—back one person, with the last person in the row giving his or her story sheet to the first student in the row. After silently reading what has been written, students add their own ideas to their new sheet. We continue to "row"tate the stories at three-minute intervals until they reach the original author again. The original author puts the finishing touches on the story and the creations are read aloud. In writing these stories creativity "row"tates through the class.

Here's an example of a "row"tated story written by some sixth graders Each indented section indicates a new author.

The Amazing Mr. Snoodle

The amazing Mr. Snoodle is a noodle who likes to live in chicken soup! His name is Snoodle because he mixed soup and noodle together.

He likes to be the only noodle in the soup and he gave the other noodles the cold shoulder.

One day he ducked out of the way of the spoon and wound up alone in the bottom of the soup bowl. It was very lonely there. He had no company.

He decided right then and there that he'd be much nicer to the other noodles if he ever got the chance.

But would he ever get a second chance?

Character Combinations

Nicholas P. Criscuolo
New Haven, Connecticut
October 1983

To inspire some unique writing projects, have your students make a composite list of several books' heroes and heroines. Then ask the children to combine story characters from different books and imagine what might happen if they met.

Some matches will be wildly disparate, encouraging story lines that would draw heavily upon the imagination—ghosts and fairy tale characters, animals and famous people. Others might evoke realistic, even scientific thinking—a blind girl and a magician, a caterpillar and a snake.

Ask the children to write original stories with illustrations using these character combinations. Some literary masterpieces will emerge!

Character Journals Aid Comprehension

Sarah A. Jossart
Elgin, Illinois
November 1988

At different times during the year, I ask students to respond to what they are reading (or hearing) by selecting a character in the story and writing a journal entry for that character. I select stopping points within a story that have descriptive action, such as the butchering scene in *Little House in the Big Woods* by Laura Ingalls Wilder.

We select a year appropriate to the text to date their entries (we use the current day, as this gives a reference to when the writing was done). The materials we use depend on when and where the story takes place; we have written on brown paper (*Little House in the Big Woods*), fluorescent paper (*A Wrinkle in Time* by Madeleine L'Engle), and notebook paper (*Tales of a Fourth Grade Nothing* by Judy Blume).

Students quickly learn that several characters could write almost identical journals. The fun begins as they work to sneak in small details that give their entry the point of view of one particular character.

After writing, the next important step is sharing the journals. We often make reading the journals into a game as the class guesses which character has written the journal entry. Everybody listens as the entries are shared because all the students want to catch the details that identify the writer. This step leads to lots of discussion.

This writing activity not only is fun but also provides a lesson in point of view, characterization, mood, inferencing, and detail.

Classroom teachers often find it difficult to launch original writing projects with children. Teachers as well as the children themselves ask, "How do I get started?" This series of articles provides both sources with which to motivate original writing and activities for making the process successful. [*Editor's note*: This single article encompasses a series that originally appeared in Volume 40 of *The Reading Teacher*, October 1986 to May 1987]. Each section focuses on the details of a particular story structure you can use as a model for children's written expression. For example, with the "wishing" story structure, students listen to and discuss a story in which wishes are a theme. Then they discuss the story's features: number of wishes, how wishes are granted, consequences of wish fulfillment, etc. Finally, the students plan and write a short story that includes these features.

When we ask children to respond in a specific way to a nonspecific writing assignment ("Write a page about something fun you did last summer"), even the most verbal child may appear to have little or nothing to write. Beginning a writing activity by reading a story with a discernible structure makes writing easier because it provides definite guidelines to follow. Guidelines produce security. (In answer to those who suggest that creativity is limited this way, we suggest that just getting started is more important at the outset. When students feel reasonably comfortable about writing using guidelines, the guidelines can gradually be eliminated.)

Each section of the remainder of this article includes a short bibliography of books or poems that can be used when teaching a particular structure. Suggested reading levels are indicated.

Story Structure: Helping Your Students Write Stories

DayAnn Kennedy
Stella S. Spangler
Buffalo, New York
Mary Ann Vanderwerf
Amherst, New York
October 1986 to May 1987

The Wishing Story

Children have always wanted wishes granted, so this story structure is a good one to use when children begin to write, because it involves a familiar situation.

Objective. Each child will write a story in which the fulfillment of wishes is realized in an unusual manner. Each author will include a specific number of wishes, show how each wish is or is not fulfilled (plot development), and tell about the consequences of wish fulfillment.

Story example. The Fisherman and His Wife is a wishing story in which a poor fisherman catches a magic fish that offers six wishes. The couple first wish for basic needs, but soon the wishes become extraordinary. Greed leads to punishment.

Procedure. Select a story from the bibliography and share it aloud with the class.

List and discuss ground rules for story writing (see *Objective*) and relate the rules to the model story.

Invite and list suggestions about characters, setting, types of wishes, how the wishes might be fulfilled, and what the consequences might be. This enables young authors to stay within the framework of the wishing story structure. Explain that the length of their stories will depend on using all of the ground rules.

You may want to have the young authors create a classroom wishing well around which stories can be displayed.

Some Wishing Stories

Bulpré, Paul. (1976). *The Rainbow-Colored Horse.* (Ill. by Antonio Martorell.) London: Warne. *Ages 6 to 9.*

Galdone, Paul. (1961). *Three Wishes.* New York: McGraw-Hill. *Ages 7 to 11.*

The Brothers Grimm. (1980). *The Fisherman and His Wife.* (Ill. by Margot Zemach; trans. by Randall Jarrell.) New York: Farrar, Straus & Giroux. *All ages.*

Ness, Evaline. (1970). *The Girl and the Goatherd on This and That and Thus and So.* New York: Dutton. *All ages.*

Waber, Bernard. (1980). *You're a Little Kid with a Big Heart.* Boston, MA: Houghton Mifflin. *Ages 5 to 8.*

Wildsmith, Brian. (1984). *Daisy.* New York: Pantheon. *Ages 7 to 10.*

The Clock Story

In the "clock" (or "ring") story structure, the characters create a kind of circle by starting and ending their adventures at the same place. With the clock form, a series of separate but related adventures unfold in a sequence that brings the story characters back to the starting point.

Objective. Students will write a short story based on the realization that circumstances always change things in some way even though a plot line may be circular. Introduce the idea that all story events can be a matter of personal imagination within a clock framework, as long as the ending is determined by the beginning.

Story example. Millions of Cats is a clock story in which a lonely couple wish for a cat to keep them company. The husband goes in search of one cat; the farther he goes, the more cats follow along. But they cannot keep all the cats! The choice about which cat to keep is resolved when the man returns home.

Procedure. Share *Millions of Cats* with the class. Lead a discussion of story beginning, sequence of events, and story ending. Help students realize that the clock story structure requires action to begin and end at the same place, although intervening events may alter the lives and attitudes of story characters.

Draw a large circle or clock face on the chalkboard and mark an "X" at 12 o'clock to show where the story begins and ends. Have a volunteer tell who the characters are and what the setting is for the story beginning. Write the answers "old man," and "old lady" and "living in a small cottage" at 1 and 2 o'clock on the circle, respectively. Then have volunteers recall the progress of events and write these at the appropriate hours on the clock face. Help students see that even though characters end up as they were in the beginning, their lives are sure to change—in the case of this story, one of the cats will live with them now.

Invite suggestions about original clock stories. Discuss characters and settings, writing them on the chalkboard. Then suggest that students write an original sequence of several events or adventures in which the last one leads back to the beginning (12 o'clock on the diagram). The first and last parts of the story must have the same setting, but logical changes in the characters may have occurred.

An art activity can follow in which each student illustrates his or her invented story event in clock form. Display these clocks in the classroom or hallway.

Some Clock Stories

Gag, Wanda. (1977). *Millions of Cats*. New York: Coward McCann. *All ages*.

Keats, Ezra Jack. (1962). *The Snowy Day*. New York: Viking. *Ages 5 to 8*.

Lewis, C.S. (1950). *The Lion, the Witch, and the Wardrobe*. (Ill. by Pauline Baynes.) New York: Macmillan. *Ages 9 to 12*.

Mosel, Arlene. (1972). *The Funny Little Woman*. New York: Dutton. *All ages*.

Oakley, Graham. (1981). *Hetty and Harriet*. New York: Atheneum. *Ages 7 to 10*.

Sendak, Maurice. (1963). *Where the Wild Things Are*. New York: HarperCollins. *Ages 6 to 8*.

The Pourquoi Story

This type of story (sometimes called a how or why tale) explains in an imaginative way how or why things happen. For example, the story might answer the questions "Why does a kangaroo have a pocket?" or "How did the whooping crane get its name?"

Objective. Each young author will create a story in which a question about the nature of things is answered. The writer will begin by asking how or why something is the way it is and progress through a short story to tell how it got that way.

Story example. Tikki Tikki Tembo is a pourquoi story that tells why some children have short names. A Chinese boy with a long name falls into a well. He almost loses his life because his brother, who tries to help him, finds his name too long to say.

Procedure. From the bibliography, select a how or why story and share it with the class. After discussing the story, list how or why questions contributed by the class. Each student selects one of the listed questions and develops a short story that must end with an answer to the how or why question.

You may want to elicit the help of the librarian in arranging a display of pourquoi stories by placing question marks on the cover of each book. After reading a book, students can write out the question that is answered.

Some Pourquoi Stories

Aardema, Verna. (1975). *Why Mosquitoes Buzz in People's Ears: A West African Tale.* (Ill. by Leo Dillon and Diane Dillon.) New York: Dial. *Ages 6 to 9.*

Kipling, Rudyard. (1974). *How the Rhinoceros Got His Skin.* (Ill. by Leonard Weisgard.) London: Walker. *All ages.*

Mosel, Arlene. (1968). *Tikki Tikki Tembo.* (Ill. by Blair Lent.) New York: Henry Holt. *Ages 5 to 8.*

Proddow, Penelope (Trans.). (1972). *Demeter and Persephone.* (Ill. by Barbara Cooney.) New York: Doubleday. *Ages 9 to 12.*

Robbins, Ruth. (1980). *How the First Rainbow Was Made.* Orleans, MA: Parnassus. *Ages 6 to 9.*

Toye, William. (1979). *The Fire Stealers.* (Ill. by Elizabeth Cleaver.) Oxford, UK: Oxford University Press. *Ages 5 to 7.*

The Cumulative Story

Clearly, children like the sound and rhythm of repetitious language—they use it often in their songs, chants, and games. The cumulative story structure uses repetition to build a story line.

Objective. This particular story structure lends itself to a small-group writing activity. Each participant in the authors' circle (three or four pupils) will follow these ground rules: (1) the story will be brief; (2) the story will have a strong rhythmic pattern; (3) each situation must occur in logical order and be linked to what happened before; and (4) all story events will repeat and accumulate until a surprise ending is reached.

Story Example. The House That Jack Built is a cumulative story in which a series of unexpected events occur after Jack has built his house.

Procedure. Tell participants in the authors' circle to listen for the ground rules of a cumulative story (as listed in *Objective*), then read aloud a story from the bibliography. A discussion follows about the ground rules as they apply to the story.

A student volunteer (or the teacher) initiates a beginning line, such as "This is the store at the end of the street." The teacher hands a roll of lined shelf paper to one student to begin the story. As the roll of paper is passed around the circle, each young author repeats all the previous lines of the story and then adds a new one. The teacher reminds writers that the rhythmic pattern must be maintained. (Younger children can write just their own line, and the teacher can write the total accumulation.)

Each author may go into the circle and act out his or her line. The rest of the circle chants the story as it has accumulated to that point.

Some Cumulative Stories

Aardema, Verna. (1981). *Bringing the Rain to Kapiti Plain.* (Ill. by Beatriz Vidal.) New York: Dial. *Ages 6 to 9.*

Adams, Pam. (1973). *There Was an Old Woman Who Swallowed a Fly.* London: Child's Play. *All ages.*

Burningham, John. (1981). *Mr. Gumpy's Outing.* New York: Henry Holt. *Ages 5 to 7.*

Byer, Carol. (1981). *Henny Penny.* Mahwah, NJ: Troll. *Ages 5 to 8.*

Galdone, Paul. (1983). *The Gingerbread Boy.* Boston, MA: Clarion. *Ages 5 to 8.*

Lobel, Arnold. (1984). *The Rose in My Garden.* New York: Greenwillow. *All ages.*

Stevens, Janet. (1985). *The House That Jack Built.* New York: Holiday House. *All ages.*

The Fable

In a fable, animals portray human characteristics. In structure, a fable is brief and full of action and always includes a lesson.

Objective. Young authors will develop a story in which the actions of animals reveal a problem. When the problem is resolved, a lesson is learned.

Story example. In Aesop's "The Fox and the Stork," a sly fox invites a stork to dinner and plays a trick on him. Then the clever stork returns the invitation and teaches the fox a lesson.

Procedure. From the bibliography, select a fable and share it aloud with the class, or have a volunteer read the fable. Discuss the boundaries or features of a fable:

- a brief story situation (approximately three or four paragraphs);
- main characters are animals;
- animals behave like humans;
- fast action usually leads to humorous ending—the tables are turned, a trick is played, or something unexpected happens;
- the last line of the story will tell the lesson the story characters have learned.

Read another fable and lead a discussion about how these boundaries apply to this story.

List story boundaries on the chalkboard and encourage young authors to include them as they write a fable of their own. With the help of the young authors, list possible animal characters and behaviors and easily communicated lessons such as "haste makes waste," "one good turn deserves another," "don't believe everything you hear," and "better late than never."

Then have students create original fables. With younger children, you may wish to rewrite a known fable, substituting children's suggestions for different animals and situations, but keeping the same lesson or moral.

As a culminating activity take common proverbs or sayings from a book like Benjamin Franklin's *Poor Richard's Almanack* and write them out on slips of paper. Insert these in fortune cookies for the group to enjoy.

Some Books of Fables

15 Fables of Krylor. (1965). (Trans. by Guy Daniels.) New York: Macmillan. *All ages.*

Aesop. (1961). *Aesop's Fables.* (Ill. by Heidi Holder.) New York: Viking. *Ages 6 to 9.*

Aesop. (1971). *Three Aesop Fox Fables.* (Retold and ill. by Paul Galdone.) Boston, MA: Clarion. *Ages 5 to 9.*

Chaucer, Geoffrey. (1985). *Chanticleer and the Fox.* (Ill. by Barbara Cooney.) New York: Crowell. *Ages 7 to 12.*

Lobel, Arnold. (1980). *Fables.* New York: HarperCollins. *Ages 9 to 12.*

Roach, Marilynne. (1975). *Two Roman Mice.* New York: Crowell. *Ages 7 to 9.*

The Diary or Journal

A diary or journal is a record of events, personal activities, or feelings about experiences, kept on a regular basis.

Entries *can* suggest a storyline, but the recorded events will *always* result in structured writing based on time and sequence.

Objective. Young authors will keep a record of real or imaginary occurrences over a specific period of time.

Story example. Diary of a Rabbit recounts the life of a rabbit from birth to parenthood. The rabbit's antics are revealed in words and photographs.

Procedure. Read aloud to the class preselected portions of *Diary of a Rabbit* or any of the other diaries or journals listed below. As you read, call attention to the sequential dates of entries.

Invite young authors to select a subject for diary keeping. Suggest a few possibilities (personal experiences, pets, friends, vacations, a new baby, a trip to outer space, colorful characters such as spies, pirates, explorers). Together, decide on the period of time each record will be kept (a day, a week, a month, or longer).

A variation on individual diary writing could be a class record-keeping project about a school pet, a school function, or a field trip. Encourage young authors to write more than a factual account by including humorous observations and personal impressions. Student volunteers may photograph the sequential events.

Some Books in Journal or Diary Form

Blos, Joan. (1979). *A Gathering of Days: A New England Girl's Journal, 1830-32.* New York: Scribner's. *Ages 10 to 12.*

Cleary, Beverly. (1983). *Dear Mr. Henshaw.* (Ill. by Paul O. Zelinsky.) New York: Morrow. *Ages 7 to 10.*

Clifton, Lucille. (1970). *Some of the Days of Everett Anderson.* (Ill. by Evaline Ness.) New York: Henry Holt. *Ages 7 to 10.*

Fitzhugh, Louise. (1964). *Harriet the Spy.* New York: Harper-Collins. *Ages 8 to 11.*

Frank, Anne. (1952). *The Diary of a Young Girl.* New York: Doubleday. *Ages 12 and up.*

Hess, Lilo. (1982). *Diary of a Rabbit.* New York: Scribner's. *Ages 5 to 8.*

Reig, June. (1978). *Diary of the Boy King Tut-Anhk-Amen.* New York: Scribner's. *Ages 8 to 12.*

The How-to Story

A how-to story is one in which directions for making or doing something are an integral part of the plot. Specific instructions may appear in the story or at its end.

Objective. Young authors will develop a story that includes directions about how to make or do something. The instructions must be written in such a way that the reader can do the activity.

Story example. In *Three Days on a River in a Red Canoe*, travelers map out in detail a short trip. Their preparations include making shopping lists, packing supplies, deciding where to go, and thinking about what they will do when they get there. During the trip the travelers give instructions for making knots, building a cooking fire, preparing camp food, and putting up a tent.

Procedure. Select a how-to book from the bibliography and share it with the class. Each young author writes instructions or directions about how to make or do something related to the story (maps, patterns, recipes, diagrams, lists, instructions for taking care of plants, pets). Ground rules include giving detailed directions (such as exact locations on maps for an overnight stay), steps for following recipes and patterns, etc.

Each student writes a paragraph telling how his or her how-to activity fits in with the model story. Authors may wish to bring in materials and invite a classmate to make or do the activity according to the instructions, which can be illustrated and made into a classroom or library book.

Some How-to Stories

Cauley, Lorinda Bryan. (1978). *The Bake-Off.* New York: Putnam. *Ages 5 to 8.*

dePaola, Tomie. (1974). *Watch Out for the Chicken Feet in Your Soup.* Englewood Cliffs, NJ: Prentice Hall. *Ages 5 to 9.*

Fair, Sylvia. (1982). *The Bedspread.* New York: Morrow. *Ages 7 to 10.*

Williams, Vera. (1981). *Three Days on a River in a Red Canoe.* New York: Greenwillow. *All ages.*

The Journey Story

A journey story is one in which characters set out with a specific destination in mind. Several adventures occur during their travels. Pursuit of the destination and adventures encountered along the way form the story structure.

Objective. Young authors will write a story in which a character or characters travel toward a destination. Some exciting adventures must occur along the way. At the end, the journey is completed and the destination is reached as planned, or adventures along the way change the direction of the journey so the destination is not reached at all.

Story example. In *The Bremen Town Musicians*, four unwanted animals join together to travel to the big city to become musicians. Encounters with robbers provide adventures during the journey. As a result of these adventures, the animals discover that they need each other's company more than they need to reach their destination.

Procedure. From the bibliography, choose a story to share. Draw a line across the chalkboard to indicate the route the characters took in the story. As students tell about the adventures and the sequence in which they took place, you mark them on the chalkboard route.

Small groups of students choose their own characters, plan the route and destination, invent adventures, and decide on a story conclusion. A group recorder lists all suggestions; from these, students write individual versions of the story to share with the class.

As an option, distribute balloons for children to send on a journey. On slips of paper, students write names, addresses, and requests for replies, and place them inside the balloons. Blow up the balloons and let children release them. Replies from whomever finds them will tell about the travels of the balloons.

Some Journey Stories

Andersen, Hans Christian. (1981). *The Steadfast Tin Soldier*. (Ill. by Thomas DiGrazia.) Englewood Cliffs, NJ: Prentice Hall. *Ages 8 to 12.*

Eastman, P.D. (1960). *Are You My Mother?* New York: Random House. *Ages 5 to 8.*

The Brothers Grimm. (1981). *The Bremen Town Musicians: A Grimm's Fairy Tale*. (Retold and ill. by Donna Diamond.) New York: Delacorte. *All ages.*

Kent, Jack. (1971). *The Fat Cat: A Danish Folktale*. San Francisco, CA: Parents' Magazine Press. *Ages 5 to 10.*

Konigsburg, E.L. (1967). *From the Mixed-Up Files of Mrs. Basil E. Frankweiler*. New York: Atheneum. *Ages 9 to 12.*

When I was a student, I found it difficult to understand why I received particular grades on my papers. As a new classroom teacher, I found it difficult to decide what grade to assign to certain papers. So I devised a more objective and efficient way for me (and maybe for you) to grade student papers. The form shown in the Figure on the next page is one I used for scoring sixth grade remedial-level paragraphs; however, it could easily be adapted for longer papers or different levels.

Students turn in their compositions in a folder to be graded in this order: rough copy, good copy, and my form containing both the student's Beginning Writing Checklist (filled out) and my parallel Writing Evaluation Form. When I grade the paper, I flip to the evaluation form and check off the correct number of points. When the students get their folders back, they can look down my part of the form to see how the

Quick and Specific Evaluations of Student Writings

Geraldine Maxwell
Brenham, Texas
February 1985

Beginning Writing Checklist

Content (what my writing is about)

____ 1. These are my own original thoughts.
____ 2. I have tried to make this story interesting for my reader.

Form (how my paper looks)

____ 1. I have my heading complete and in the right-hand corner.
____ 2. I have left a blank line after the title and indented the first line of my story.
____ 3. I have a title I made up on the top line. It has the first and all important words capitalized
____ 4. I have used my best penmanship and tried to keep the paper as neat as possible.

Structure (how my paper reads)

____ 1. Every sentence expresses one complete thought, begins with a capital letter, and has end punctuation.
____ 2. I have tried to make improvements between my rough copy and my best copy.
____ 3. I have tried to spell every word correctly.
____ 4. I have not used any word excessively (e.g., and).

Writing Evaluation Form

____ Content—35 points

Comments:

```
┌─────────────────────┐
│   Total Score       │
│                     │
│                     │
│                     │
└─────────────────────┘
```

Form—25 points

____ 1. Your heading is complete and in the right-hand corner. (5 points)
____ 2. You have left a blank line under the title and indented the first line of your story. (5 points)
____ 3. Your title is original and on the top line. The first and all important words are capitalized. (5 points)
____ 4. You have been neat and used good penmanship. (10 points)

Structure—40 points

____ 1. Every sentence expresses one complete thought, begins with a capital letter, and has end punctuation. (15 points)
____ 2. You have shown attempted improvement between your rough copy and your best copy. (10 points)
____ 3. You have tried to spell every word correctly. (10 points)
____ 4. You have not used any word excessively. (5 points)

paper was graded and to note particular strengths and weaknesses.

Under the Content section, there is room for comments. I try to make one positive comment and one suggestion for improvement focused strictly on content. This is often subjective—I look only at what the student had to say and score it on a scale of 1 to 35. Under the Form section, I give either partial or full points. For example, with number 2, if the student leaves a blank line under the title but fails to indent the first line of the story, she or he will get three points instead of the full five. I take a similar approach to the Structure portion.

This system is not entirely objective, but it does weigh those elements set as performance objectives by teachers for particular students. Using the form has cut the time it takes me to grade papers in half.

Chapter 8

Learning about Literature

Using good literature in the reading program allows children to enter the world of books. Literature is what encourages children to be readers. Picture books, poetry, folktales, myths, epics, fantasies, fiction, biographies, multicultural literature, and information books are genres recommended for inclusion in the elementary language arts curriculum. These books can cover a vast range of topics—from asteroids to zebras—and lure reluctant readers and skilled readers alike into learning from literature. Basal readers limit children to the topics within them, but libraries have books, books, and more books to expand children's worlds. Professional journals contain a wealth of ideas to guide teachers who want to use these books in their classrooms.

The benefits of using literature in the classroom are many. In a review of research on how literature influences children's reading achievement, Tunnell and Jacobs (1989) found that literature helps students learn basic skills earlier and improves their attitudes toward reading. In addition, reading fluency increases when children are surrounded by books and are encouraged to read often. Research indicates that using literature in the classroom benefits children's oral language development (Chomsky, 1972; Teale & Martinez, 1986). Teale and Martinez have documented the value of reading and listening to literature in vocabulary development. As children hear and read literature, they absorb language from it and begin to use that language themselves. In addition, children who have been read to frequently before beginning school show greater success in beginning reading programs than do children who have not been read to (Wells, 1982). In the later grades, reading literature to children has been shown to improve their progress in reading comprehension and vocabulary development. (Cohen, 1968). In sum, children's overall achievement in reading appears to be greater when they are involved intensely with quality books.

Children who experience a literature-based curriculum also have better attitudes toward reading and value reading more than children who are not regularly exposed to literature (Cullinan, Jagger, & Strickland, 1974). Generally, children who interact with literature often are inclined to appreciate excellence in writing and illustrations, to select books that meet their needs and interests, to interpret and evaluate literature, to write in a variety of literary forms, to communicate with an expanded vocabulary and in complex sentences, and to appreciate and accept the cultures and beliefs they encounter in their reading (Hennings, 1986).

Literature benefits more than just the reading program. Writing, for example, is also affected. Children who participate in discussions about structure, characters, plot, themes, and setting of exemplary pieces of literature are likely to pay attention to these elements when they write their own stories. The meager diet of stories in many basal readers surely does not provide children with the depth, breadth, and richness needed to inspire them to write in a variety of genres and styles. In the content areas, supplementing textbooks with biographies, information books, narratives, or poetry about the topics under study provides different perspectives on those topics. Since no two texts are exactly alike, each experience with an additional piece of literature provides new information.

In a literature-based curriculum teachers can organize instruction around a genre, a theme, or a literature set (multiple copies of a book that children can read in small groups). Children are often encouraged to select the books that they want to read. They read and discuss the books, as well as write about their reading in journals or logs to which the teacher and other children can respond. A variety of activities usually accompany and enrich the experience. When instruction is organized around a genre or theme, children can read different books that fall in the same category—say, appropriate fiction and nonfiction books about insects or a variety of books from the literary genre of historical fiction.

In sum, integrating literature into the language arts curriculum or using it as the foundation of that curriculum is important in children's elementary education. Literature is increasingly seen as the preferred material from which to teach reading and writing. Literature motivates and interests children. It increases their reading skill, provides models for writing, and teaches about the world. The following activities are suggestions for teachers to consider as they look for ways to use literature in their classrooms.

References

Chomsky, C. (1972). Stages in language development and reading exposure. *Harvard Educational Review, 40,* 287-307.

Cohen, D.H. (1968). The effect of literature on vocabulary and reading achievement. *Elementary English, 45,* 209-213.

Cullinan, B.E., Jagger, A., & Strickland, D. (1974). Language expansion for black children in the primary grades: A research report. *Young Children, 29,* 98-112.

Hennings, D.G. (1986). *Communication in action: Teaching the language arts* (3rd ed.). Boston, MA: Houghton Mifflin.

Teale, W.H., & Martinez, M. (1986). *Teachers reading to their students: Different styles, different effects.* Paper presented at the 14th Southwest Regional Convention of the International Reading Association, San Antonio, Texas. (ED 169 754)

Tunnell, M.O., & Jacobs, J.S. (1989). Using "real" books: Research findings on literature-based reading instruction. *The Reading Teacher, 42,* 470-477.

Wells, G. (1982). Story reading and the development of symbolic skills. *Australian Journal of Reading, 5,* 142-152.

Further Reading

Au, K.H., & Scheu, J.A. (1989). Guiding students to interpret a novel. *The Reading Teacher, 43,* 104-111.

Cullinan, B.E. (1987). Inviting readers to literature. In B.E. Cullinan (Ed.), *Children's literature in the reading program* (pp. 2-14.) Newark, DE: International Reading Association.

Cullinan, B.E., & Strickland, D.S. (1986). The early years: Language, literature, and literacy in classroom research. *The Reading Teacher, 39,* 798-806.

Lehr, S. (1988). The child's developing sense of theme as a response to literature. *Reading Research Quarterly, 23,* 337-352.

O'Brien, K., & Stoner, D.K. (1987). Increasing environmental awareness through children's literature. *The Reading Teacher, 41,* 14-21.

Rogers, W.C. (1985). Teaching for poetic thought. *The Reading Teacher, 39,* 296-300.

Sullivan, J. (1987). Read-aloud sessions: Tackling sensitive issues through literature. *The Reading Teacher, 40,* 874-879.

Wilson, P.J., & Abrahamson, R.F. (1988). What children's literature classics do children really enjoy? *The Reading Teacher, 41,* 406-411.

Mother Goose Is on the Loose

Cheryl M. Haake
West Seneca, New York
January 1990

Many small children begin acquiring a love of poetry when Mother Goose rhymes are first recited or read to them. By the time children come to school, they have heard many of these rhymes, have seen numerous books of them, and can easily recite a few. These rhymes can become an important feature of a whole language classroom and can easily be adapted for use at any grade level because they lend themselves so easily to the content areas. Listening, speaking, writing, and reading as well as social studies, science, and mathematics all play an important role in a Mother Goose unit.

A good way to start is by examining different Mother Goose books. Verses tend to differ a little, and the illustrators' interpretations of the verses are worth comparing. A few of the favorites in my classroom are *Tomie dePaola's Mother Goose* because of his animated illustrations and *A Treasury of Mother Goose* published by Ariel Books. Many of the rhymes lead naturally into interpretive drama, modern nonsense verse, and narrative poems.

The following activities based on Mother Goose lend themselves to various content areas. They are easily adapted to any grade level.

Research. Who was Mother Goose? Find out the origin of Mother Goose. Were various editions written? How does history play a role in the rhymes?

Categorization. Make a list of rhymes about people ("Mary, Mary Quite Contrary," "Little Miss Muffet," "Jack Be Nimble," "Little Jack Horner," "Old King Cole"), animals ("Baa Baa Black Sheep," "Jenny Wren," "This Little Piggy"), counting rhymes ("One, Two, Buckle My Shoe," "As I Was Going to St. Ives"), weather ("Rain, Rain Go Away," "January Brings the Snow"), days of the week ("Solomon Grundy"), and tongue twisters ("Peter Piper").

Fractions. Children enjoy guessing how many parts Humpty Dumpty broke into when he fell off the wall. This can lead to a discussion of fractions.

Time. "Wee Willie Winkie," "Ten O'Clock Scholar," and "Hickory Dickory Dock" all help introduce or reinforce the notion of telling time.

Measurement. Read "Jack Be Nimble." Then have children measure various candlesticks in inches or centimeters.

Parts of a plant. Read "Mary, Mary Quite Contrary." Then have children plant seeds, learn what a plant needs to grow, and learn the parts of a plant.

School rules. Read "Mary Had a Little Lamb." Then discuss what school was like in the past and compare it to the present. The beginning of the school year is a good time to use this as a discussion starter for presenting classroom rules.

Counting. Read "One, Two, Buckle My Shoe," "Going to St. Ives," and "One, Two, Three, Four, Five."

Women's roles in the community. Two of our units in social studies are about community helpers and the family. After the children have completed reading "Peter, Peter, Pumpkin Eater," we discuss the possibilities of jobs for Peter's wife.

Days of the week. Teach recognition of the days of the week by reading "Solomon Grundy." The rhyme follows the sequence of days by describing what happened to Solomon on each day. The children enjoy the rhyme and also learn to read the days of the week.

Superstitions. Halloween is a perfect time to introduce children to superstitions, and what better way than by reading the rhyme "Pins" to them. We discuss what good luck and bad luck mean and then talk about other superstitions.

Cooking. Children like to search for rhymes that deal with food, such as "Hot Cross Buns" and "Davy Dumpling." After reading the rhymes and enjoying the patterning, we define dumplings and hot cross buns and talk about their origins. Discussions usually follow about whether any of the children have tried this type of food. Then we talk about various ethnic dishes.

Often the children become so familiar with the patterning and repetitive sentences in the poems that they begin to create their own rhymes. I have used Mother Goose as a whole language experience in my first grade classroom for many years. The children are always overwhelmingly enthusiastic. I am also fortunate to have a guest who comes to my class each year, dressed up as Mother Goose, to act out and recite rhymes with the children.

Using Fairy Tales with Younger Children

Christopher W. Sparks
Gainesville, Florida
April 1984

The stories young children hear most often, like "Little Red Riding Hood" or "The Gingerbread Boy," are folktales. They are short, repetitive stories filled with the personification and characterization small children love. Using folktales in a beginning literature program is always a good idea. You gain much, however, by broadening the program to include fairy tales.

Fairy tales make more use of magic than do folktales. This fosters children's abstract thinking by conveying events that cannot be explained or illustrated in concrete terms. Fairy tales arouse many of the same feelings that folktales do and help children understand and deal with those feelings. Two of the most valuable features of fairy tales are that they help children learn to predict outcomes and infer characteristics and they introduce the concept of justice.

To be of optimum benefit, fairy tales should be repeated at least four times. The repetitions allow the child to (1) listen for pleasure and concentrate on the story; (2) listen again with knowledge of the outcome and without having to pay attention to detail; (3) listen once more, this time picking up on the less apparent twists and turns of plot and story structure; and (4) listen with the confidence and understanding that comes from complete familiarity with the story. During this fourth telling, children's fears are allayed as they fully identify with the central character who began his or her adventure at great disadvantage, only to emerge victorious and receive just rewards.

Telling fairy tales rather than reading them is preferable unless a particularly well-written version can be found. Among the best are *East of the Sun and West of the Moon* by Mercer Mayer and *Beauty and the Beast* as retold by Marianna Mayer. *The Grimm's Complete Fairy Tales* (Doubleday) is a good collection that includes many popular selections: "Rapunzel," "Sleeping Beauty," "One-Eye, Two-Eyes, and Three-Eyes," "Rumpelstiltskin," "The Fisherman and His Wife," and "Hansel and Gretel." Many tales are also available on record, tape, or CD.

These stories, like folktales, lend themselves to dramatization, puppetry, and flannelboard activities and are excellent for developing vocabulary and accurate language patterns.

For some wonderful insight into fairy tales, Bruno Bettelheim's *The Uses of Enchantment: The Meaning and Importance of Fairy Tales* is recommended.

Success with Silverstein

Jamie Reiser
Beaverton, Oregon
February 1989

I have found an effective method for my fourth graders to practice oral expression using Shel Silverstein's poems. My students love Shel Silverstein, and if they have any free time during class, they are often found reading one of his books. I decided to use this love and enthusiasm to motivate them to perform his poems. They were excited by the opportunity.

I read through *Where the Sidewalk Ends* and *A Light in the Attic* and selected poems that would be fun to learn and perform. Next I let the children pick out their favorites. Everyone chose one poem to perform alone, and then the students were encouraged to learn and perform poems with partners or small groups. The next day, we discussed oral expression: enunciation, volume, speed, and tone of voice. We brainstormed different hand and body motions that would fit with different poems and shared some simple prop and costume ideas. The students went home, worked on their poems, and came back ready to practice in front of the class. Afterward, we shared compliments and constructive suggestions. The originality of each presentation was exciting.

Now the class was ready to put together a performance for other students and parents. I wrote up a short narrative on Shel Silverstein's life, and we selected a narrator. The students picked a title for the program—"Blast off with Shel Silverstein"—and made a backdrop of stars and a rocket with an enlarged picture of the poet and his books. We performed twice for parents and twice for different grade levels. I was amazed that students had learned each other's poems, which provided support and encouragement for all participants.

The success of this program, along with the variety and wide popularity of Shel Silverstein's poems, suggests that this activity could be adapted for any grade level.

Experiencing October

Karen S. Henderson
Carpentersville, Illinois
October 1985

Children's literature and the language experience approach should be integral parts of every elementary curriculum. In October, I decided to combine some common experiences of autumn with some books on the same topic, all the while developing a number of the children's skills.

The first session, developed around the colors of autumn, emphasized listening and remembering details. We began by discussing what colors we saw most often in the autumn. We looked around outside, then decided on orange, yellow, brown, and black.

I told the children that *Hailstones and Halibut Bones* by Mary O'Neill (Doubleday, 1961) contains a poem about each of these colors. I read each of the poems to them, then asked them to close their eyes and think about one thing that was mentioned for each color.

Next I gave the children drawing paper and asked them to fold it into quarters. Using their orange, yellow, brown, and black crayons, the children wrote the name of one of the colors in each quarter, then drew the object they remembered from the poem about that color. We discussed their drawings, then listed on the board the objects they mentioned for each color.

In the second session, we moved on to a story to develop the children's story comprehension. The goals were to have them listen to and retell the story, then individually dictate similar stories and share them with the class. We began by talking about small animals that live in the woods. In particular, I asked the children what animals have to do to get ready for the winter. Then I read *Mousekin's Golden House* by Edna Miller (Prentice Hall, 1964). After the reading, the children eagerly remembered Mousekin's winter home and all the things he had to do to prepare for the winter.

Next, I asked the children to imagine what another little forest animal might do to prepare to spend the winter in a jack-o-lantern. I told the children that each of them would be telling me a story about his or her animal, then putting the story into a golden house. Using orange and black construction paper and lined story paper, I had the children make booklets in the shape of pumpkins. While they glued on black paper cutouts to make jack-o-lanterns, I went from child to child, listening to their stories and recording them on the lined paper. The children were delighted with the activity, and were even more delighted when they shared their stories with others with little or no help.

In the third session, I wanted to emphasize story prediction, key vocabulary, group retelling of a story to enhance comprehension, and individual dictation of language experience stories. Before I read *Strega Nona* by Nomie dePaola (Prentice Hall, 1975), I asked the children if they had ever been told not to do something, but had done it anyway. With that in mind, we looked at the book cover and talked about what the story might be about. Then I read the book to them, stopping at key points to ask what might happen next. After I finished the book, we retold the events.

To encourage thinking, I asked the children to imagine that Strega Nona had more than one magic pot. What might be magic about it? What might come out of another pot? Using the same procedures as for session two, I had the children draw a picture of what might come out of a magic pot and used that picture to make a booklet for a language experience story. As the children worked, I went around the room and wrote down their dictated stories. After we were finished, I had each child copy his or her story before sharing it with the group.

The last session was based on an adaptation of Don Holdaway's shared book experience (*The Foundations of Literacy*, Ashton Scholastic, 1979). The book I used was Mary Lystad's *The Halloween Parade* (Putnam, 1973). Before reading, I talked with the children about Halloween customs and costumes and told them to listen to find out the main character's ideas about various costumes and what he would need to wear each costume. We followed the reading with discussion on what had happened in the story.

I had each child dictate a story about one of the costumes Bob had thought of wearing, and I recorded the story on large chart paper. Then I gave the paper with the story on it to the child to illustrate. While they were doing this, I circulated and had each child dictate another story about what she or he would need to make her or his own Halloween costume. The children also illustrated those stories. I read the finished stories with each child several times.

Next, we put all of the stories together to make a Big Book, designed a cover, and bound the book together. Finally, we read the finished book.

Our October experiences were a great success. The children enjoyed all of the books, and they had a chance to listen, write, speak, read, and experience success at every step.

A Week with Millions of Cats

Donna Angeron Browning
Spring, Texas
April 1989

Whenever the subject of cats is mentioned at a neighborhood gathering, at the veterinarian's office, at the grocery store, or in a classroom, children and adults alike reveal definite opinions about the purring felines. With this thought in mind, I set the stage in my first grade classroom to present Wanda Gag's story *Millions of Cats*.

Picture children walking in on a Monday morning and discovering two very famous cat personalities sitting in the big easy chair in our sharing circle. Excitement and curiosity is apparent in their voices as they exclaim: "The Cat in the Hat! Why is he here?" "Are we going to read that story?" "May I hold him?" "Look at Garfield! Did he bring Pookie and Odie?" "I have one just like that!"

Day one. On the first day I start with the first verse of a poem called "What in the World?" by Eve Merriam, which poses a sort of riddle. The discussion that ensues should provide the answer to that riddle: a cat. It is at this point that I mention the two cat celebrities, who help me introduce the Feature Book of the Week.

While listening to *Millions of Cats*, students start to anticipate passages in which they may start an impromptu choral reading. After the first reading of the story, I guide the children in discussing the describing words (adjectives) that were used about the cats. I record responses on the cat-shaped chart paper that will hang in the room for the week. Words like *little, fluffy, prettiest, fuzzy, beautiful, brown and yellow stripes, gray, thirsty, hungry, frightened, thin, scraggly, homely, soft, shiny,* and *plump* are from the text. If the students suggest other descriptive terms that apply to cats, such as *spotted, calico,* or *huge,* I write those on the chart as well.

Then I draw the children's attention to Dr. Seuss's *The Cat in the Hat* and a comic strip of Garfield and ask them to describe each of them. *The Cat in the Hat* has a hat and an umbrella that need to be included in the description. Garfield is striped and orange with no articles of clothing. When I am satisfied with their responses, I hand each child a piece of drawing paper. Each is to draw and color a cat, real or imaginary, on which they put a special distinguishing item to help identify it. When the children are finished with the drawings, I collect these and put them away.

We begin each morning of the week in our sharing circle with cat poems selected from sources such as *The Random House Book of Poetry* and *Read-Aloud Rhymes for the Very Young.* If students bring in any of their own favorite toy cats (and they do), we take this time to talk about them, too.

My listening center includes tapes of stories about cats (along with the corresponding books) that children may go to hear. Books and stories available in the reading corner include *I Can Read with My Eyes Shut* and *The Cat in the Hat* by Dr. Seuss, *The Color Kittens* by Margaret Wise Brown, *Three Little Kittens* by Lorinda B. Cauley, *Whiskers and Rhymes* by Arnold Lobel, *Fat Cat* by Jack Kent, *Fire Cat* by E. Averill, *Puss in Boots* by Paul Galdone, *Millions of Cats* by Wanda Gag, and Tomie dePaola's *Favorite Nursery Tales,* which includes the stories "Belling the Cat" by Aesop, "Owl and the Pussy Cat" by Edward Lear, and "The Cat and the Mouse" by Joseph Jacobs.

Day two. On the second day, before reading aloud *Millions of Cats* again, I ask my students to tell me the different number words that are used in the story. Responses should include "hundreds," "thousands," "millions," "billions," and "trillions." After these number words are named, I ask if someone would like to volunteer to hold the number cards that I've prepared (see Figure on the next page). Each time one of these number words is used in the story, the volunteer steps forward, holds up the card, and says the number. Usually the entire class chimes in. With the use of these cards, children develop knowledge of place values up to the trillions with amazing comprehension and understanding. Volunteers to hold the cards are plentiful as the story starts again.

After this activity, the children write a description of the cats they have drawn. I encourage them to use adjectives from the chart as well as invented spelling to complete their descriptions. I walk around to confer with each author to make sure they are not neglecting important details. On this piece of writing, I usually do the editing for the children to incorporate into their rewriting.

Day three. On Wednesday, I ask for volunteers to be the little old man and the little old lady to tell the story of *Millions of Cats.* For the old lady, I have a scarf, and for the old man, a pipe and an old felt hat. The number cards are used as props. If someone wants to hold the toy cats that have been gathering on the table, she or he may do so. This presentation sets up a series of sequencing activities that are part of the story. I ask the children to relate the sequence of action: at the nice clean house, over sunny hills, through cool valleys, the cat-covered hill, the old man with cats following, at the pond, grass-covered hills, back to the house. During the day, I ask the various groups which point of the story they would like to illustrate to go along with the next storytelling of *Millions of Cats.*

This third day is also the day set aside for students to rewrite their cat descriptions. While they are rewriting, I again walk around to confer and make suggestions. I put the completed descriptions aside with the drawings until the end of the week.

Day four. My students devote this day to storytelling; they present their interpretations of *Millions of Cats*, accompanied with props and scenery. The whole class gets involved in this "drama," conducting choral readings, drawing pictures of the sequence of events, and assuming the roles of the little old woman and man. At this point children are ready to take their play outside of the room to perform for another first grade class or a kindergarten class.

Day five. To culminate the week, I have a special kind of "Hide and Go Seek" game that involves the drawings and descriptions of cats that the students prepared earlier. When the children enter the classroom on Friday, they immediately notice that all of their drawings are hanging up. The names are on the backs so the students don't know who drew most of them. The children have ten minutes to study the drawings for details.

When the children have finished, I explain the game of "Purrfect Cat." I ask for a volunteer to find each "Purrfect Cat." Clues come from the descriptions the children wrote. As I read the descriptions, the seeker tries to find the author's drawing. If the author did a good job, the seeker will be able to identify the correct drawing. If by chance the description needed more details, the seeker will have difficulty in finding the cat. If this happens, I ask the author to collaborate with me by adding more clues. This type of collaboration spares children embarrassment and allows them to edit their work without fear of failure. If the seeker still fails to find the correct drawing, I ask the author to point it out. Then I ask the class to participate in sharing ideas about things that could have been changed to help us find the "Purrfect Cat."

On occasion a student puts something in the description that is not on the drawing, thus throwing the class off the track. Then we ask the student to modify the drawing to match the description. Once the description and the drawing are matched, the artist becomes the next seeker. We proceed until all of the works are matched.

These pictures and descriptions are mounted and bound to form a class book of "Purrfect Cats." I place it right beside the other cat books in the reading corner. The children read it repeatedly with amusement and pleasure.

Using one book like *Millions of Cats* can help students write accurate descriptions, create artwork, improve oral language, learn to sequence events, participate in choral reading and theater arts, edit their writing, listen to various types of poetry, and learn about place value skills in math. The activities are adaptable to most first graders: the quicker learners give more details in descriptions; slower learners participate with fewer clues but with satisfactory results.

Millions of Cats provides the quality of reading material teachers need to transcend basal readers while still providing meaningful learning experiences.

Gold Coins Entice Students to Read and Write Poetry

Pat Scofield
Houston, Texas
December 1985

Students often have a negative attitude toward poetry. To improve this attitude, I developed a six-week unit for my fifth graders that I hoped would motivate them to read and write poetry. The unit had three important features: a stimulating environment, a good gimmick, and teacher enthusiasm. The lessons were designed to be about 20 minutes long and to be incorporated into the regular elementary language arts block.

To begin the unit, I collected as many poetry books as possible and displayed them in activity centers. The purpose of these centers was to allow students to read books on their own, to create their own poems, and to share poems with others. Each center had a theme such as animal poems or food poems. Other centers featured popular poets such as Shel Silverstein; in these centers, I displayed the poet's picture, books by the poet, and biographical information about the poet. There was also a listening center with recordings of poetry and a tape recorder for taping poems.

The bulletin board in my room displayed a leprechaun sitting on a pot of gold with the caption "Win Gold Coins." This was the gimmick to entice the students to read and write poetry. It was also a good device for measuring the level of poetry activity. The students received gold coins cut from yellow paper as rewards for reading a poem to a partner (one coin), memorizing and reciting a poem (two coins), and writing an original poem (three coins).

On Fridays, the students cashed in their coins for various rewards: 30 coins gave them a homework pass; 25 coins meant they could chew gum in class one morning the following week; 20 coins entitled them to 10 minutes of free time; and 10 coins got them a few stickers. The coins students earned by reading had to be initialed by the person who listened to the poem; the poems also had to be at least eight lines long. This gimmick worked extremely well. Some students earned as many as 100 coins a week.

Fridays were also used as sharing days when students recited poems they had memorized, read their favorite poem, or read a poem they had written.

Themes, Books, Props, and Activities

Theme	Books	Props and Activities
Food	*Poem Stew* (Willliam Cole, HarperCollins, 1983) *The Random House Book of Poetry for Children* (Jack Prelutsky, Random House, 1983)	Display and discuss unusual foods (like prunes or artichokes), then read poems about them. Make something to eat after reading a poem about it, such as chicken soup, peanut butter sandwiches, or pancakes.
Animals	*Zoo Doings: Animal Poems* (Jack Prelutsky, Greenwillow, 1983) *The Baby Eggs Are Hatching* (Jack Prelutsky, Greenwillow, 1983)	Bring in blown-out eggs, pictures of animals, or an empty bird cage to display while reading poems. Have students bring a favorite stuffed animal to class and write a poem about it.
Pigs and people	*The Book of Pigericks* (Arnold Lobel, HarperCollins, 1983) *They've Discovered a Head in the Box for the Bread and Other Laughable Limericks* (John E. Brewton and Lorraine A. Blackburn, HarperCollins, 1978)	Bring in pictures of pigs and funny-looking people. Read poems aloud while wearing a pig nose and pig ears.
Music		Play the record *Really Rosie* by Carole King (a collection of poems by Maurice Sendak put to music). Play popular songs and discuss their lyrics. Write acrostic poems using the names of students' favorite songs.
Scary poems	*Nightmares: Poems to Trouble Your Sleep* (Jack Prelutsky, Greenwillow, 1976) *The Headless Horseman Rides Tonight* (Jack Prelutsky, Greenwillow, 1980) *Ghost Poems* (Daisy Wallace, Holiday House, 1979)	Turn out the lights and light a candle or wear a scary mask while reading poems from these books.
Humorous poems	*Oh, Such Foolishness!* (William Cole, HarperCollins, 1978) *Where the Sidewalk Ends: Poems and Drawings* (Shel Silverstein, HarperCollins, 1974) *A Light in the Attic* (Shel Silverstein, HarperCollins, 1981) *The New Kid on the Block* (Jack Prelutsky, Greenwillow, 1984)	Dress in a silly costume or wear a silly wig. Have a backward day when the activities are done in reverse.

The daily lesson plan included my reading aloud (with attention-getting props) to model a poetic form, guided practice with the students, and independent practice for them to write their own poems. I chose a weekly theme for the poems to read aloud and matched the theme with a poetic form. Themes included food (cinquain), animals (diamante), pigs and people (limericks), music (acrostic poems), scary poems (free verse), and humorous poems (pupils' choice of form). (The Figure on the previous page shows these themes, books to use for each theme, props to use while reading, and additional activities.)

On the first day of each week I introduced a poem and modeled the structure, and the students wrote poems as a group. During the rest of the week, I read at least one poem aloud each day and the students created their own poems. While the students were doing independent work, I held conferences to check their progress.

To keep the students organized, I prepared a poetry packet that explained the different kinds of poems and gave examples of each kind. Each student was required to write at least one poem for each of the forms. Because I wanted the students to read a variety of poems, I prepared a list of different kinds of poems and different poets for them to read. The students had to read at least one poem of each kind and one by each poet. This packet was to be completed by the end of the six weeks.

At the end of the unit, the students' poems were published in a class newspaper and distributed to the rest of the school. Each student who completed the poetry packet satisfactorily got a certificate granting him or her a "poetic license." Judging from the numerous gold coins the students earned, the quality of their poems, and their eagerness to read and write, I feel this poetry unit was a tremendous success.

Shakespeare for Excitement in the Elementary Classroom

Kim M. Richardson
Huntingdon, Pennsylvania
March 1987

We know that exposure is an important stage in the learning sequence, and in the elementary grades we expose children to many concepts and skills we expect them to master in later years. The following activity exposes children to the work of William Shakespeare. It helps them become familiar with the plot and characters in *Macbeth* and gives them limited exposure to the language and poetry of the play. In addition, the choral reading part of the activity provides a successful reading experience for all the children and an opportunity to practice reading with expression. While the activity is intended for grades three to six, it has been used successfully in the first grade as well.

The story of Macbeth, with its witches, ghosts, blood, and mystery, has surefire appeal. Read a modern version aloud to the class. An especially rich and exciting retelling is found in *Favourite Tales from Shakespeare* by Bernard Miles (Hamlyn, 1983), in which the stories have been rewritten in prose especially for reading aloud to children. The illustrations by Victor Ambrus capture the stories' spirit.

Then, to expose the children to Shakespeare's own language and poetry, use an excerpt of the witch's song from Act IV, scene I of the original for follow-up study. The day after reading and discussing the Macbeth story, ask the students to close their eyes and picture a cauldron bubbling over a fire in a cavern in Scotland. Tell students you will read them one of the witches' songs from *Macbeth*, the song the witches sang when Macbeth went to see them in their cave to find out the dangers he would have to face. Ask the children to listen for the things the witches put in the cauldron to make three spirits appear (eye of newt, toe of frog, and so on). Read the poem out loud (with witchlike expression, of course).

After reading, list the items put into the cauldron on the chalkboard as the children name them. Distribute copies of the poem to each child and have them underline the items on the chalkboard and find in the poem any items they failed to mention. Review vocabulary as needed (words such as *sweltered, fenny, newt,* and *howlet* may be difficult for the children).

This poem lends itself well to choral reading. Have the children read it in unison several times to become familiar with the words. Then work on expression, tempo, rhythm, and voice. Elicit from the children the way they think a witch should sound when making a charm. The tempo and rhythm for the first part of the poem should make you think of a chant. In the second part, it may sound like the witches are checking off their list of ingredients. In the third part, the witches are quite satisfied with the bubbling charm.

After experimenting with expression, try additional variations. For example, a group of children may repeat the line "Round about the cauldron go" as the others chant the rest of the poem. A group of witches may be formed to recite selected lines. Individual children may be assigned to one ingredient each and the class as a group could then read the other parts of the poem. As a follow-up, the children may write their own recipes for charms and indicate at the bottom of the recipe the type of spell for which it is useful. Bind the recipes in a black cover cut into the shape of a cauldron.

Once you've introduced the children to Shakespeare, you'll find them eager to hear the other stories in Bernard Miles's book. If children get pleasure from the work of Shakespeare when they are young, they may approach his plays with greater enthusiasm in high school. They will also understand the plots and be able to concentrate more fully on the poetry.

It's Better Than a Book Report!

**Sarah S. Krouse
Nancy G. Hamlin**
*North Manchester, Indiana
February 1986*

Having tried everything from card files to individual conferences as a means of monitoring children's independent reading, we finally developed the Circle of Books project for our second graders. In addition to recording a sample of children's reading, we have found this tool to be particularly useful in encouraging independent reading, promoting peer interaction, and communicating with parents.

Early in September each child is given a 5" x 7" index card (about 12 cm x 17 cm) on a 2" loose-leaf ring (one of those rings that snap open and shut easily). This is the Circle of Books title card, which the child labels as such, decorates, and identifies with his or her name. We tell the children that throughout the year, they will get additional cards each week to add to their circles. On each card they will be asked to tell something about a book they have read that week during independent reading time at school or at home. On one side of the card, children record the following information: the title of the book; its author; their name; the date; and an original drawing for the cover of the book. The other side of the card is available for the week's activity, which is assigned by the teacher.

The project's success lies in picking an activity that requires the child to zero in on a particular aspect of a book. Without this structure, children are easily overwhelmed, not knowing where to begin telling about their books. Circle of Books has worked especially well in our classrooms because of the varied approaches we have used each week to keep the children's interest level high. The space-limited 5" x 7" card format ensures that the activity will be within each child's ability to complete and precludes the anxiety and tedium of the traditional book report.

The activities described in what follows can be adapted to a range of grade levels. Using a wide variety of them will give children a broad foundation from which to analyze books in lengthier reports when desired. Keeping the activities crisp and brief is one of the keys to sustaining children's interest through the year. Some activities in the project may even invite

206

peer response, thus encouraging children to "write to be read" and to read others' comments purposefully. Here are the activities we have found to be particularly successful:

- Write to a friend and tell why he or she should not miss this book.
- Tell an exciting part and end with "Read and find out more!" (Don't give the ending away!)
- Divide your card in thirds. Tell something from the beginning, the middle, and the end of your book.
- Send a Valentine to your book telling it why you like it.
- Choose ten words from your book. Use them in four sentences about it.
- Find five rhyming words in your book and use them in a poem.
- Choose one character and write five sentences describing him or her.
- Tell five new facts you learned from a nonfiction book this week.
- Tell something funny that happened in your book.
- Tell something that surprised you in your book.
- Choose a character and tell why you would like that character for a friend.
- Choose a character and tell why you would have done something different from what he or she did.
- Choose a character and write five questions you would like to ask him or her.
- Write a note to the author of your book.
- Tell another way the book might have ended if....
- Write what you think could be the first five sentences of the next chapter of your book.
- Think about where events in your book take place. Describe an interesting setting from your book.

When the circles are not in use, we display them on hooks near the classroom library corner where they are available for everyone's enjoyment. At the end of the year, children take home a complete Circle of Books on their loose-leaf ring representing their reading for the year and telling their thoughts and feelings about the books they have read. While the Circle of Books may not record in detail every book the children read, it does give a representative sample of their year in reading and a peek into the joy discovered. Best of all, children look forward to their weekly Circle of Books activity; that's something we never saw with book reports!

Novel Trivia

Donna Frank
Fairfax County, Virginia
December 1987

It's so important to motivate children that last year during our statewide special reading month, I decided to play "Novel Trivia" with the entire school. I hoped that asking questions about books would encourage more children to read and use the library.

Questions were created for two categories: easy fiction for use in kindergarten to grade two and the regular fiction shelf for grades three to six. Questions for the easy fiction included these:

- In what Caldecott Award winner do we find Max, who gets sent to bed without his dinner?
- In what book does the man with the yellow hat first appear?
- Name the book in which a little boy goes for a walk with a crayon and draws himself some wonderful adventures.
- (Answers are Maurice Sendak's *Where the Wild Things Are*, H.A. Rey's *Curious George*, and Crockett Johnson's *Harold and the Purple Crayon*.)

Questions for the regular fiction shelf included these:

- In what book does Milo find himself in the Lands Beyond, an enchanted world with some of the craziest creatures ever imagined?
- In what Newbery Award winner by Ellen Raskin do we find 16 heirs attempting to become instant millionaires?
- Name the author who wrote seven books dealing with Narnia, an imaginary land you enter by passing through a wardrobe.
- Name the author of the book *House with a Clock in Its Walls*, in which Lewis must foil Isak Izzard's plan to end the world.
- (Answers are *The Phantom Tollbooth* by Norton Juster, *The Westing Game*, C.S. Lewis, and John Bellairs.)

Each morning during the school's announcements, I asked a question for the easy fiction and then one for the regular shelf. Each classroom teacher helped the children decide on the answer most of them believed to be correct, and that answer was written on the board. At the end of the day, I announced the answers. Children cheered when they were correct, and those cheers floated out of the classrooms and gave everyone a boost.

The results of this simple trivia game were wonderful. Teachers noticed that the students who knew the answers couldn't wait to share how much they enjoyed the books and why they should be read by a certain classmate or the teacher. This produced an immediate run on the library as students wanted to find and read the books in the trivia game as well as other books by the same authors.

Character Mug Sheets

Trevor H. Cairney
*Wagga Wagga (now Kingswood), NSW, Australia
December 1987*

Character mug sheets enable children to reflect on the personalities of the characters in any text. Their use encourages children to consider not only the personality traits of the character but also the relationship of different characters to each other. While many students (especially avid readers) need little help to concentrate on characterization in texts, this technique encourages them to reflect on the characters in a different way.

Mug sheets can be used with any narrative text that children have listened to or read. The composition of the mug sheet may be varied, but I have found the format shown in the Figure to be useful. Before asking children to complete their own mug sheets, you should model the construction of one

Sample Mug Sheet

[drawing of character]	Name: _____ Alias: _____ Age: _____ Address:_____ Description: _____ Special features: _____ Major goal(s) in life: _____ Unusual or interesting habits: _____

for a character they all know. It is also useful to show your class how the mug sheet for any character can take a number of forms. For example, I often demonstrate the construction of a mug sheet based on fact and one that involves stretching the truth.

It matters little whether the children decide to create mug sheets based purely on the traits and the events contained in the story or to present a lighthearted interpretation of the character. In both cases, the reader needs to know the character.

Once children have created their own mug sheets, they should be given the opportunity to share them with other members of the class. This is not only extremely enjoyable, but it gives students a chance to hear how other children have represented different characters from the same book, or even the same character.

Spinning a Prereading Lesson

Ginny Hoppes
Littleton, Colorado
February 1989

I use semantic webbing for myriad purposes in my classroom. During a unit on books that are animal fantasies, I found it especially beneficial for activating background knowledge, increasing organizational skills, focusing on topic, and notetaking. To introduce the unit I had my fourth graders read an excerpt from *Charlotte's Web* by E.B. White. To activate background knowledge before reading, the children and I made a semantic web of all we knew about spiders. After reading the selection, they were to use what Charlotte told Wilbur about spiders to make their own semantic webs. This required them to identify factual details within the narrative. Then I had the children read an informational selection on spiders. From it they extracted new information to add to their webs. They were able to see that facts can be obtained from both nonfiction and fiction. They also had an opportunity to confirm their items.

Next, as a group we looked at the original web and added or deleted facts based on the information gathered from the reading. From the initial web, we categorized the facts into satellite webs on food, habitat, looks, habits, and enemies.

As a prereading strategy for Roald Dahl's *James and the Giant Peach*, I extended the spider activity. Each child was to research one creature that appears in the novel (ladybug, grasshopper, earthworm, centipede, silkworm, or glowworm). I gave each child a 3" x 5" (8 cm x 13 cm) matrix on which to write down facts (see Figure). Then I modeled how to take notes (i.e., how to write a few words and not copy sentences). I had purposely designed small spaces so only notes, not sentences, would fit on the cards. The children were to research four topics pertaining to their creature: food, habitat, looks, and habits. An interesting fact that did not fit could go under the heading "Other." The children were to use at least two sources to gather information.

Fact Chart: Silkworm

	Food	Looks	Habitat	Habits	Other
Source 1:	mulberry leaves	creamy, smooth	no longer wild		
Source 2:	mulberry leaves	horn on tail, 3½"	incubates in boxes	spins long thread	

After reading about their creatures and taking notes on the fact chart, the children put their information into a written report. I modeled the concept of paragraphs in a minilesson using the information from two of the satellite webs on spiders, writing each as a separate paragraph. This showed how paragraphs focus on different topics.

As a final step before reading *James and the Giant Peach*, I gave each child a large piece of chart paper on which to transform the written report into a visual display as a web. Children who had researched the same creature could work on a group web. These resulting webs were displayed on the walls and served as references when we read *James and the Giant Peach*.

Since Roald Dahl gave his characters personalities based in part on their natural traits, I felt it was imperative for the children to have background knowledge of all the creatures. In addition, when writing reports, children tend to include everything they read. Semantic webs help teach them how to focus their topic, as well as how to take notes without copying information.

Books Come to Life

David C. Hayes
Berwyn, Pennsylvania
November 1985

"Hello, I am the book *Jane Eyre*...." This simple introduction soon transported a class of fifth and sixth graders to 19th-century England and the world of Charlotte Brontë. As the day went on, *Moby Dick, The Black Stallion, Shadow of a Bull,* and other classics appeared before us.

This special activity for our annual Book Week celebration was based on Ray Bradbury's futuristic novel *Fahrenheit 451*. This book is set in a time when all printed material is outlawed and systematically burned. In order to preserve the truly great literary works of the past, a group of individuals seclude themselves in a remote area to memorize these classics. Each "rebel" becomes a book, learning it from cover to cover and repeating it continuously, hoping that someday it will once again be written down. Bradbury thereby confronts the reader with a thought-provoking and somewhat frightening prospect.

Using that novel as our inspiration during Book Week, we, too, "became" books. Each student picked out an acknowledged "classic" piece of literature, memorized a significant passage to present orally to the class, and began with the format "Hello, I am [name of book] by [name of author]." Although most selected the book's introductory lines to share, several students picked a favorite passage. Younger, inexperienced readers needed assistance in selecting an interesting or appropriate selection. Length and vocabulary varied with ability, but motivation never lagged. Once students had practiced their oral presentations, we videotaped each presentor, providing for the all-important self-evaluation step.

The goal for the activity was not merely to have students commit a passage of exceptionally fine writing to memory but to whet their appetites for further reading of the books presented. It proved to be one of the most interesting activities of the year and one to which the students responded very positively. So the next time a great white whale appears in your classroom, don't be alarmed. It's just a student "becoming" a book.

Novels for Group Reading

Shirlee R. Morris
Tarzana, California
October 1983

Most of us know what it is like to find a book so compelling that we can hardly put it down. I wonder, though, if children have this experience in school.

Several years ago, I decided that basal reader stories are often too short and too controlled to involve children's emotions, curiosity, and imaginations. I began looking for novels that would be exciting and compelling for my fourth

212

graders. The novels I found were written by such notable authors as Roald Dahl, Betsy Byars, Katherine Paterson, Madeleine L'Engle, and E.L. Konigsburg. The topics ranged from science fiction to fantasy to realistic stories.

The first surprise for the children in my new reading program is that they are offered a choice of three novels. For the first time, they can read the novel that they find the most appealing.

Along with his or her own paperback book, each child receives a kit containing projects and related assignments. The children may respond to the literature in a variety of ways. A group of children who read *From the Mixed-Up Files of Mrs. Basil E. Frankweiler* by E.L. Konigsburg may construct a model of the first and second floors of the Metropolitan Museum of Art and take the class on a tour through the eyes of the two children in the book. A group that reads *Chocolate Fever* by Robert K. Smith may decide to take a chocolate survey, devising questions for the class to answer after tasting four different types of chocolate. Reading *Cricket in Times Square* by George Selden may lead to research on subways and Time Square Station in New York and ultimately to building a two-tiered model of Times Square itself. This group also may make fortune cookies and write original fortunes to go in them.

In addition to group projects children can complete individual projects and present them to the class. One student designed a stuffed dragon after reading *My Father's Dragon* by Ruth S. Gannet. The characters in *James and the Giant Peach* by Roald Dahl were brought to life by another student in "animated" cut-outs of the animals in the book. Another student took the class on a journey through space by means of a filmstrip for *A Wrinkle in Time* by Madeleine L'Engle.

On completion of the novels, a class may get involved in creative writing projects. Letters to the author are first. (The children become so aware of communicating with authors that many of them will write to authors of other books they are reading as well.) The children may also write poems and stories, which can be typed on duplicating masters, proofread, illustrated by the children, and finally compiled into a book for each student in the class.

One of the most valuable aspects of my novel-reading program is the daily group discussion. The discussions reveal how involved students really are in the stories and how much their interpretations of the events and characters' motivations vary. It's not surprising in these discussions to hear children "confess" that they knew they weren't supposed to read the next chapter but they just couldn't stop! Children reading *A Wrinkle in Time* may argue constantly about the meaning of each of Mrs. W's roles. They may try out a few Chinese accents while they read *Cricket in Times Square*. An awareness of grammar may bloom among students who read *From the Mixed-Up Files of Mrs. Basil E. Frankweiler.*

Answering written questions and looking up vocabulary from the novels is certainly more tedious and less exciting than the discussions, art projects, dramatizations, and creative writing, yet the exercise is far more relevant than the vocabulary tests in language books and comprehension pages in workbooks.

Each year my program expands. More novels are available and some of the books get made into movies. With the help of videotapes, children may see a movie based on a novel they have already read and be asked to compare the two versions of the story.

When the novels are completed, the students have copies of the class's creative writing compilation, their art projects, and their letters to (and sometimes from) the authors. They have intangibles, too. They have the experience of participating in a group with a common interest, and they have that sense of satisfaction that comes when we turn the last page and say, "That was great!" How often do teachers hear that when a basal story is over?

Book Webbing across the Curriculum

Jan Donaldson
Orting, Washington
January 1984

The remarkable tale of *Lafcadio, The Lion Who Shot Back* by Shel Silverstein (HarperCollins, 1963) is a gold mine for any teacher interested in using a book to its full potential and, at the same time, developing an integrated curriculum. This can be achieved through "book webbing."

What is book webbing and how does it work? Those familiar with theme development are probably aware of the webbing process. A thematic web is a chart of possible avenues of study within a particular topic, displaying alternative ways to approach the topic and teach basic skills at the same time. A web can record a teacher's brainstorming of possible teaching ideas. It is not likely that all the ideas listed in the web would be used, but having a variety of directions to choose from gives a teacher a great deal of flexibility.

The notion of webbing implies an integrated curriculum, one that connects the various subject areas. As students study a specific topic in depth and across various interrelated curriculum areas, they gain a broader perspective of that topic and can apply the new knowledge in a multitude of ways. If possible, work with at least one other teacher when using this

214

process. The adage that "two heads are better than one" certainly applies here.

Step 1. Screen several books that may be appropriate for the class. Choose books that can be read chapter by chapter. Look for those that are appropriate for reading aloud, that students will enjoy hearing, and that contain portions relating to many curricular areas (language arts, math, science, social studies, art, music, physical education, and health). Narrow your choice down to one book to start off with.

Step 2. Read the whole book. Get a feel for the author's style and the main story line. Think of this as pleasure reading and try to imagine how a child would react if the book were read aloud.

Step 3. Read the book again after two or three weeks. Take a blank piece of paper for each subject area and, as you reread the book, record ideas from it that apply to each curricular area.

Step 4. Compare your ideas with those of another teacher. Discuss these ideas and the techniques you might use in instruction. Think about both whole-class instruction and individual needs.

Step 5. Develop the web. Make as many connections as possible with different subject areas. (The Figure on the next page shows a web developed for *Lafcadio*. Notice how well it lends itself to work in all the curricular areas.)

Step 6. Develop specific lesson plans from the web.

Step 7. Begin reading the book aloud to the class, a chapter or two each day, implementing the ideas and activities you've developed in related subject areas. (In selecting specific activities from the web, deliberately cover as many curricular areas as possible.) Each time you work with part of the web, be sure to solicit and record on the web additional ideas from the students. Be prepared to discuss what is happening in the book before, during, and after reading aloud each day.

Follow up each day's reading with good comprehension questions. They can be answered orally or in writing and should vary in level of difficulty from recall to interpretation and evaluation.

Step 8. Take careful notes as each book is used, documenting successes and failures with particular ideas. Take the time to compare results with those of another teacher and see if there are different ways to approach some areas to produce the desired results.

Step 9. When the book is finished, give students many follow-up activities. Drama and art may be particularly motivating at this time.

Step 10. Carefully think through the next book to select to read aloud. Try to find a book whose main theme has features in common with the book you've just read so it will extend students' thinking.

When one begins to examine a book critically to draw as much information and ideas out of it as possible, many different avenues open up. This is where the concept of webbing can be so helpful.

A Web of Possibilities

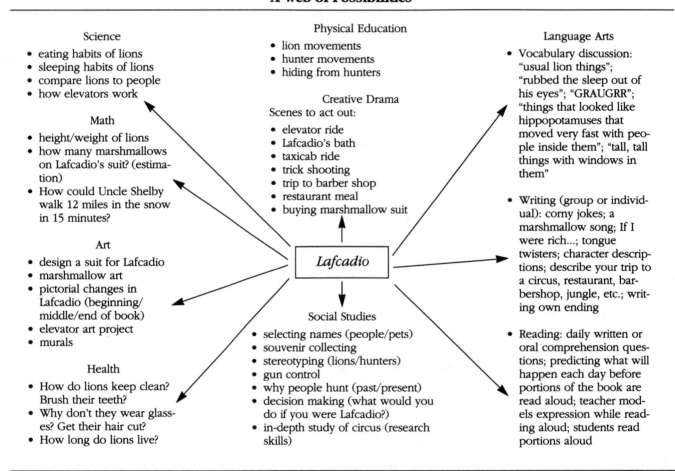

Science
- eating habits of lions
- sleeping habits of lions
- compare lions to people
- how elevators work

Math
- height/weight of lions
- how many marshmallows on Lafcadio's suit? (estimation)
- How could Uncle Shelby walk 12 miles in the snow in 15 minutes?

Art
- design a suit for Lafcadio
- marshmallow art
- pictorial changes in Lafcadio (beginning/middle/end of book)
- elevator art project
- murals

Health
- How do lions keep clean? Brush their teeth?
- Why don't they wear glasses? Get their hair cut?
- How long do lions live?

Physical Education
- lion movements
- hunter movements
- hiding from hunters

Creative Drama
Scenes to act out:
- elevator ride
- Lafcadio's bath
- taxicab ride
- trick shooting
- trip to barber shop
- restaurant meal
- buying marshmallow suit

Lafcadio

Social Studies
- selecting names (people/pets)
- souvenir collecting
- stereotyping (lions/hunters)
- gun control
- why people hunt (past/present)
- decision making (what would you do if you were Lafcadio?)
- in-depth study of circus (research skills)

Language Arts
- Vocabulary discussion: "usual lion things"; "rubbed the sleep out of his eyes"; "GRAUGRR"; "things that looked like hippopotamuses that moved very fast with people inside them"; "tall, tall things with windows in them"

- Writing (group or individual): corny jokes; a marshmallow song; If I were rich...; tongue twisters; character descriptions; describe your trip to a circus, restaurant, barbershop, jungle, etc.; writing own ending

- Reading: daily written or oral comprehension questions; predicting what will happen each day before portions of the book are read aloud; teacher models expression while reading aloud; students read portions aloud

216

Chapter 9

Reading for Pleasure

Recreational or pleasure reading is reading that children (or adults) do because they want to. When children choose to read rather than, say, watch television, they have become *readers*! Unfortunately, the results of most studies of children's (and, for that matter, adults') reading habits are quite gloomy. For whatever reason, many children simply do not rate reading as an activity of choice (Anderson, Wilson, & Fielding, 1988; Walberg & Tsai, 1984). While teachers have limited or no influence on home activities, they do have a great deal of control over the activities that are scheduled in their classrooms. Children sense what teachers value by what teachers ask them to do. Recreational reading can occur in school as well as at home; teachers should promote this activity in order to foster a love of reading in their students.

Spiegel (1981) provides an excellent guide for teachers who want to create a recreational reading program within their existing curriculum. She also points out that reading time is precious for all children and should not be used as a reward—or worse, a time-filler—for children who finish other work. Certainly such a program has many benefits—not the least of which is probable improved performance in reading and related school tasks, including standardized tests. Children who read extensively are likely to have positive attitudes about reading which, in turn, lead them to read even more. A school day that includes periods of time for pleasure reading encourages those positive attitudes; moreover, such attitudes are likely to carry over into the home. Wide reading also helps children expand their knowledge of the world, builds vocabulary, strengthens comprehension, and improves fluency—all of which, in turn, make reading more pleasurable.

Teachers need to remember that if the reading habit is to spill over outside of school, children need access to public libraries and must develop a pride in ownership of books. Inexpensive paperback books are available through book clubs; children's magazine subscriptions are reasonable for most families; and some nonprofit groups provide books for children. If families cannot afford reading material, parent-teacher groups or other organizations may be able to supply funds.

A time to read, a teacher who values reading time for all children, and a wide variety of books and other materials with a range of reading levels.... What better classroom could a child wish for or a parent hope for for his or her child? The activities in this chapter focus on ways to encourage recreational reading. (Note that many activities described in Chapter 8 also foster reading for pleasure.)

References

Anderson, R.C., Wilson, P.T., & Fielding, L.G. (1988). Growth in reading and how children spend their time outside of school. *Reading Research Quarterly, 23,* 285-303.

Spiegel, D.L. (1981). *Reading for pleasure: Guidelines.* Newark, DE: International Reading Association.

Walberg, J.J., & Tsai, S. (1984). Reading achievement and diminishing returns to time. *Journal of Educational Psychology, 76,* 442-451.

Further Reading

Berglund, R.L., & Johns, J.L. (1983). A primer on uninterrupted sustained silent reading. *The Reading Teacher, 36,* 534-539.

Fielding, L.G., Wilson, P.T., & Anderson, R.C. (1986). A new focus on free reading: The role of trade books in reading instruction. In T.E. Raphael (Ed.), *The contexts of school-based literacy* (pp. 149-162). New York: Random House.

Gambrell, L.B. (1978). Getting started with sustained silent reading, and keeping it going. *The Reading Teacher, 32,* 328-331.

Madden, L. (1988). Improving reading attitudes of poor readers through cooperative reading teams. *The Reading Teacher, 42,* 194-199.

Mork, T.A. (1972). Sustained silent reading in the classroom. *The Reading Teacher, 25,* 438-441.

Morrow, L.M. (1987). Promoting inner-city children's recreational reading. *The Reading Teacher, 41,* 266-275.

- When there's a library corner in the classroom, children read 50 percent more books.

- Children use library corners that have easy access and that are quiet, partitioned off for privacy, and located where children can see them.

- A good corner has comfortable seating for six or more children at a time and includes pillows and rugs.

- Children are attracted to library corners that have story props, such as flannelboards, taped stories with headsets, role movies, and attractive displays.

- The corner should have about five items (books, magazines, whatever) per child, and the items should be changed frequently.

- Library corners are more popular when the children have helped plan and arrange them, including picking a name for the area, putting up a sign with the name, and helping decorate and maintain the corner.

- Children use the library corner more when their teacher also reads to them, tells stories, uses storytelling props (feltboard stories, puppets, filmstrips, tapes), gets children to discuss literal and critical issues in stories, and so on—that is, he or she uses literature as part of instruction.

Teachers will be glad to know that all of these have been verified by studies analyzing children's movements into and use of library corners.

Facts about Library Corners in the Classroom

Lesley Mandel Morrow
New Brunswick, New Jersey
November 1984

We had accumulated a wealth of books for our second graders: fine fiction from picture books to novels, nonfiction on topics from dinosaurs to Booker T. Washington, and shelves to separate the two categories. We even had attractive book nooks. Nevertheless, for many children, our wealth of books seemed to be an overwhelming jungle of choices offering many more chances to be disappointed than delighted. A child-oriented system of organization was needed. To solve this problem while helping children become responsible for as much of their learning and classroom life as possible, we devised a color-coding system that not only organized the books but also could be maintained by the children.

Organizing the Classroom Library

Sarah S. Krouse
Nancy C. Hamlin
North Manchester, Indiana
January 1986

Dividing fiction and nonfiction one step further, we decided on five subclassifications and a color for each. A small strip of colored tape purchased at the hardware store marked the lower spine of each book. A simple color chart that displayed the five divisions hung in the book nook for reference. The nonfiction classifications were blue for history and biography, yellow for science, and white for other nonfiction.

Fiction was more difficult to classify, requiring a subjective judgment of each book's difficulty for children. Red was for "Red Light Book"—harder fiction that demanded the reader go slowly and spend some time to complete. Green meant "Green Light Book"—easier fiction that everyone should be able to read quickly. In explaining the fiction classifications to the children, we were careful to stress that their choice of a red or green book might be a matter of mood: red books were not "better" than green books; they just offered a different type of reading.

To help keep track of each book's whereabouts, we glued a pocket to the inside front cover and placed in it an index card with the book title written across the top. On a chart hung in the book nook, we glued pockets with each child's name. When children borrowed books, they were to remove the cards and place them in their personal book pockets. They returned the cards to the books when they finished. This was a tremendous help in locating lost books and in determining at a glance who did or did not have a book in progress. Students quickly caught on that they should try not to be caught with their pocket empty.

To keep the books properly arranged on the shelves and avoid clumsy bookends, we used cardboard boxes covered with adhesive-backed plastic and marked on the edges with the appropriate color tape. These we set on their sides on the shelves. Blue books stood in blue boxes, and so on; fiction and nonfiction boxes stood on separate shelves with signs pointing them out.

Finally, to make the system truly manageable by students, we created a "librarian's supply box" to house extra colored tape, glue, a pair of scissors, book pockets, and cards. A child, appointed classroom librarian for a week, carried the responsibility of preparing any new books for the shelves with colored tape and book pockets, replacing lost title cards, and straightening the shelves at day's end.

The initial classification and color coding of a collection was done in a few extra hours as rooms were prepared for summer storage. As the new year began, the system's effectiveness quickly became apparent. Students approached the book nook more purposefully, as if they already had in mind the sort of book they wanted and were confident of finding it.

Browsing became more fruitful and little time was required to locate particular books. Reshelving was no longer a problem. There could be no doubt as to the placement of a book in its correspondingly colored box. The classroom librarian could quickly spot misplaced books with their telltale colored tape clashing against properly placed books. Even the number of books placed upside down and backwards decreased as children realized that the tapes showed at the bottom when a book was properly shelved.

This color coding system can easily be adapted to a variety of classrooms and grade levels by further subdividing the book classifications or eliminating some classifications for younger children. Alphabetical lists of the books in each category can be kept for quick reference. The student librarian's task can be diminished, or increased and assigned to partners or teams.

In our classroom, color coding brought order to our books so that students could use them effectively. It freed the children of reliance on excessive teacher assistance, making them more confident and independent in their learning and in their lives at school. Color coding is a practical tool that eliminates many of the mechanical problems of classroom life so that education may proceed.

Making Safe Reading Environments

Anne Heasley Billica
Baton Rouge, Louisiana
October 1984

Good readers seem to flourish in any reading environment but for other children, early failure means reading is no fun. Poor readers desperately need to feel comfortable when trying to read books on their own level. How can we create a safe reading environment? Here are some ideas.

Tell adults about safe reading environments. Well-meaning adults often encourage children to select "hard enough" books (with more words and fewer illustrations). Reading becomes unsafe when children are concerned that their selections be "hard enough." Explain to parents and other adults the value of reading "easy" books. When children read books at their independent reading levels, they are practicing and applying their new skills. We may have to bite our tongues a few times to avoid judging a book as "too easy." The tongue-biting becomes less painful when the goal of recreational reading is kept in mind—to develop the habit in children of turning to books as a source of enjoyment. Encourage concerned adults to make positive statements about "easy" books children have selected. "Looks like a great book!" can be all that's needed.

Talk to students about safe reading environments. Reading becomes unsafe when children criticize each others' selections. Explain to them that "easy" books are an essential ingredient in everyone's reading diet. Discourage them from making negative judgments about another child's selection. Children will stop making negative comments when they hear adults approving "easy" selections. They'll soon be reinforcing each other in unrestricted selections.

Establish routines that safeguard the reading environment:

- ***Lower-grade reading buddies.*** It's hard for children in third grade or higher to cross the invisible line that marks the primary area of the library. If older students have beginners as reading buddies, the library's barrier can be safely crossed. The older buddy selects and reads aloud books that the younger student will enjoy. Both benefit.

- ***Reading aloud.*** Books the teacher reads aloud become top choices with all the students. When good books with readability levels lower than the grade level are included, children soon realize it's the book that is important, rather than the number of pages or words. Use books with a variety of topics and formats so children can expand their interests within a wide range of teacher- and peer-accepted materials.

- ***Classroom library.*** The reading materials available in the classroom are a major factor in a safe environment. Books, magazines, newspapers—anything readable—should present a full range of topics, formats, literary genres, and difficulty levels. Introduce some of each type. A book talk may mean only holding up an item and making a few tantalizing comments about it. Rotate the materials often to keep interest high.

- ***Sustained silent reading.*** The safe environment is reinforced when the teacher also reads many different sorts of materials. Follow Beverly Cleary's lead: The teacher in *Ramona Quimby, Age 8* has a special time during the day called "D.E.A.R.": Drop Everything And Read.

When safe reading environments prevail in classrooms, children can explore materials with success and enjoyment, happily selecting and reading any book—even an "easy" one.

Book-a-Day Club

Mary P. Melvin
Oxford, Ohio
January 1986

Bridging the gap from beginning reading to independent reading is a major step in the primary grades. Any youngsters who don't close the gap by the end of third grade are likely to become totally frustrated, faced with the conflict between their desire to read "hard" books like their peers and the need to stick with easier books to get the practice they need. An appealing response to this problem is a Book-a-Day Club, which ensures that students read independently every day and that they experience constant success.

Establishing and directing a Book-a-Day Club is simple.

1. Identify a limited number of students who have one or more of these characteristics: lack confidence in reading, are reading below grade level, have difficulty selecting books for independent reading, need an extra dose of teacher attention.

2. Invite these students to join the Book-a-Day Club. Send them each a personal letter through the mail. The students respond either by signing and returning the Book-a-Day Club agreement (see Figure) or by choosing not to join.

Sample Letter and Agreement

Dear Friend,

This is a very special invitation for you to join a very special club—the Book-a-Day Club. This is a new club that is being organized for people like you—people who can read, but who want to read more!
    What will members of this club do?
1. They will read at least one book each day.
2. They will keep a record of all books they read.
3. They will attend Book-a-Day Club meetings twice a week.
4. And, best of all, they will become readers who really read!

The first meeting of the Book-a-Day Club will be in Room 145 on Monday, September 20, at 8:45 a.m.
    Don't miss this opportunity to become a fantastic reader. Just sign the agreement form below and return it to Ms. Melvin. And be sure to show up for the first meeting on Monday, September 20.

- -

Agreement Form

I wish to become a member of the Book-a-Day Club. I understand that the club leader will help me select books that I can read easily in one day. I promise:

1. to read a book each day.
2. to keep a record of all books I read.
3. to attend meetings twice a week if at all possible.

_____
Signature

_____
Date

3. At the first meeting, talk with the club members about the rules and decide on regular meeting times. Students choose books from a collection you have assembled.

4. Students read a book every day and keep a record of each.

After the Book-a-Day Club is established, students should attend meetings regularly. Structure these meetings to suit their needs. You might encourage them to tell about books they have read, discuss how they feel about reading a book every day, read favorite parts of their books out loud, read a certain kind of book (e.g., animal story, mystery, poetry) for the next meeting, plan a way to share their books with classmates who are not in the club, or share books with younger children.

Reading a whole book every day has several important advantages for eight-, nine-, and ten-year-olds who haven't reached a comfortable level of independence in reading. They get practice in reading every day. It makes the reading of short, easy books legitimate. (After all, even good readers don't read a whole, long book every day!) It lets them enjoy a feeling of success in reading.

A Book-a-Day Club can be very useful for a few months. After that, enthusiasm may wane. Some students will be ready to tackle more difficult material; some will need a different motivational emphasis. This would be a good time to ask students to suggest appropriate next steps. They may have ideas about another format for a club, or another way to get the support they need for gaining independence in reading. Encouraging students to assume responsibility for developing a new approach is, in itself, an excellent way to support their steps toward becoming independent readers and learners.

A Book for a Book

Pamela Beth Heukerott
Scarsdale, New York
November 1987

The more students read, the more proficient their reading becomes. To spark my class's independent reading, I enroll each child in the Critics' Book Club in September. During the first week of school, I introduce the children to the rules governing membership in the club: the book chart, the project forms, the project box, and independent reading time. The reading corner is explained as a focal area in the classroom.

We hang up the book club chart, which is made of heavy white posterboard or poster paper, with horizontal lines drawn to represent one "bookshelf" for each participant. All the students' names, along with my own, are listed in a column on the left. (Allow 1½"—about 5 cm—for each name for grades four to six; for younger children, allow 2" to 3", or about 10 cm.)

When a student completes a book, she or he selects a project from the Critics' Book Club project filebox, which is kept in the reading corner. The activities are simple, fun, and motivating, so the children do not become discouraged about having to do a task on top of reading. Successful projects have involved puppet shows, taped dialogues from the book, dioramas of story settings along with brief summaries of the events that are occurring, letters to authors, board games, crossword puzzles, interactive computer programs to inform others about the book, and dramatized scenes from the story.

When a project is completed, the student fills out a Critics' Book Club project form that asks for his or her name, the book's title, its author, the type of book (mystery, poetry, biography), the project completed, and an opinion about the book. The appropriate rating box must be checked: VG (Very Good), G (Good), F (Fair), or T (Terrible). The T rating is uncommon since such books are rarely read in their entirety. The project form, along with the project, is then submitted to me for evaluation. I write comments on the project form and then hold a short conference with the student. The project form is then filed in the student's reading folder.

At this point, the student receives a small "book" to hang up on the book club chart next to his or her name. These are made of small rectangular pieces of light but brightly colored construction paper folded in half to resemble a book. On the front, we print the title of the book and its author. On the left inside flap, we put the type of book; on the right inside flap, the book's rating. As the weeks go by, students see the tiny bookshelves next to each name fill up with books. Students enjoy reading the chart to check what books their classmates are reading. Often this leads to discussions about books and recommendations about what to read. When the bookshelf next to a student's name is filled, the minibooks are removed so that they can be taken home, and a gold minibook (made from foil wrapping paper) is put in their place. On the inside right-hand flap is written the number of books it signifies.

To ensure that students do read independently every day, I set aside ten minutes at the beginning of reading period for silent reading. I also have surprise "free reads," which are given at my discretion. A special display in the reading corner acquaints students with recently published books and books on different or unusual topics. Newspaper and magazine reviews of children's books are posted on the reading corner bulletin board. Periodically, I give out bookmarks to help the children keep their places.

At the end of the school year, each student receives an award for being an active member in the Critics' Book Club. Then we cut up the book club chart so that each student can take home his or her bookshelf.

Adopt-a-Book

**Catherine Lapsansky
Teresa McAndrew**
Pittston, Pennsylvania
May 1989

Children dressed in jogging outfits, picnicking in the halls on junk food and teddy bear drinks.... Children wearing Hershey bars as badges.... Children wearing blue ribbons inscribed with a special word to describe themselves.... How do these images relate to books? Each is part of a schoolwide event that lets children and teachers share books in a wonderfully exciting way. The children will long remember *Albert the Running Bear*, *The Chocolate Touch*, and *Charlotte's Web* because of the positive experiences they shared when these books were read.

These were only a few of the many creative ideas generated in our school district's Adopt-a-Book program, which was based on the idea that the best way to bring books and children together is through children's literature. Adopt-a-Book transformed the halls into a museum of children's literature. Each class displayed a colorful work of art promoting its favorite book. A tour of the building would surely entice anyone to read one of the newly adopted books.

Each elementary class formally "adopted" a favorite book to promote during Book Week. Applications for adoption were filled out, and each class then received an official adoption certificate that was signed by the students and teachers and officially sealed by the reading department. These certificates were displayed at the Adoption Center in the main hall, so that visitors would be encouraged to visit the classroom displays.

Throughout the week, classes promoted their adopted book through advertisements, presentations, badges, invitations, and so on. These promotions encompassed all the language arts. The focal point for the promotion was the door and hall outside each classroom. Oral activities included plays, discussions, and original songs. Written activities included webbing main story words, listing main elements of the story, writing about the best part of the story, writing ads to entice future readers, and writing poems and summaries. Some of the artistic activities included making models of buildings described in the adopted books, making costumes, and much more. Creativity was evident as a multitude of displays and promotions filled the school with book titles and authors everywhere.

On Friday the most creative projects from each grade level were selected by public librarians from the area. Each winning class received a framed certificate, and each student in the class received a personal copy of the adopted book. Every class received a classroom copy of its book, and library copies were affixed with a permanent label on the front cover, so that new students would always know that this book was recommended by their peers.

As a culmination, the classes were paired up on Friday to share their promotions with other students. Teachers commented that this was the highlight of the week. The ideas generated in these sessions were as diverse as the displays themselves as the students discussed why they liked their adopted book and encouraged others to read it.

Books definitely had center stage during this celebration. Because of its success, Adopt-a-Book has become an annual event.

It was Friday night and the library began to fill up with children and sleeping bags. Favorite television shows were forgotten as third, fourth, and fifth graders reached for Ramona, Paddington, and Great Brain books. These students had won the prize of coming back to school to spend the night at a Read-a-thon. How had this come about?

Our state's governor had declared December to be reading month. The state Department of Education sent a proclamation to all the schools along with a pamphlet of suggested activities and slogans. The school's two reading specialists and librarian began to plan reading activities for our 925-pupil elementary school. The reading month activities emphasized three things: (1) encouraging students and parents to read a lot; (2) inviting community leaders to the school to read to individual classes; and (3) publicizing December as reading month in our state.

To inform parents and students about reading month, we prepared a six-page pamphlet. The cover illustration encouraged students to read, read, read! Page one was a photocopy of the governor's proclamation. Page two was a letter to parents, informing them of a school reading contest. The

Forty Books Wins Forty Winks

**Margaret V. Blackmon
Pamela E. Douglas
Julie W. Harris**
*Fredericksburg, Virginia
February 1984*

centerfold was a December calendar with a space for recording the number of minutes each child read or was read to each day and the number of books and pages read. Each child was to have a parent sign the calendar before turning it in on December 16. Page five was a list of "Dos and Don'ts of Reading Aloud." Page six had the slogan "Give a Gift of Love... Read a Child a Story" and included three lists of six books that were especially recommended for children in kindergarten to grade one, grades two to three, and grades four to five. The back cover bore slogans made up by the students—"Reading is always right/Reading is dynamite!" was one.

Once the reading pamphlet was prepared, the reading teachers and librarian met with the school board to inform them of the planned activities: Community Readers, Reading Contest, and Read-a-thon.

The Read-a-thon was a reward for the children in grades three to five who logged the most reading time on their calendars. Of the 78 children invited, 68 showed up at 7:00 p.m. that Friday, wearing comfortable clothing and carrying bedrolls. Also on hand were two fathers, five teachers, one college professor, the principal, and a school-board member who volunteered to read to the children during scheduled breaks.

The children signed in, found comfortable spots, and were off in search of a book to begin their reading. Quickly and quietly they began to read. After about an hour there was a break during which the principal and school board member provided reading entertainment. Midway through the evening there was an apple and filmstrip break featuring *A Wrinkle in Time* by Madeleine L'Engle. Then it was back to reading until lights out at 11:00 p.m. After roll call it was *Goodnight Moon* for everyone.

Before the sun rose on Saturday, the principal, one father, and two cafeteria volunteers were rustling up breakfast for the Read-a-thoners. The menu consisted of "Runaway Pancakes," "Johnny Appleseed Apple Juice," and "Curious George Bananas." By 8:00 a.m. breakfast had disappeared, the cafeteria was clean, and all the children had been picked up by their parents.

The Reading Contest winners in kindergarten to grade two received paperback books as prizes. We felt that these students were too young for the all-night Read-a-thon. After we explained our purpose, a local bookstore let us purchase books at a discount. We typed a short note to the parents and inserted a copy in each book. We allowed each winner to choose from a variety of books presented on a large tray; many were Caldecott or Newbery award winners.

Throughout that month school-board and city council members, local school administrators, doctors, lawyers, librarians, businesspeople, and retired persons were invited to read to classes. These Community Readers could choose a convenient day and time, as well as the age group preferred. If an individual had a favorite story, she or he was encouraged to read that to the class; otherwise, the school librarian would offer suggestions. On a sign-up sheet in the faculty lounge, the reader's time was divided into several 15- to 30-minute blocks so teachers could choose readers to fit their daily schedules.

This experience showed the children that adults other than teachers valued reading, and the 32 Community Readers became aware of the importance of preparation in working with students. They learned that reading and storytelling require a certain amount of expertise. All the readers enjoyed the opportunity and many came to read more than once. At the end of the month, each Community Reader received a thank-you letter.

Classroom teachers and their students contributed to the program via several activities. Many upper-grade students chose books and short stories to read to classes of younger students. Primary grade students did choral reading. Book reports took such forms as posters, shadow boxes, and mobiles. One class produced, taped, and then aired a play over the school PA system. Students enjoyed cooking treats related to book themes and making puppets of book characters.

In addition to presenting our ideas and plans to the school board and faculty, we made other efforts to inform the community of reading month. Our six-page pamphlet was sent home with every child. The principal's weekly newsletter and the school menu contained reminders to parents to read to and with their children. The school system further publicized reading month in its quarterly newspaper mailed to students' homes. An article pictured the chair of the school board reading to a kindergarten class. The librarian asked a local radio station if students might tape one-minute announcements to be aired during reading month. After writing and rehearsing radio scripts with six children from grades two to five, the reading teachers and librarian took the children to record their spots and slogans. The librarian also persuaded the local bank to display reading slogans on its electronic sign. Many people commented on seeing the slogans as they drove through town. The local education association sponsored a reading day at a nearby mall, where 30 teachers took half-hour shifts reading to students who sat at their feet. Parents delighted in seeing their children enjoy stories, and passersby saw teachers giving their Saturday time to read to children.

Local and major state newspapers provided the most exciting publicity. In response to a call from our principal, a reporter from a nearby city came to the school. He interviewed students and wrote an article headlined "40 Books Wins 40 Winks for 68 Students." A reporter and photographer from our local newspaper came along, too, and talked with dozens of our Read-a-thoners. The Saturday edition carried a story plus photographs that took up nearly a full page of the newspaper and told the whole community of our reading month's success.

Children as Storytellers

Susan A. West
Frederick, Maryland
November 1987

Storytelling has often been regarded as a method for motivating students to read. It can be an even more powerful learning tool when the students become the storytellers. During Children's Book Week, the children at my school became totally immersed in storytelling and, through it, familiarized themselves with a wide variety of reading materials. Even poor readers and beginning readers were able to participate actively.

The week began when a local storyteller visited the school and spent half-hour periods with different grades. In addition to entertaining the children with stories, the storyteller gave tips on how to tell stories (enjoy your story, use facial expressions, use props, use movement, and be able to improvise).

During the next several days, reading classes were transformed into storytelling workshops. To find stories they wanted to tell, the children had several options: look through familiar and unfamiliar books for stories, write original tales, or practice known favorite stories (such as family legends or folktales). After the students had chosen their stories, they spent time practicing their storytelling techniques, either in small groups or with the teacher. They were encouraged to practice at home, using their families as audiences and critics. Thus, learning about public speaking and accepting constructive criticism were additional benefits.

On Thursday, the students performed as storytellers in front of their classes, and each class voted, by secret ballot, for the top storyteller of its class. The performances were polished and creative. Some students had devised puppets, some used various props, and many were adept at using facial expressions and movements to tell stories.

On Friday, the top storytellers in each class shared their stories with the whole school at a morning assembly. Noting the positive reactions of all the children, storytellers and audience alike, the teachers have decided to incorporate student storytelling into the curriculum more frequently.

Index of Contributors

234

Also available from IRA...

The International Reading Association has a longstanding commitment to publishing books that will make reading teachers' lives easier. Here are just a few recent publications that are full of practical suggestions for teaching at the elementary level:

- *Invitation to Read: More Children's Literature in the Reading Program*, edited by Bernice E. Cullinan, is full of ideas for using outstanding children's literature in all aspects of literacy instruction—from preschool to middle school. (Publication #371, US$18.00/US$12.00 IRA members)

- *Beyond Storybooks: Young Children and the Shared Book Experience*, by Judith Pollard Slaughter, shows how reading aloud from Big Books can lead to activities for learning across the curriculum in the preschool through early elementary years. (Publication #377, US$15.00/US$10.00 IRA members)

- *Teaching Reading Skills through the Newspaper*, by Arnold B. Cheyney, is a handy guide—now in an all-new third edition—to using this inexpensive, widely available, topical, and flexible resource for helping students at all levels learn about reading while studying the world around them. (Publication #236, US$6.00/US$4.00 IRA members)

With new books like these to complement bestsellers like *Children's Literature in the Reading Program* (Bernice E. Cullinan, editor), *Emerging Literacy: Young Children Learn to Read and Write* (Dorothy S. Strickland and Lesley Mandel Morrow, editors), *Semantic Mapping: Classroom Applications* (Joan E. Heimlich and Susan D. Pittleman), and *Responses to Literature, Grades K-8* (James M. Macon, Diane Bewell, and MaryEllen Vogt), IRA is clearly the source for elementary teachers to turn to when they're looking for professional resources. For information about these publications or to place your order, call 1-800-336-READ, ext. 226 (outside North America, call 302-731-1600, ext. 266). Visa and MasterCard accepted; postage included on prepaid orders.